T0374285

Also by John Sager

A Tiffany Monday – An Unusual Love Story WestBow Press, 2012
*Joan's Gallery, 50 Years of Artistry by Joan Kohl
Johnson Sager,* Blurb Inc., 2013

UNCOVERED

My Half-Century with the CIA

John Sager

WESTBOW
PRESS
A DIVISION OF THOMAS NELSON

WestBow Press books may be ordered through booksellers or by contacting:

WestBow Press
A Division of Thomas Nelson
1663 Liberty Drive
Bloomington, IN 47403
www.westbowpress.com
1-(866) 928-1240

ISBN: 978-1-4497-8972-5 (sc)
ISBN: 978-1-4497-8971-8 (hc)
ISBN: 978-1-4497-8973-2 (e)

Library of Congress Control Number: 2013905514

Printed in the United States of America.

WestBow Press rev. date: 6/11/2013

A nd you shall know the truth, and the truth shall make you free.

John 8:32, inscribed on the floor of the main entrance of the CIA Headquarters Building, Langley, Virginia

O ur father told us about Christ's disciples being fishermen, and we were left to assume, as my brother and I did, that all first-class fishermen on the Sea of Galilee were fly fishermen and that John, the favorite, was a dry-fly fisherman.

Norman Maclean
A River Runs Through It

Dedication

For Scott and Mike—who probably wondered, but were smart enough not to ask—just what *was* their Old Man up to? Now you can know.

Table of Contents

Preface

A few days before Memorial Day of 2012, the chaplain at my Covenant Shores retirement community asked me to deliver a brief homily at the up-coming Memorial Day service, to be held in the community's Fellowship Hall. He explained that, traditionally, such homilies discuss some aspect of America's military history or other activity. This time, he offered, my experience as a CIA intelligence officer could provide some examples of our nation's "silent service," to remind the congregation of the contributions of other-than-military men and women.

In that homily I offered three examples of intelligence operations that I had been a part of or knew something about. Two of them are recorded in these pages.

After the service, a number of people told me how much they had appreciated my presentation: It was different, interesting and informative. They suggested I should recount more stories about my service, especially now that I had uncovered myself and was able to discuss heretofore "hush-hush" events.

I thought about those encouraging remarks and decided to put my thoughts to paper. That experience morphed into this book. It is an autobiography. It covers the first 83 years of my life and I'm optimistic to think that, by the grace of God, I may have a few left before I join my beloved Jo-an in that Better Place.

I lived about half of those 83 years as an Operations Officer in the

CIA's Clandestine Service. It was an exciting and rewarding career and I have tried to bring to these pages the more memorable parts of my work, as best I can recall them.

Retired intelligence officers who write books about what they have done over the years are always faced with a problem: How to tell the story without saying too much about sources and methods. "Sources and methods" covers a lot of ground and that is why this book has been scrutinized by the CIA's Publications Review Board. What you read in these pages has been reviewed by that group of conscientious men and women and, while I have not always agreed with their decisions, I have been required to accede to them. Readers should understand that the Board has insisted I omit from these pages a considerable portion of the description of my five-year service in Iran, operational activity which they consider to be too sensitive to write about, notwithstanding that all of this happened more than 50 years ago.

I appealed the Board's decision through the office of the Agency that administers the Freedom of Information Act, and that appeal has been denied, a decision with which I am obliged to comply, even though I believe it to be wrong.

Having said that, the reader will see that I have been careful to write only about operations and, yes, sources and methods, that were in play a very long time ago—most of my text deals with events no more recent than 20 years ago and most of them much older—and I am comfortable with knowing that no one still living is in any danger of being uncovered by what I have written. In a few places, as Sergeant Joe Friday used to say, "The names have been changed to protect the innocent." These occasions are rare but I have included them to give readers a closer look at the often mundane details that are part of any successful intelligence-gathering operation.

This, then, is the story of just one man who served his country in its "Silent Service." There have been thousands of others, many of whose accomplishments far exceed my own. But my hope is that by uncovering my career, the reader will gain a better appreciation of what goes on—unread and unnoticed—as our intelligence services attempt to ensure that we Americans remain strong and free.

John Sager
Mercer Island, Washington
May, 2013

Acknowledgments

It seems likely that anyone who undertakes to write, and then publish, an autobiography would want to get it right the first time, despite the fact that he/she may have had limited experience with such an endeavor. This most certainly is where I have found myself—needing help, and lots of it.

I have been blessed to find that help from my far-away cousin, Kitty Katzell—one can hardly be farther away from Mercer Island, Washington than Medford, New Jersey. She has been an encouraging critic, pointing out alternative word choices, punctuation glitches and the other nitty-gritty that would otherwise diminish the final product. Although well into her senior years, Kitty has mastered the mysteries of computers and is now a whiz at the edit-by-email process.

My early attempts to choose a catchy title for the book were met with polite scorn. Eventually, we decided to go with *Uncovered*, which in a way says it all. Through this months-long process, I've come to realize that Kitty is not only my cousin but she has become a close friend, like a real sister. So—thank you, Sis.

Another indispensable helper would be Bob Wallace, a friend and former co-worker who has helped me navigate (for me) the uncharted shoals of the CIA pre-publication review process. That process at times seemed unfairly demanding as, not surprisingly, I was required to repair the many redactions that the reviewers believed necessary to protect classified information. Bob, himself an author of two books about CIA operations, (*Spycraft* and *The Official CIA Manual of Trickery and Deception*) provided invaluable counsel on how to "get it done," without which this story never would have seen print.

A third helper in this project has been my beautiful step-daughter, Janice Bornstein. Janice brought a younger-generation wisdom to many parts of the story, while patiently out-lasting me as we struggled to arrive at a suitable title. Readers won't notice the differences she has made in the final manuscript, but I certainly do.

Part One – The Early Years

Chapter 1

Friends

Because I'm an old guy, eighty-three years as I begin to write this autobiography, I would hope the reader might consider what real friendships can mean over the course of a long lifetime. None of us grows up in a vacuum, and without friends, none of us, likely, would be very happy.

My wife Joan, for example—and about whom I will say a lot more—had tons of friends, many of them quite close. She was just that kind of person, beautiful to look at, with a smile that would stop a train, and a soul-deep kindness beyond words. She would sometimes grow impatient with her grown kids, of course, what parent does not, but other than those two exceptions I doubt I ever heard her say a harsh word to or about anyone. In any conversation that might be heading toward a bit of tension she could diffuse it instantly, just a knack she had that I never did.

But I digress. I could probably number on two hands those friends who were really influential in my life, probably because people who were not close enough to be influential are not so well remembered. I suppose many people see themselves the same way.

I should write a few words about these folks right now, as they will have important roles in this story.

My two parents, of course, would be at the top of any such list. I was an only child and my father, I eventually decided, was determined that I not become a spoiled kid. He was a lawyer and from what I heard later of him, as a young adult, a very good one and I think some of his court-room persona came home with him each evening after work. He was stern but fair—that I also determined later, when I figured out what "fair" meant—and he could stare at me without a word and I knew that whatever was at issue was his to call.

He never hugged me or told me "I love you." That was pretty common in those days, something I also learned later. For some reason, during the Great Depression of the 1930s, a lot of dads were not very sentimental toward their kids, sons *or* daughters.

My mom made up for that, she was a sentimental and tear-prone woman of Swedish descent, always there for me. A lot of moms in those days were stay-at-home, even though family incomes were mostly tight, and she was among the best of them. She had been a high school English teacher before she married my father, and without my being aware, she passed on to me a love of our language and an appreciation of its many nuances. I vaguely remember coming home after school one afternoon, probably eighth or ninth grade, with an English language homework assignment that I just couldn't handle. I actually broke into tears in front of her. She gently sat me down at the dining room table, went over the whole thing with me, pointed out stuff I should have known or remembered and, bingo, the tears stopped and in a couple of days I got an "A" on the ensuing report.

I remember my parents having a fight, in my presence, only once, and I lived with them for seventeen years, so that's saying something. My dad said something to Mom about her not having enough money to be a "snob." She got up from the kitchen table, crying, and told him it was the most unkind thing he had ever said to her. She went into the bedroom, closed the door, and left my dad and me sitting there in the kitchen. He was not a happy camper. He may have apologized to her, but not within my hearing, and I know he regretted what he had said.

As a man of few words—with me, not in the court room—I do remember a brief chat Dad had with me when I was about to enter the University of Washington, age 17, as a freshman, in the Fall of 1947. I was walking along the street in front of our home and he intercepted me, so I sensed that what he was about to say was important and that he didn't want Mom to hear it. I don't remember his exact words but they had to do with a young guy's attitudes about young gals. He made a couple of points that I've never forgotten. Without saying it in so many words, he let me know that if I ever became responsible for a girl becoming pregnant, that would be my boat to row, with no one available to toss me a lifeline.

But that was not his main point. He wanted me to understand that *respect* for the opposite sex, of any age, but especially for the college girls I would meet, was an absolute must, in his book. He hammered home this theme in just a few words, but I've never forgotten: Any woman deserves a man's respect and gentle treatment, no exceptions. Which leads me to another idea about my father.

My reading of the Bible, the whole story of God's love for us undeserving sinners, seems to make it pretty clear that God wired us humans so that the *man* is the one whom He expects to be the leader. We men are expected to care for our women, at least with common-sense kindness and courtesy, if not the deeper love that we should have for wives, daughters and, often, relatives and close friends.

Harry and Crystal Sager

So my dad seemed to understand this idea very well and he wanted to make sure that I did, too.

Dad was not a religious man, or at least so he said. He had been raised in a Catholic family, in western Montana, one of eight brothers. Like his siblings, he went to the Missoula Catholic school, grades one through twelve. Then, a sea change. He enrolled at the University of Montana Law School and received his degree four years later. He chucked Catholicism. He never told me why. He worked his way through those four years selling encyclopedias. Later, after graduating with his law degree, he worked in Yellowstone Park as a tourist bus driver. It was there that he met my mom, she (as I've said) a young school teacher. They met on the dance floor at one of the large lodges then (1927) so popular with tourists from all over the country. Apparently it was love at first sight. They were married soon thereafter and came to Seattle on their honeymoon. My dad had always wanted to be "near the ocean," as he put it, only to discover that Seattle was still some one hundred miles from his goal.

There were other people who had great influence on me, especially during my growing-up years. The Sumner school system, small as it was, was blessed with a number of very good teachers, nearly all of them women, who had been in the system for many years and, in that small town, were part of the larger "family." The Schlauch sisters were a prime example of this. The elder of the two, Emmaline, taught all the math courses and chemistry. Her sister, June, taught typing, girls' physical education, and debate and public speaking. I was on the debate team and did some extemporaneous speaking in competitions and I got to know "Miss June" very well. We spent hours together traveling with the other debate team members, all over Washington State. Those quiet conversations, with a dedicated teacher like June Schlauch, really add up in a young guy's maturation.

Then there were two young professors at the University of Washington who were important to me. One of them taught American political history, the other was my political science advisor. Both had served in World War II but were still young enough to relate easily to their younger students. These two men had fought for their country and they seized on the opportunities they were given to instill in their students a fierce patriotism, something we never would have understood absent their vivid experiences in the military. I've often thought about those two men, especially nowadays when I'm reminded of the "soft liberalism" that seems to have infected our colleges and universities.

Another man whom I greatly admired was Livingston Blair, the adult leader at the two Junior Red Cross conventions I attended as a high school junior and senior. (More of this, later.) He spoke passionately about his experiences in Western Europe, immediately following the end of hostilities in the Summer and Fall of 1945. He was there as a representative of the American Red Cross, taking stock of the urgent needs of the survivors of that conflict. Because I was on one of the leadership teams at the two conventions, I was able to hear him describe, in small-group discussions, his recollections of the terrible suffering still going on in Germany, France, Belgium and the Netherlands. I was only a 17-18 year-old kid but "Mr. Blair" taught me much about sacrifice and sharing. And years later, when I became a Christian believer, his dedicated life made even more sense to me.

On this short list, last but certainly not least, would be my long-time and very good friend, John Aalto. A lot more about him as we move along.

Chapter 2

Sumner: A Big Fish in a Very Small Pond

During most of my grade school years, what little I remember of them, I seem to have been watching Joan Kohl, the prettiest thing I could imagine. She had deep brown eyes and hair to match and she always was dressed as well as or better than any of her classmates. And she seemed to be the most talented kid in my class, maybe in the whole grade school. She could draw, paint, sing, she eventually played the clarinet in the grade school orchestra; and she was smart, as the report card sharing, which we all did a few times each year, easily showed.

Aside from falling in love with Joan Kohl, as a six-year-old, my most vivid first-grade memory has to do with a funeral parlor; no kidding.

During the year that my grandmother lived with my family, we lived in an old house that was sort of "on the other side of the tracks."

To get to school—and I lived too close to school to be able to ride a school bus—I walked up the narrow lane that led to our home, then across the Stuck River bridge, and then right by one of Sumner's two funeral parlors.

The Voiles family owned and operated the funeral home and Ronnie Voiles was the youngest of its three kids. He, too, was a first-grader and because we often walked to school together, we became good buddies. "Good buddies" meant that we were inclined to do what a lot unsupervised six-year-olds do: get into trouble.

One day, on our way home from school, Ronnie told me that his dad was preparing for a funeral and the deceased's body was lying in an open casket. The service wasn't to take place until the next day. Had I ever seen a dead body? No. Would I like to see a dead body? Of course!

Ronnie swore me to secrecy, knowing that if anyone—especially is father—found out about this he would be in deep trouble for a very long time.

Our first challenge was to get into the viewing room without anyone seeing us. Ronnie either had a key, or the door was unlocked, I was too scared to remember which, and we crawled on our hands and knees up to the casket. He gave me the "hush" sign with his forefinger over his lips—as if we were likely to waken the man in the casket—and we stood up to have a look.

I think I was disappointed: The man looked as though he was peacefully sleeping, probably just what his family wanted him to look like. And probably a tribute to Ronnie's dad, doing what a good undertaker should do.

Over the years, when I think about this prank, I can excuse it by thinking "boys will be boys." But something about it bothers me just a little bit because I had invaded some very private space.

Other than Joan, my most vivid recollection of grade school centers on an "incident" I created in Mrs. Cook's fifth-grade home room. In those days, in the midst of the 1930s Great Depression, it was a common thing for a man or woman to come to the grade school with some kind of entertainment: a magician, a juggler, a story-teller. These entertainers, of course, came to the school because they were paid for whatever they did. Usually, to attend one of these performances—they were held in a large assembly hall—each student had to pay five cents, one nickel. The home-room teacher collected those nickels the day before the performance.

At that time, and since then for that matter, I've never thought of myself as a prankster, but for some reason I decided to try something "cute" in Mrs. Cook's classroom. Maybe it was because she was hands-down the toughest and most strict of all the teachers in the school: a very-unlike-me "I'll show *you*" attitude.

A few days earlier a friend had shown me a "device" which his parents had given him the year before, with which to help celebrate July Fourth. It was a small, spring-loaded cap "pistol." You put a couple of cap-gun caps in this gadget, held it closed inside your clenched fist and when you opened your fist you released the spring and the caps exploded, loudly. I asked him if I could borrow it for a few days.

So I'm sitting there at my desk, with my fist clenched as Mrs. Cook approaches to collect my nickel. She already had a handful of nickels, from the other kids; perfect. As she reaches for my nickel I open my hand and, CRACK!. Suddenly, nickels are flying all over the classroom, but nobody is laughing, certainly not Mrs. Cook. She ordered me to pick up all the nickels and to meet her in her room after school.

I think that was the only time I ever had to stay "after school," a punishment not quite as severe as having to go to the principal's office. Mrs. Cook wasn't kidding. I reported to her for five consecutive days, the worst part of it being that I had to explain to my mother why I was coming home late from school. During those excruciating thirty-minute sessions with Mrs. Cook she talked to me about all kinds of things, trying straighten out this misguided child. I don't recall the subjects of her admonitions but I'm sure they didn't hurt.

I shared this story years later, at high school reunions with many of the same now-adults who had been inwardly giggling as I picked up those nickels off Mrs. Cook's home-room floor. Oddly, I thought, none of them remembered the incident. But I imagine that Mrs. Cook did.

When, finally, in September 1941, we sixth-graders moved to the junior high school, a few blocks away from the grade school building, we all thought of this as a big deal; we were now seventh graders and "on our way." Our enthusiasm was dampened just three months later, on the morning of December 8th, 1941, when our principal called all of us, plus the eighth and ninth graders, into the large study hall to listen to President Roosevelt's "day of infamy" address to the United States Congress.

Sumner, Washington lay in the midst of the Puyallup Valley, a fertile flat landscape that extended from the base of Mount Rainier northward toward Seattle. That valley produced much of the fresh vegetables that were sold in Puget Sound market places. The farms that produced those vegetables were owned and operated, mostly, by Japanese-Americans, Nisei as they were known.

Several of our classmates were children of these Japanese-American farm families, a few of them were friends and Joan and I counted one of them, Frank Sato, as one of our best friends.

Within a month or so, following the December 7 attack on Pearl Harbor, the word came down from Washington, DC that all these Nisei families were to be rounded up and sent to "relocation centers." We seventh graders hardly understood what was happening, only that our friends were being forced to move away. Their "interim stop" was at the Puyallup Fairgrounds, a large "county-fair" space with plenty of room, just three miles from Sumner. Joan and I, years later, well-remembered going to that fair grounds and, after some searching, finding our friends, including Frank Sato, behind barbed wire. It was a searing vision that neither of us ever forgot.

The irony of ironies, I've thought in recent months, is that Frank Sato came to Joan's memorial service at Mercer Island's Presbyterian Church, just a week after she died in June 2011, and delivered the most eloquent eulogy of all those we heard that day. A true friend, to the very end.

So all the kids in the Sumner school system spent the rest of the World War II years without their Nisei friends. Many of them had been the smartest students and I often thought, years later, that I would never have become the school's valedictorian, on graduating in June 1947, had Frank Sato still been in my class.

As an afterthought about Frank, readers should know that when he returned to a normal lifestyle, after World War II had ended, he enrolled at the University of Washington and received a degree in accounting. To say he "worked his way up the ladder" would be putting it mildly: Years later he was appointed by President Jimmy Carter as the Department of Transportation's first Inspector General, the first Japanese-American to achieve a sub-cabinet level position. Later, President Reagan named Frank to be the Inspector General for the Department of Veterans' Affairs. Not bad, for a kid from lil' ol' Sumner!

By the time I began my sophomore (tenth) year in high school I apparently had decided to take school more seriously than I had up to that time. I don't remember making a conscious decision about this, but the courses had become more interesting and I worked harder to understand what they were teaching. I took Latin, for example; most of the kids who took a foreign language preferred German or Spanish. (We all knew that admission to the University of Washington, just thirty miles north in Seattle, required at least one credit in a foreign language.) My father already had told me that if I did well in high school he would help me with the money needed to get a college education.

Chemistry and physics had great appeal and I was good enough in math that the math teacher did a one-hour tutoring class just for me, in the morning before regular classes, in spherical trigonometry. I also took a full-credit course in typing, got so I could do sixty words a minute and that course, probably, was the most "practical" of any of them because, later at the "U-Dub," I could do all my term papers on a typewriter, something not many of my contemporaries could handle.

One day, just as I was about to leave my Latin class, the teacher asked me if I might be interested in getting involved with the American Junior Red Cross. I was aware of what the organization was doing in the post-World War II environment, collecting and sending overseas the simple things that the war-torn kids in Europe could not afford or find: soap, tooth brushes and tooth paste, a comb, a Hershey bar, sewing kit, that sort of thing. The AJRC was contacting high schools all over the country and asking students to pitch in and help.

I thought about it and decided sure, it's about time I learned more about what was happening to kids my age who had just survived the most awful disruption imaginable. That brief chat with my Latin teacher opened up a whole new world for me, as I would soon learn.

Mrs. Stevens, the Latin teacher, asked me to go into Tacoma, ten miles away, and report to the Red Cross office. There I would be interviewed by Edith Ackerman, the woman in charge of the JARC in the Puget Sound region. When I arrived for the interview I learned there were four or five other kids, from nearby high schools, all in their eleventh year (as was I), who would also be interviewed. After a 30-minute chat with her I went back to Sumner to wait for her decision. I remember thinking at the time that if there were four or five other kids in this "competition," my chances for being chosen were pretty slim. The other high schools in that area were much larger than Sumner's, whose student-body population was about thee hundred. The two large Tacoma high schools probably had at least three times that many, and across-the-river-from-Sumner rival Puyallup high school, twice as many.

About a week later Mrs. Stevens asked me to stay after her

class for a few moments. When the other kids had filed out of her classroom she told me, much to my surprise, that I had been chosen to represent the AJRC's Pacific Northwest Region of its Western Division. I had already learned that the organization was divided into geographic groups, to ensure common-sense administration by the adults. The AJRC was a relatively new sub-set of the American Red Cross, organized soon after the end of World War II specifically to focus its relief efforts on Europe's children, many of whom were having a very difficult time. Some had lost one or both parents and those who still had homes to live in were the more fortunate.

I learned within a week or so of being chosen that I would soon be going to San Francisco to meet with four other high school juniors who had just gone through the same selection process. The kids in this group represented northern and southern California, Arizona and Utah and, collectively, we would be known as the AJRC's "Pacific Area Advisory Council." Pretty heady stuff for a 16-year-old kid from little ol' Sumner.

The meeting in San Francisco required me to get there, of course, so I took my first-ever commercial airline flight. I had been given a cash advance to cover the cost of my hotel room, meals and "incidentals," but no one had told me how to get from San Francisco's airport to my hotel, which was downtown. So I took a taxi; big mistake. I don't remember what the fare came to but it ate up a lot of my pocket money. This is how kids learn, isn't it?

The meetings were interesting because the five of us shared our experiences as high schoolers in parts of the country that none of us had yet visited. We also learned a lot about what the AJRC was doing in Europe and what would be expected of us in our "advisory council" role. The most exciting news to come out of these meetings was that we would fly to Philadelphia, as soon as school was out in early June, to participate in the American Red Cross' annual convention. Its organizers had decided to hold its first separate convention for the new "Junior" group. At the convention, to which more than a thousand youngsters would flock from all over the country, the adult leaders would arrange for the selection of an AJRC National Advisory Council, to represent each of the organization's five geographic regions: East, Southeast, South, Midwest and West. "My" Pacific Area Advisory Council would be one of five such groups and together we would select one member from each regional group and those five would become the AJRC's first national advisory body.

The flight to Philadelphia would have been unremarkable but for the fact that it was the first time I became air sick. The airplane I flew on was a United Airlines DC-4, in those days without a pressurized cabin, and it could not fly more than 10,000 feet above sea level. While we were crossing the Rocky Mountains, eastbound out of Seattle, the air became very rough, another new experience for me. Fortunately the man sitting next to me sympathized with what was happening next to him. I survived, but the experience was another one of those things one remembers for a very long time.

Philadelphia was an event none of its participants ever forgot. We were jammed into hotel rooms fitted with World War II surplus bunk beds and the close quarters required us to get to know each other quickly. That was the best part of it. My bunk-bed partner was a Mormon kid from Salt Lake City and over the course of the next few days he told me about his plans for going to Africa, for one year, as a missionary. That was a routine experience for young Mormons but it was something I had known nothing about.

During one of the breaks between convention sessions, our regional groups got together to elect one from each of the five. That one person, along with the four others so chosen, would then constitute the JARC's National Advisory Committee. My group chose me, an honor that really surprised me, I suppose because coming from one of the smallest school systems represented at the convention it would have seemed a long shot.

When I returned to Sumner, after the convention shut down, school was already out for the summer so I didn't have to say anything to my classmates about my experiences in Philadelphia. However, the local newspapers had picked up the story and so, to my embarrassment, my picture and an article about the convention appeared in Tacoma's

daily *News Tribune*, and in Sumner's two weekly newspapers. I think
my parents were pretty proud of their only child but my dad, in
character, said very little to me about my experience. Maybe a "Well
done, Kiddo," but for me that was more than good enough.

That Fall, when school began again, the first thing I noticed was
that Joan Kohl was "missing," nowhere to be seen. I learned from
mutual friends that she had moved to Tacoma with her family and
was already enrolled at Stadium High School. Although I never had
the courage to ask her for a date, I was sure I would miss her presence
in my classes and in the school's hallways. But with my new "job"
with the AJRC, I had plenty to do to keep me busy; and I had been
elected student body president for the 1946-47 school year, another
task that would compete for study and homework time.

Football was another competitor. As a junior I had played back-up
center on the Sumner Spartan football team and we didn't do very
well, losing five, tying two and winning only two. As a senior I would
be the starting center, all 147 pounds of me. This was a much better
season and we breezed through our first seven games, outscoring our
opponents by about thirty to three. But arch-rival Puyallup, from
just across the river, beat us at home on the traditional Thanksgiving
"Turkey Day" game, 27 to 6. The team had a chance to at least tie
for the conference championship, playing its last game at Renton.
An unlikely November snowstorm scrubbed the season's scheduled
final game and the make-up, played a week later, saw the two teams
sloshing around in wet snow and water, pretty much between the
twenty-yard lines. Eventually we lost, 6 – 0, on a last-minute blocked
punt. Something about "character-building," as I recall.

My American Junior Red Cross "job" required me to visit the
region's high schools and talk about the AJRC's philanthropic work
in Western Europe. Most of the high school kids, and their teachers,
knew little or nothing about the program, so I found myself in
the role of a sort-of salesman. The schools would arrange for large

groups to hear my talks and, like it or not, I had to get used to "public speaking" in front of audiences I had never seen before. It was good practice and I like to think I made a small difference in the understanding of the real hardships kids were experiencing in Europe.

My senior year at Sumner High ended in June 1947 and I was pretty excited at the prospect of entering the University of Washington, in just a few more months. But first, I had to attend one more AJRC convention, this one in Cleveland, Ohio.

That experience produced two surprises that I've never forgotten.

The organizers arranged for the many hundreds of convention goers, kids from all over the country, to hear talks by Bob Feller and Lou Boudreau, the two best-known players on the Cleveland Indians' baseball team. Both of these men were heroes to any kid who loved baseball, as I did. Boudreau would be named the American League's MVP the following year and Bob "Rapid Robert" Feller already was a legend in his own time.

The other surprise really caught me off guard. The AJRC's adult leaders, who really ran the convention behind-the-scenes, asked me to give the plenary session's main address. In it I would review all the work that the AJRC had been doing in Europe since the end of WW II. I had one evening to prepare my talk and I'd be lying to say I wasn't a bit nervous, standing in front of a microphone and speaking to all those young people.

However, there was a serious downside to my AJRC experience and that came about four years later. While at the University of Washington, I had stayed in touch with some of the kids I had befriended at the two conventions and, especially, with the program's adult leaders. These were the most influential adults I had yet come to know, outside my own family and some of my college professors. But when I went to Washington, DC, the Headquarters city of the American Red Cross and its AJRC affiliate, my new job with the CIA required that I go "under cover" and not reveal my real employment to anyone. As I thought about this, I could not bring myself to "fib" to these men, so I just dropped out of sight and never contacted them again, even though they were just a phone call away. I've always felt a bit uneasy about that.

It was during that summer of 1947 that I first met Betty Jean Cleaver. Her older sister, Shirley, was just a year behind me in high school, Betty Jean (BJ, as she would become known as an adult) two years further back. She was 14 at the time, I was 17; at that age, a huge difference.

Shirley was a very attractive girl and a popular student. She had lovely blonde hair and a dazzling smile. She was part of the school's newspaper staff and one day she asked me if I would be willing to sit for an interview. By that time I had been elected ASB president for the 1946–47 school year and she wanted an "inside story."

Thinking back on it, I believe it was that interview that persuaded Shirley that I should meet her little sister. But before that happened, Shirley had offered to teach me to dance. She was a very good dancer and she knew that I was not. So we met at the kids' recreation hall, located on Sumner's Main Street, and spent a few evenings on the dance floor. As all kids do, we talked about what interested us most, usually other kids, who is dating whom, etc.

I don't remember this for certain but I would bet a lot of money that it was during one of those "dance-lesson" chats that I told Shirley about my "life-long" (about 10 years, to that time) love affair with Joan Kohl. And I'm just as sure that Shirley passed this "news" to Betty Jean.

Toward the end of that summer, Shirley telephoned me—she was not shy—and asked if I'd like to meet her sister. I agreed, not knowing exactly where this was going because I was only vaguely aware of Betty Jean's existence. At that time she was visiting an aunt who lived in Auburn, just ten miles north of Sumner, so I borrowed my dad's car and found the aunt's home. Of course Betty Jean knew I was coming and we took a long walk along a wooded path, sort of a getting-to-know you conversation. I quickly learned that she was a cute kid, maybe a little bit shy in the company of this big-shot-about-to-go-to-college guy, but charmingly pleasant. We got along, liked each other, and I asked her for a date.

We dated several times that summer, before I went off to the U-Dub and we wrote a few letters back and forth. But as I became involved in my fraternity house and my studies, BJ slowly slipped into the background. What I didn't realize at the time was that she had fallen in love with me. She may have been only 14 but it was a love that was to last a very long time.

Chapter 3

The U-Dub

In Fall 1947, I enrolled in the University of Washington's Arts and Sciences department, declaring a "pre-major," which meant that I was still unsure about what courses I wanted to take and, for that matter, about my future. I knew my father wanted me eventually to become a lawyer, as he was, but he never expressed this wish to me, having decided I should choose my future without a lot of influence from him.

I had received good grades in high school but like all entering freshmen I was required to take an entrance exam. (This was before the SAT tests that high school kids now prepare for.) As it happened, that entrance exam took place in a large auditorium on a very warm September afternoon. The auditorium's windows were wide open and I was sitting next to one of them. About two minutes into the exam a bee stung me on my upper leg and the pain was severe. I had no way to "fix" the situation but that bee certainly messed up my test-taking.

About a week later, when I reviewed the test scores with my counselor, he told me that based on the test results I would probably have a tough time in most of my classes and did I really want to stay in school? I wasn't about to alibi about my bee sting and decided to do the best I could, poor test scores or not.

I had already pledged the Zeta Psi fraternity and was assigned to room with a returned World War II veteran. There were many of these much-more-mature men enrolled at the university and my being able to live with one of these men for three months was one of the highlights of my university experience. Stan Reece taught me more about the things a young guy should know than I could have imagined possible, beginning with how to tuck my shirt into my pants before going out in public.

Stan also was a stickler for making wise use of study time and he brooked no foolishness from me during study hours, seven to ten each week-day evening. We both had our noses in our books and, as our room was at the end of one of the hallways, we soon acquired a reputation, among our fraternity brothers, as "the quiet ones."

This discipline paid off. In those days the university had a policy which required that a student's grade sheet be sent to his/her parents, rather than directly to the student. In the case of a fraternity-member student, the university knew that each fraternity had a study chairman and that the fraternity's freshmen would be "graded," each freshman's grades tallied and the "house average" published in the campus newspaper. This put pressure, wisely intended by the university's leaders, on each fraternity to make sure that its entering freshmen paid attention and studied hard.

When my grade sheet reached the fraternity's study chairman, he was pleasantly surprised to see that I had a four-point-oh grade sheet, "A's" in each of my five classes. I realized then that there was "nowhere to go but downhill," but it seemed logical enough that I continue to try to do the best I could. My dad was footing the bill and I owed him, and my mom, my best efforts.

My entrance exam bee-sting test results notwithstanding, I was invited to take a "competence test" in the English language. Every entering freshman understood that the university insisted he/she take some kind of English language course. There were three levels, "bone-head," standard and advanced. About ninety percent of the freshmen took the standard course, a few unfortunates the "bone-head" version, and a few the advanced. Apparently my high-school public speaking experiences qualified me for the advanced English course.

I mention this only because the advanced class to which I was assigned was taught by an instructor who eventually was fired by the university for his pro-Communist views. I think that most of the students in this class were as naive about international politics as I was, at that time. Over a period of several months the instructor had us believing that Joseph Stalin—who was alive and well at the time and still very much in charge of the Soviet Union—was really a pretty nice guy, doing good things for his mostly-peasant countrymen. At that time the world had yet to learn of the purges, Stalin's murderous assault on his own military officer corps and his other evil deeds.

One of the assignments in this advanced-English class required that each student give a speech, on whatever topic he or she chose, to demonstrate what we had learned in the class. Each speech was recorded, taking advantage of the then-new technology that made it possible to record speeches in a classroom.

I've long since forgotten the particulars of my speech, but I do remember giving the recording to my mother who, after listening to it, was aghast at what her young son was learning at the university. She never played it back to me but she did ask me if I really believed what I was being taught about world Communism.

That experience—it happened during the second quarter of my freshman year—may have been a blessing in disguise.

While I was still in high school, in 1946, I learned of Winston Churchill's famous "Iron Curtain" speech, delivered at Westminster College in Fulton, Missouri. Churchill described in vivid detail what had happened since the end of World War II, just one year earlier, how the Soviet Union had indeed built an "Iron Curtain" between itself and the rest of the world. Churchill's message stuck in my mind and when I had finished my advanced English class, just 18 months later, it seemed to me that, given what Churchill had said, the United

States would be either fighting with or, one would hope, trading with the Soviet Union.

It was then that the light bulb came on: Why not study the Russian language, Russian culture and history and be prepared to "participate" in America's future with the Soviet Union, as either friend or foe?

I asked my advanced-English (pro Communist) instructor: Where/how would I be able to learn the Russian language? He may have believed he had a "convert" in his class, and he told me how to reach the university's Russian language department, of which I knew nothing.

A few days later I was in the office of the head of the Russian language department, a man named Gershevsky who had escaped from the Soviet Union, via China, during World War II. He told me that his language-teacher staff included five former Soviet citizens, each of them sharing a similar experience, escaping Soviet communism for a life of freedom in the West. His department would be happy to have me become one of its students.

Thus encouraged, I enrolled in the university's Russian-language school. It was purposefully an intensive course, ten hour-credits each quarter. That meant two hours of Russian language each morning, plus one other class, for as long as I wanted to stick it out.

And stick it out I did, eventually accumulating sixty hours of Russian language training. The last course included translating into English articles from *Pravda* and *Izvestia*, the two principal "news" sources in the Soviet Union. In Russian, "Pravda" means "truth," and "Izvestia" means "news." The usual joke was that neither of them contained either.

Part of my Russian-language training included an opportunity to live in the on-campus "Russia House," which was really a few rooms in the women's dormitory building that had been set aside for this purpose. Six of us chose to do this, so I moved out of my fraternity house, just for the summer, and lived with the other Russian language students. Several of our language-school instructors came to the "house" each day and we tried to do all of our speaking in Russian.

It was awkward, to be sure, but it certainly helped us to get a feel for the real thing, "spoken" Russian.

It was during this summer that I met Colleen Wolfe, she also a Russian language student. Colleen, a year later, would become president of the Sigma Kappa sorority, at the same that I was elected president of my Zeta Psi fraternity. The two houses already had connections because a couple of Zetes were engaged to women at the Sigma Kappa house, so it was natural enough that Colleen and I became "an item."

Early on, after our first date or two, Colleen told me that she had been in love with, and engaged to, a university student. He was a member of the Chi Psi fraternity, right next door to Colleen's Sigma Kappa house. Soon after war broke out in Korea he was sent there, I believe as a naval aviator, and was killed in action. Colleen's grief by now had passed but she made it clear to me that her former fiancé would always be "number one" in her heart.

I received this news with a kind of inward satisfaction because— and I told Colleen this—Joan Kohl already was "number one" in my heart, even though we had never had a date, that I had been in love with her for many long years and, implied, it would be unlikely that Colleen could ever "replace" her.

So Colleen and I solidified our romance with a kind of mutual understanding about our "private loves," hers past and mine on-going, that in the future should best go unmentioned.

Speaking of Joan, at that time I was totally unaware of her presence at the university and had not heard from or about her for more than three years. She had dropped off my "radar screen" after moving to Tacoma for her senior year at Stadium High School. Little did I know that she had been enrolled in the university's art department, taking courses in painting, sculpture, art history and many other things. To make the irony even deeper, Joan had pledged the Alpha Phi sorority, as a freshman, and her sorority house was situated no more than three hundred feet from my fraternity house, on the same street. Yet we never ran into each other because her walk to her classes took her by a different route than did mine to my classes.

Every fraternity and sorority house at the U-Dub had an aggressive social program, most of them designed to make it easier for their young men and women to meet one another. (I had heard, while in high school, that that was the reason most young women went to college, to find a smart young guy to marry.) The Zetes, like all the other fraternities, arranged "exchanges" with the other sorority houses, usually after-dinner get-togethers where the guys would swarm all over the sorority house to which they had been invited. I had had no reason to wonder why the Zetes hadn't arranged an exchange with the nearby Alpha Phi house because I didn't know that "my" Joan had been living there for the past two-plus years.

Then, one evening, it was the Zetes' turn to "exchange" with the Alpha Phis. I walked into the living room and could hardly believe my eyes: There was Joan, more beautiful than ever, sitting on a couch. She was as surprised as I and I had to resist the instant urge to throw my arms around her. We had a wonderful "catching-up" chat and she agreed to go out with me, our first-ever date. Finally, that obstacle had been overcome!

I honestly don't remember what we did on our date, but because neither of us had a car we probably walked to a near-by movie theater, had a Coke and then walked back to the campus. What I do remember, in spades, is that she let me kiss her good night on the steps of her sorority house. Wow, two "barriers" broken within a week's time!

Although I was elated at my good fortune to have "found" Joan, I could not be sure, then, that we were really the kind of match that would last. Joan was very close to her family and had shared many heartaches with them. Would she *really* be happy with a husband who likely would take her as far away as Washington, DC and probably to far-off foreign lands?

Colleen, I knew, was anxious to get away. She knew that my

Russian language training (and hers, too) had prepared us for unknown but exciting overseas adventures. So that even though in my heart of hearts my feelings for Joan were so very strong, I concluded that I had best not try to win her love. It was the toughest decision I had made up to that point in my young life.

But Joan and I had one more "date" while we were at the university. She and I, as high school classmates, were invited to an informal gathering at the home of one of our Class of 1947 friends. I had agreed to drive Joan home after the party—I had borrowed my dad's car for the occasion—and when we got there we sat in the car and talked for a long time. By then, she was pretty well committed to her eventual husband Cliff Johnson and I was on my way to marrying Colleen. So we agreed that we were on separate paths, even though we were the best of friends. I kissed Joan again that evening, as far as I knew then it was a farewell kiss. She would tell me many years later it was the sweetest kiss she could remember.

Of course my four years at the university included much more than Russian language immersion. I was enrolled in the Political Science department and took courses in constitutional law, international trade, Soviet/Russian history, Russian geography, American political history and economics. The university required all its students to take at least two courses in the "hard sciences," and since I had already studied chemistry and physics in high school, I chose astronomy and meteorology.

The astronomy class was one I've never forgotten. I took it in winter quarter and chose for my term paper to do a "tracking" of the moon's elliptic, its path through the night sky. To do this, I stood on the fire escape of my fraternity house, two floors above the ground and facing south, and sketched the moon's position each week, for three winter months. Sometimes it was too cold to remain outside for long but my paper eventually earned me an "A" for the course.

My other "hard science" course was in meteorology. Growing up in the Pacific Northwest gives anyone an opportunity to be curious about weather, as unpredictable as it often is. Little did I suspect it at the time, but this training would become very useful, only a few years later, when balloon flight became a major part of my life in the CIA.

Graduation from the University of Washington in Spring 1951 was uneventful and not especially memorable, except that I did manage to achieve a 3.5-plus grade point average and the Phi Beta Kappa key that came with it. That academic record, including my sixty hours of Russian language experience, would help a great deal when I applied for work with the Central Intelligence Agency.

Part Two – The CIA Rookie

Chapter 4

Getting Started

When I moved my small family from Arlington, Virginia to far-off Tehran, Iran, in April 1955, I had already been working for three-plus years in the Near East branch of the Soviet Division of CIA's Clandestine Service. As a lowly desk officer, I had learned a lot about our operations program in Iran, some of it in pretty good shape, some not.

The CIA's Soviet Division ("SR," in the vernacular of that period) was one of several "area divisions," as one might expect, covering the globe: Near East, Far East, Eastern Europe, Europe, South America, Africa. An assignment to SR was considered a pretty good deal because the Soviet Union, after all, was our country's greatest threat. And, it should go without saying, there was tremendous pressure on the Division to "do something, anything" to help the president and his national security team steer a course short of war or the serious threat thereof.

It was only seven years later, in October 1962, that the world trembled for a week or so during the Cuban Missile Crisis, when war with the Soviet Union seemed an all-too-likely possibility. We'll talk later about my involvement during that scary time.

Within the Division, there were other area branches, in addition
to my Near East branch: Baltic, Far East, Eastern Europe, those
regions surrounding the Soviet Union. And throughout all the
divisions of the Clandestine Service, there was something we called
compartmentalization: You were not supposed to know, or try to
find out, what was happening down the hall or even next door, if
what was going on belonged to another branch. The idea was that if a
CIA officer got into trouble or, worse, decided to quit and talk to the
press, or worse yet, defected to a foreign power, his/her knowledge
would be limited to only that acquired in the course of normal work
responsibilities.

That was fine with me. I can be as curious as the next guy, but
not in those circumstances. Besides, I had more than enough to do
without wondering what "down the hall" was up to. In fact, my
colleagues and I put in a lot of overtime in those days, trying to keep
up with the work load.

I remember well my first few days on the job, right after I entered
on duty on September 24, 1951. Every CIA person I ever knew
remembered his/her EOD date.

I was to report to a several-months-long training program, but
until the next cycle was ready for me, my branch chief put me to
work poring over World War II aerial photographs of the Soviet
Union, looking for possible drop zones for the agents we hoped to
parachute into the country. My area was limited to the Georgian and
Armenian republics, because the Division believed its aircraft could
fly north from Turkey, reach a drop zone in one of those areas and
have enough fuel to get back safely to base. By doing it that way,
the aircraft would be over Soviet airspace for only a few minutes
and could probably avoid being intercepted by Soviet fighter planes
stationed at one of their military airfields. And this was a safer route,
probably, than flying from somewhere in Western Europe, over
Eastern Europe, to reach Soviet air space.

What fascinated me most about this job—remember, my very
first work for the Agency—was that the maps I was using had been
taken by WWII American aerial reconnaissance cameras so that they

overlapped and when I examined them through a three-dimension viewfinder, the "ground" seemed to jump right off the photo's surface. Pretty heady stuff for a twenty-one year old green horn! And they were detailed enough, I seem to recall, that I could see on-the-ground details such as gravel pits, clearings in the woods, crop lands and such.

My branch chief knew a lot more about this than I did and he briefed me carefully on what a drop zone should look like: proximity to roads, not too close to populated places, away from likely power lines, no rivers or streams for the agent to cross while quickly leaving the DZ; common-sense things like that.

Eventually I found what seemed to me to be two or three acceptable DZs and my boss agreed that they were okay. So we sent that information to the appropriate field station, knowing that they would look just as carefully as we had. This was my first up-front exposure to compartmentalization: I never learned if my work was used in a real overflight operation. I learned a good lesson from that experience: A lot of effort goes into the planning and execution of any clandestine operation and its contributors often, maybe usually, never have the satisfaction of knowing if their work has paid off.

Early in my assignment to the branch, my chief told me an interesting, and personal, "what if?" story. When my application for employment was circulated through the Division, this same branch thought I would be a good candidate to send to a small Near East city situated within 150 miles of the Soviet border. This was before the interview with one of the branch officers, detailed below, which revealed my intent to marry just before going to work for the Agency. But, as a brand-new recruit, my pay grade was not high enough to support the transportation and funding of dependents, even a new bride, so my assignment to that place never materialized. The "what if" part of this tale, of course, is how my career might have progressed had I signed on with the CIA as a young bachelor. With 20-20 hindsight I'm glad things happened as they did.

While doing this very interesting work with aerial photographs, my branch chief introduced me to some of the grunt work expected of all new recruits: running name traces.

One of the largest, and most important, divisions in the Clandestine Service was RID, the Records Integration Division. In the 1950s, this division occupied a huge amount of space in one of the old World War I "temporary" buildings in Washington, DC, strung along the southern edge of the Reflecting Pool, just east of the Lincoln Memorial.

Running a name trace seemed to me, at that time, to be pretty boring because the names being "traced," in most cases, had nothing to do with the work I was involved with. But it was a cardinal rule that no person would be considered for operational use, or for any kind of discussion, without first being traced. The Agency insisted on this procedure not only for security reasons, to see if the person had already come to the attention of the police or security forces, anywhere in the world, but to generally understand who the person was, his/her background, associates and all the rest.

Names of people, from all over the world, were constantly pouring into the area divisions as the Agency in those days gradually expanded its operational reach. Of course many times a name would pop up that was exactly the same as another name already in RID's massive file system. So it helped a great deal if that name came along with a DOB, date of birth; even better, DPOB, date and place of birth.

The importance of this name tracing procedure hit home, indelibly, one day when I was involved in a discussion about a name that had just come in from one of our field stations. I've long forgotten the specifics, but my boss asked me if I had run a trace on the name. I had not yet had time to do it but nonetheless received a good chewing out for my oversight. I think the boss knew what he was doing for this rookie, me, because I never again forgot about name tracing.

After a month or so of this kind of "desk work," I went off to the training program that I knew was ahead of me. For the first time I found myself in a large classroom with perhaps 30 other newbees, men, and a few women, who were, like me, brand new to the CIA and its Clandestine Service. I discovered almost immediately that these were very sharp people, a few of them wearing their Phi Beta Kappa keys, a bit too conspicuously I thought, having one myself that I rarely displayed.

Most of the instructors, all of whom belonged to the Office of Training, had served during World War Two in the OSS, the Office of Strategic Services, at one time under the leadership of "Wild Bill" Donovan, a legend in his own time. These instructors really knew what they were talking about, each one of them having been involved in wartime operations of one kind or another. Some of them had returned recently from overseas assignments with one of the area divisions, others had come from other assignments.

For me the curriculum was a fascinating one. We learned about "tradecraft," a term that covers many sins in the spook business: The art—and it really is an art—of spotting and assessing a potential agent, how a CIA officer knows what to look for and how he/she then decides if that person is likely to be willing to work for the CIA and if so, what kind of agent he/she is likely to become? Clearly, simply being willing is not enough.

That approach assumes the person being spotted and assessed knows that the CIA is the recruiter. Another kind of recruitment— much more difficult, as we learned—is known as the "false flag" recruitment, wherein the targeted agent is purposely led to believe that he/she is being pursued by another government, or in some cases a non-governmental entity of some kind. Anything to conceal the CIA's hand in the recruitment. This is one of the several reasons the Clandestine Service was/still is referred to, by its detractors, as the "Department of Dirty Tricks."

We were taught the how-tos of writing classified reports, much more to it than one might expect to have learned in a college English writing class. Clarity and brevity, to be sure, but much more. For one thing, we learned about EEI's, the essential elements of information. When writing reports, the author must assume that his/her reader, sometimes down the hall, often in a far-away CIA field station, is a very busy person, usually at a higher grade level than the writer. So be brief, clear, get the subject matter out in front and then back up what you have to say with facts, figures, whatever you need to make your case. Just because your report may need to be classified Secret or even Top Secret, don't believe for a minute that that makes any difference. You must assume that anyone, even the director of the Clandestine Service, might for some reason you never expected read what you have written.

The cardinal rule above all others: When writing any report, think for a moment if what you have to say describes a potential or actual threat to the safety and security of the United States.

With that in mind, we were taught how to decide what kind of urgency we should assign to each report: Routine, Priority, Operational Immediate, and Flash. These assigned priorities were essential in order for the Agency's communication center to know how quickly to process, and deliver, the thousands of pieces of "mail" that it handled every day.

The training program's curriculum included a number of other tools of the trade. Some of us elected to learn about photography, how to take good pictures with the then-available 35 millimeter cameras. We learned how to work in a dark room, how to develop and print our own film. Obviously, dark rooms are not available to a case officer working in many environments in the field, so we learned how to use a "dark bag," how to develop film without being able to see it, then dry it and print it, or, sometimes, send it to Headquarters as a developed strip film. (I used that technique, eventually, in a successful aerial photo operation in Tehran, the subject of another chapter in this book.)

Secret writing was another thing about which we learned. How to put a message into an innocuous letter, assuming a hostile intelligence service might intercept that letter and read it. There were a number of ways to use SW, a simple weak solution of lemon juice and water being the easiest to use, and the easiest to detect. When heated, the paper immediately shows the writing, so this technique was used only as a training tool. There were other, much more difficult-to-detect methods. In all my years with the Agency I never was in a position to use SW but I did have occasion to teach it to others.

Coded, or encrypted, communications was another topic, of great use to me, eventually, because I was assigned the onerous job of using a one-time-pad (OTP) at our station in Moscow. The system is a very old one, known to every intelligence service in the world, but if used correctly it is virtually impossible to break. The one time pad contains many pages, each with a series of randomly-selected letters, five letters to a group. Above each of these letters, the to-be-encoded message's letters are inscribed and those two letters are two legs of the "triad," the third being one of the twenty-six letters in the English alphabet. I eventually memorized these twenty-six combinations which made using an OTP much quicker and a lot more satisfying.

Today, of course, all of this encoding and decoding is done by computer, is lightning fast, and no one thinks much about it. But in the 1950s, 60s and 70s it was still a big deal and any intelligence officer worth his salt needed to know about it.

Agent Communications was another part of our training curriculum. How to safely and securely communicate with someone who, often times, has agreed to betray his own country to help the CIA learn whatever it is that the agent knows.

There are many ways to communicate, of course, but most of them won't work for a person who has already taken this risk. The chief principle is to avoid linking the agent with the Agency in any way that might reveal the relationship to someone not already in the loop.

My branch chief gave me some on-the-job training in this kind of work. The Near East branch had on its payroll two young men who were not allowed to come into the CIA buildings. They had been hired for especially sensitive assignments and the Agency wanted to do everything possible to avoid their being connected. Being seen coming to work in one of those "temporary" buildings along the Reflecting Pool, for example, was a sure way to be linked to the Agency.

So my job was to meet with these two men, separately of course, as they did not know each other, and arrange a communications link with each of them. The first thing to be "communicated" would be their monthly pay envelope, a check written on a local bank, not attributable to the Agency. I remember seeing some raised eyebrows when I first discussed this arrangement, but they understood and in any case they had no choice in the matter.

The communication method was to be a "dead drop," one of the oldest known ways of linking to an agent. In this case, I instructed each man to go to a certain public rest room, at a certain time, and retrieve his pay envelope which would be taped to the underside of a specific wash basin. The timing was important and this taught these new employees something about punctuality. I would place the taped envelope myself at a certain time but neither I nor the "payee" wanted that envelope to be there any longer than necessary, nor did I want to be seen by either of them, again avoiding contact with me in a public place.

I've forgotten how long these two men received their monthly paychecks in this way, but long enough to have given both of them, and me, something to remember about being careful, being punctual, and trusting each other.

Surveillance was another big item in the training curriculum. The simple act of following someone, as everyone knows, is as old as humanity. But in the intelligence business, it is best to learn how to do it without "the rabbit" becoming aware. This is not as simple as it might seem, when on foot. It is even more difficult when in a moving vehicle.

When I was stationed in Moscow, in the 1960s, every American who worked in our embassy was followed, some frequently, others sporadically, by the KGB "goons" who were assigned this boring task. In that environment, however, it was very important that we knew how to evade a surveillant without him/her being aware of what had happened. It was crucial, if we were about to meet an agent, in that hostile environment, that the "tails" never saw the person we needed to contact. It was quite literally a life-or-death event. It required very specialized training, later in my career, to perfect this essential skill.

What was probably my most unusual "training" experience began in the Agency's cafeteria. The cafeteria was a huge dining area, with many tables and a natural place in which to meet CIA officers who worked in other divisions, men and women I would have no reason to get to know or know about.

At one of these lunch "bull-sessions," where people talk about what's going on in their lives, I learned about a training program that was being sponsored by another division but that was open to anyone who wanted to apply. The two guys who were talking about it used the words "E and E," as in "evasion and escape." What in the world is *that?*, I wondered.

They explained that during World War II and more recently in the Korean War, too many American Air Force personnel found themselves on the wrong side of the enemy's lines, usually because they had been forced to bail out of their aircraft. Most of them had survived the parachute jump but too often had been captured while trying to walk back to their own units. And after their capture they were interrogated, sometimes roughly, where the Geneva Convention rules were never in play.

Thus, "evading" this kind of treatment and "escaping" back to friendly territory had become an important idea in the minds of those responsible for training CIA's young officers. Even though the officer himself might never face such an ordeal, it would be good for him to know how to teach the fundamentals of "E and E" to someone else, say an agent who might be tasked to go behind enemy lines.

After hearing all this at the lunch table, I thought about my upcoming assignment to Tehran and decided that "E and E" training would be a good thing to add to my "resumé." I found the telephone number of the officer who had told me about this and asked him how I could apply for the training. He described the application procedure and I then prepared an official request. This, of course, had to be approved by my division chief who, I soon learned, was unaware of the program. When the application landed on his desk he called me to his office and asked me what kind of "boondoggle" was I thinking about, going out to Idaho to "play in the snow," as he put it.

I wasn't accustomed to standing in front of the division chief's desk, all by myself, and responding to such a direct question. But I thought I detected in his question a sincere interest in the program and so I explained it to him as best I could: In Iran I might be required to know some of this stuff, to teach it to others, and the training in Idaho's mountains would likely be about as realistic as any training could be. The division chief smiled, signed the application and asked me to tell him "all about it" when I returned.

A few weeks later I found myself at an abandoned U.S. military base, not far from McCall, Idaho. It was mid-November and an early-winter storm already had blanketed the nearby Sawtooth Mountains in deep powder snow. When the trainees, about 30 of us, got together for our indoctrination, our instructors pointed to the snow-covered mountains and told us they would be our home for the next week. The instructors were outdoor-savvy guys, each with a number of years in the U.S. Air Force, now retired from active military duty and working for the Agency. One of them was an expert on bears and he told us about bear habits in the Sawtooth Mountains. There were a few Grizzlies, he said, but mostly Black Bears who would avoid us. As it was November, there would be no danger from mother bears with cubs. Still, he warned, when walking into the wind, make enough noise to be heard. With the wind at your back, he explained, the bear will catch your scent and be long gone.

Our instructors then explained what the training would try to simulate, to make our evasion and escape experience as realistic as the climate and terrain would permit.

When an airman is required to leave his aircraft, either after a crash landing or, more likely, by escaping with his parachute, he finds himself on the ground with a survival kit (part of his parachute pack) and his parachute. With those bare necessities he will be expected to try to get back to friendly territory, eventually to rejoin his unit.

The instructors then told us about the contents of a standard survival kit: a G-I aluminum mess kit, a shiny metal signal mirror, a pocket knife, a small compass and flashlight, some freeze-dried fruit and several bars of pemmican. And then there is the parachute. The nylon canopy can be cut into pieces, to serve as a tent and/or a wrap-around "blanket," if the weather is cold enough to require extra warmth at night. The hundreds of feet of parachute cord will have many uses, not the least of which is to make bindings and cross-hatches for the snow shoes we trainees will fashion from pine boughs.

We were shown how to use the small-diameter nylon filaments from the parachute cord to fashion snares, how to stomp out a "rabbit run" in the snow, how to bait a deer trap.

The instructors then moved their attention to the "escape" part of the evasion and escape training. Evasion, if successful, means only that one has evaded capture. Escape is another matter. Every Iron Curtain country's frontier is guarded by a fence, usually patrolled at night by armed sentries, often accompanied by dogs. An American who is apprehended while trying to escape through that fence is certain to be regarded a threat and then interrogated by his captors. While the Geneva Convention requires such a "prisoner" to reveal only his name, rank and serial number, the world knows that hostile interrogators pay it little heed.

Before we trainees were sent off into the snow-covered foothills of the Sawtooth Range, we were given some words of encouragement, and incentive: Any trainee who managed to escape, at the end of the training exercise, would be allowed to listen in to the interrogations of those not so fortunate. Those instructors were clever: No trainee would want his buddies to listen to him squirm in an interrogation room but every trainee would welcome the chance to listen.

Early the next morning our instructors marched us as far into the forest as they dared, single file and over a route designed to confuse us. When the instructors left, after telling us we were on our own for the next three days, our first task was obvious enough: Make a pair of snowshoes and then figure out which way is "back home." Most of us had remembered to check our compasses but, failing that, it seemed logical enough that "home" had to be "downhill," following the several creeks that would lead back to McCall, or close to it. We also knew, however, that somewhere between "here" and "home" we would run into a fence, patrolled by guards and dogs. This would require some stealth and planning.

One of the young officers in our group of 30—I'll call him Jack—was from my Division at CIA Headquarters. We had not known each other prior to meeting in McCall but decided we might as well consider ourselves a two-man team, to look out for each other if the "survival" part of the training should become more than we wanted to handle alone. This partnership paid off almost immediately: Neither Jack nor I had ever tried to make a pair of snowshoes out of parachute cord and pine boughs. Finding the right kind of bough was not so simple; most of them broke in half before they could be doubled back to form the necessary "loop." We both had been Boy Scouts, so it was easy enough to use the right kind of knots to tie the parachute cord in its criss-cross pattern. We discovered almost immediately that binding the snowshoes to our boots was no easy trick; it was, for sure, a two-man job. Then, walking on these improvised snow shoes required some practice. Soon enough, Jack and I were among the first of our group to "master" our new-found skill and we went plodding off through the snow, listening to a few cat-calls from our friends still struggling behind.

We spent our first night under a hastily-rigged tent, part of one of the two parachutes we had been issued by our instructors. We pitched the tent under a large pine tree, on a patch of bare ground. Our instructors had told us how to make a bough bed, something Jack and I remembered from our scouting days, and it was a good thing, too, as the ground was damp and lumpy and we did not have sleeping bags, just the parachute material. I kidded Jack, as he lay there before going to sleep: He looked like a mummy.

The next morning, we awoke to nearly-empty stomachs. Our

instructors had issued us not quite enough pemmican to get us through our time in the woods. They expected us to try to "live off the land" and that meant catching, cleaning, cooking and then eating either a squirrel or a rabbit. Jack and I had read a few of Jack London's stories about this kind of "outdoor life," but we quickly discovered that the real thing was something else. Jack was determined to succeed and he set out a snare near the base of a pine tree in which he had spotted a squirrel. While I was away from our camp, trying to determine the best escape route, Jack's snare did its job. When I returned an hour or so later, there was Jack, roasting "his" squirrel over a small fire.

Our GI mess kits contained small amounts of salt and pepper, with which we would season Jack's roasted squirrel. We both had to admit that that "meal" was probably the worst either of us would ever eat: tough, stringy and virtually without flavor. The pemmican and dried fruit saved the day, as it would for the remainder of the exercise.

Our last day in the woods brought us close enough to the fence that we could hear the barking of one of the guard dogs. There was enough cover that we could see the fence without being seen by the uniformed sentry. We noticed that he was dressed in a Soviet militia man's uniform, something we had not expected, and he was carrying a rifle, adding even more realism to our exercise. Jack and I timed the guard's movements, figuring we would have at least five minutes to work our way through the fence without being seen or, we hoped, smelled by the dog. We decided to wait for nightfall, early enough in November. It would be a moonless night, another advantage.

While we were waiting we heard, barely, a commotion going on a few hundred yards away, probably along the same fence. It seemed certain that one or more of our trainee-colleagues had just been captured while trying to cross the fence. Without saying a word to each other, Jack and I determined we would not meet that same fate.

Our immediate problem, when it became dark enough to make our escape, was to get close enough to the fence to be sure of the sentry's pattern. Fortunately, only a slight breeze was blowing and it was coming toward us, so the dog likely would not catch our scent. As soon as the sentry and his dog had moved about 100 yards away from us we made our move. The fence was made of tightly-strung barbed wire, its strands about eight inches apart. It was too tall to scale so we skidded under the bottom strand, taking turns stretching the wire far enough above the snow-covered ground. We realized that when the sentry returned he would see our skid marks in the snow but we had been told earlier by our instructors that once beyond that fence we were to consider ourselves "home free."

And home free we were. We used our flashlights to follow a road that led from the fence to a small cabin. Inside the cabin, enjoying their beer and pretzels, we found our instructors and two other trainees who had just escaped. When the exercise was over we learned that of the 30 trainees, only Jack and I and the two others had made it through the fence without being caught.

Our instructors asked us if we would care to go next door to listen to one of the ongoing interrogation sessions. We decided to decline the invitation and, instead, to take a nap.

The next day, back in one of McCall's modest motels, I had my first shave in more than a week, and a hot shower. The "boondoggle" was over. A day or two after returning to Headquarters I visited my division chief and told him all about it. He agreed: It was an experience that likely would be one of the most memorable of my CIA career.

After I finished the prescribed training curriculum, I returned to my branch and did a brief stint in the United States Navy, to meet my Selective Service obligation. From there I returned to the same group of young officers and awaited my turn to go overseas. That was where the action was, and the eventual promotions, as everyone knew. It was time to reflect on how I became a CIA officer, not all that long ago.

When I first applied for employment with the CIA, in 1950 and as a wet-behind-the ears junior at the University of Washington, I had only a small inkling of what I was about to get into. Several of my fraternity brothers were recently-returned veterans from World War II and they knew about my Russian language studies and my interest in the Soviet Union. One of them had been with the OSS and he suggested that I would do well in the "intelligence business." So I wrote a letter to the "Office of Intelligence" in Washington, DC, not even knowing the CIA's official name.

A few months later I returned to the Zete house from one of my on-campus classes and to my surprise found a man waiting for me in my room. He introduced himself and told me he knew of my application for employment and wanted to talk to me about it. We had a very pleasant conversation and I learned that he, too, had learned Russian at the university some years earlier. He was serving in the SR Division and, as I later decided, the Division had asked him to look me over. Nothing like an "eyeball" assessment of a would-be CIA recruit! And while he was waiting for me in my room he spotted on my desk a photograph of my fiancée she, too, a Russian language student. He told me that at one time he had wanted to marry her, but for reasons he never gave, decided not to ask her.

As I look back on these events, they seem an unlikely prelude to a career that eventually spanned more than a half-century. As I have told many friends about my career, I cannot remember a single day in which I did not look forward to the work ahead. Not many can honestly say that.

Part Three – Overseas at Last, Tehran

Chapter 5

J.A.

I first met John Aalto when I stepped off a Pan American 707 at Tehran's Mehrebad Airport, in late summer 1958, returning for my second tour, having arrived there, the first time, in April 1955. My family was with me, all three of them, my wife Colleen and our two kids, Scott and Mike. Mike was born in the American military hospital there, the year before, in October 1957, Scott in the naval hospital at Bethesda, Maryland, in December 1954, just three months before we flew off to Iran to work there for the next five years for the CIA.

As I look back on this event, I have to admit to a rather audacious attitude about travel. Colleen and I had decided, while we were in the States on home leave between tours in Tehran, that our kids should have a swing set, something beyond imagination in any of Tehran's bazaars or shops. So we bought one, at Sears, and had them box it and label it for shipment to me. It qualified as "excess baggage" and so the government paid for its shipment, just as though it were an odd-shaped suitcase. It arrived on the same Pan American 707 with us, but almost beyond recognition, tied together with (probably) German (stopover) twine, but all the pieces were there, long blue steel pipes and yellow swing seats, waiting for me to put it all together, in the front yard of our home in suburban Tehran.

John Aalto had arrived in Tehran while I was on home leave and he already had been assigned to our Soviet operations section, as was I. To avoid the confusion of having two "Johns" in the same group, he came to be known as "JA." I, of course, was "JS."

John was waiting at the bottom of the PanAm jet's stairway. No jetways in those days, certainly not in almost-pre-historic Tehran. He greeted us with a huge smile and a Texas "Howdy." His own family, wife and three kids, one younger even than Mike, little Tommy, were close behind. So the nine of us had a kind of family welcoming party right there on the blistering summertime tarmac at Iran's one and only international airport. A pretty good beginning for a friendship that still, today, more than fifty years later, is as strong as ever.

JA had a vehicle waiting for us, something spacious enough to haul the Sager family, plus the swing set, to our already-waiting home on *Kutche Sheybani*, about half way up the "hill" from Tehran's simmering capital toward the much cooler hills beneath Mount Tochal. (*Kutche* is the word, in Farsi, for a small street, or alleyway.)

Tehran lies at the southern base of the Elburz mountains, most of the city at about 3,000 feet above sea level. That's not high enough to avoid sweltering days in the summer or chilly nights in winter. Like most cities in hilly or mountainous climes around the world, the folks who are financially better off live higher up, where it's cooler and, sometimes, the views are much better. So it was with *Kutche Sheybani*, a walled compound within which lay the house we had rented before we went home for our between-tours leave. The Sheybani family, a big name in Tehran business and society, was our landlord. The brick house, large and spacious, had a swimming pool out front, and an employed gardener who, like all Iranian gardeners, got his watering can out every day and from a pool, or a *jube*, watered all the lawn and flowers within reach. The pool was huge and, usually, the water too cold to really enjoy for swimming, coming as it did from the snow melt in the mountains a few miles to the north of our home.

A word about the *jube*. This is a man-made construct crucial to the lives of millions of Persians, maybe others in that part of the world. It is an open ditch, almost always tiled with stone or concrete slabs, usually no more than two feet deep, a foot wide, completely open at the top, and at the surface, right along the street or the sidewalk. Through these *jubes* flows the water for the entire community, drinking, washing, whatever.

The source of this water is another uniquely Persian construct, the *quanat*. The *quanat* is a tunnel, dug below the surface at a depth of as much as twenty feet, bored downhill and parallel to the surface above, from the base of the snow covered mountains, with a vertical access shaft every two or three hundred meters along its route. The deposited earth from the digging of these tunnels and their associated vertical shafts leaves a large mound, or cone, around the top of the shaft and from the air, as in a jet passenger Pan Am 707, on the bare desert floor below, it appears as a precise bombing run from World War II, little pock marks in remarkably straight lines. When the newcomer arrives in Iran and sees this "watery lifeline," he understands how primitive peoples have made do, over the centuries, with what they have.

I have not been back to Iran since 1960 and assume that, at least in the cities, the water supplies are much more refined and reliable, certainly cleaner. The story about *quanats*, in the 1950s, was that the many shepherds in the fields would take their dead and dying animals and toss them into the nearest *quanat*, to hide from the owners of the flock the evidence of mishandling or nature's demands. That folklore was the reason nearly everyone then living in Iran boiled his water before drinking it.

But back to J.A.

John had graduated from Texas A & M, receiving a degree in electrical engineering. He signed on with the CIA in 1950, the year before I did, and was immediately assigned to a group of brand new and very young intelligence officers known as the "PMs," the paramilitary group. These young men were sent to Fort Benning, in Georgia, and pushed through its training program that the Army ran for its own people. Jumping out of airplanes was the most notorious aspect of what these men were taught, knife fighting and other tricks of the trade included, a guerilla warfare program designed for and by the CIA

I had heard about this group and was quietly happy to learn that I would not be joining them. The idea, of course, was that the CIA, in those days, needed officers who could train others to parachute into the Soviet Union, real spies who would then—if they were fortunate enough not to get caught and shot—would report back to the Agency on their small RS-1 short-wave radios.

I learned later that only a few such operations ever made it off the ground, literally, so difficult was it to find men, former Soviet citizens themselves, who were willing to return to their native land under such difficult circumstances.

But in order to train those few former Soviet citizens who were willing to try, the trainer had to know the Russian language. And it was not easy for the CIA to find young men, who were American citizens and therefore up to the scrutiny of the Agency's security clearance procedures, who already spoke Russian well enough to use it, face to face, with an agent who was about to risk his life going back to the Soviet Union by parachute.

So the CIA had a very skillful cadre of foreign language instructors, none better than those who taught Russian. And my friend J.A. happened to have an aptitude for such. I never did, and whether John realized this before he entered the language-training part of his career I don't know. But I do know that he came out of that training program with a working capability in Russian that still amazes me.

And, as we'll learn later in this story, he used his Russian language skills, in retirement and many years later, in a very different and helpful way on the Kamchatkan Peninsula, Russia's most remote province, eight time zones east of Moscow—fly fishing for steelhead trout.

The Swing Set

Chapter 6

Working on the Railroad

As I've said, very early in my career at CIA Headquarters, I spent a lot of time as a desk officer in the Near East branch of the SR Division, poring over maps of the Soviet Union. And I remember noticing, for me the first time, how close one of the major Soviet railroad lines came to the Iranian border. I knew by then that I was probably going to be posted to Tehran, my first overseas assignment, and I was already thinking about what I could do at that post that might make a difference to the CIA's mission in Iran.

Before leaving for Tehran, I had discussed with my branch chief the possibility of photographing that rail traffic. I had done pretty well in the photography course, part of the curriculum during my stint in the months-long training program. It seemed to me, at least in theory, that a good camera could capture on film that railroad traffic that passed, every day, within a thousand yards or so of the Iranian border.

So, as the CIA bureaucracy required, and with my branch chief's help, I wrote a "Project Proposal," a formal proposal for a specific project, with details about cost estimates, risk evaluations, the required logistics support and a number of other things. These proposals, as I soon learned, were pretty serious stuff, requiring as they did the expenditure of real money, the taxpayers' money, and the Agency's budget office was never inclined to buy a pig in a poke. I had to hand-carry this proposal to any number of branch chiefs, section chiefs, at least two Division chiefs (SR's and the chief of the Near East Division) and, eventually all the way to the "top man" in the Clandestine Service, the DDO himself (Deputy Director for Operations), collecting their signatures along the way.

Apparently, as I look back on it, none of these "higher ups" had previously considered what my proposal might actually accomplish, a systematic photographic record of Soviet rail traffic along a major rail line servicing the Soviet Union's vast Central Asian land mass.

My Project Proposal included a map, showing that this rail line passed within a thousand meters of the Iranian border and, that with help from the Iranians, with whom our Tehran station already had established an effective working liaison, we should be able to photograph that rail traffic.

One problem I had yet to face: The CIA did not have a camera, ready-to-go, that was capable of doing what my project required.

So I contacted the Agency's Technical Services Division, or TSD. They would build the camera. I explained to them the exact situation, showed them the maps, and explained to them what I had learned about the topography and climate at that point on the earth's surface.

That "point," by the way, was very near the village of Lutfabad, a tiny community located less than one kilometer from the Iran-Soviet border. Our Iranian liaison officers had told us that there was an Iranian border guard post sitting within a hundred meters of the actual border, and, of course, at least one Soviet watch tower a few hundred meters on the other side of the line.

In between were the typical Soviet border "trappings": a barbed wire fence, a twenty-meter wide "plowed strip," raked over with a mechanized harrow every few weeks to reveal the footprints of anyone foolish enough to try to enter, or, more likely, to escape from the Soviet Union. There were trip wires, to send flares into the night skies, and the ubiquitous watch towers, every kilometer or so, a hundred meters back from the border, with at least one Soviet border guard soldier constantly on the alert, armed with a rifle and binoculars. (I was impressed to learn that this "fence" was at least ten thousand miles long, extending from Finland to China, Joseph Stalin's monument to his beyond-belief paranoia.)

All of this meant that our rail traffic surveillance camera had to have several special characteristics: It had to run silently, because the Iranian troops who manned the Iranian post would not be made aware of what was going on inside their adobe hut, heretofore their place of rest and tea-drinking. They would be told only that something "special" was going on and that it was none of their business. The hut had two rooms, each with its own entrance, one of which they would continue to use, the other would be home to our camera and its supporting equipment.

Second, the camera had to be capable of operating, on its own, for at least one month, as that was the minimum interval we believed possible to service the camera without arousing suspicion by those Soviet watch tower occupants, who could see everything happening on the Iranian side.

Third, it had to run, reliably, on batteries that could be replaced every month by a non-technical guy, me.

What TSD came up with was a modern marvel for its day. They designed and produced an electronic-eye "trigger," common enough nowadays in garage-door openers and other such "gadgets," but in 1956 something very new. This "trigger" had to respond to the movement of freight trains about 1,000 meters distant; not so simple. The camera itself used a standard reel of 35 millimeter film, but "Hollywood" style, one thousand feet long. As each frame would be no more than three-eighths of an inch deep, that one thousand feet of film would last one month, easily. The trigger mechanism actuated the camera the instant a train's locomotive broke through its "view," and stopped the camera when the last car had passed by.

A serious problem, we discovered, after Headquarters developed our first 1,000 feet of film, was that the constant desert sun, over that arid landscape, produced the normal heat waves, or "shimmering" that we all know about, and some of the images were not sharp enough to read the painted numbers on the individual rail cars. The line-of-sight path from the camera's lens to the targeted rail cars was little more than two or three meters off the ground, so the "shimmering" problem was one for which we had no answer. And it was those numbers that were critical to the success of the collection operation: The numbers, the direction the car was going and its likely cargo were the indicators that the analysts in Headquarters needed to evaluate the rail traffic's contribution to the Soviet military-economic well-being of its Central Asian region.

Another problem—and this was one of the very few times that I was aware of a TSD "miscalculation"—was that the chemical composition of the wet-cell batteries, lithium hydride, ate through aluminum with amazing speed. And the camera's battery "box" was made of aluminum, to save weight. This problem was serious enough that TSD sent one of its technicians to Tehran and I escorted him to the border guard post. He had never been out of the United States before and, needless to say, he was a bit nervous as we spent a night, in sleeping bags, on the dirt floor of that Iranian border guard post, barely a few hundred meters from those Soviet watch towers.

He concluded, after looking over the entire camera set-up, that the camera would have to be rebuilt. There was no alternative to the batteries' composition. By the time it would have taken for a re-build, Headquarters had decided that the "take" was not significant enough to justify the re-build.

So the success of this operation was marginal but the idea had been sound enough. In Winter, with little or no "shimmering," the camera and its pictures were just fine, but the analysts at Headquarters needed year-round coverage to fully evaluate the product.

During the year or more that our railroad photography operation was in place, the Near East branch of SR Division (my "home away from home") decided to take advantage of what they now knew to be a "comfortable" relationship between the Tehran station's officers and the Iranian military commander at Lutfabad. The branch had known for years that it might, someday, be possible to dispatch an agent, overland, through the border at Lutfabad. A properly-documented agent could walk to the nearest railroad station, about ten kilometers distant, and from there "blend in" with his Soviet surroundings.

But to be able to persuade an agent that such an overland crossing was possible, the branch needed a scale model, in three dimensions, which would display the terrain, the Soviet border defenses and, of course, the railroad itself.

The branch asked the station if it thought we could do this: Could we do an accurate survey of the two-kilometer-square area near Lutfabad?

The branch already knew that my colleague John Aalto and I had developed a "can-do" attitude about operational possibilities in Iran, certainly in the vicinity of Lutfabad, and the station told the branch that we would give it a go.

First, however, we would need two pieces of specialized equipment. One would be a camera with a powerful telescopic lens, the other an accurate range finder. It would be impossible for John and me to pace distances on foot, even at night, with a manned Soviet watch tower just a few hundred meters away on the other side of the border.

Within a month or so of our "give it a go" response, the station received a range finder, a U.S. Army "Mark One" model from World War II. John and I tried it out on the desert a few kilometers from our homes in suburban Tehran and found it to be so inaccurate as to be useless in its present condition. But, as I've said, we hadn't developed a "can-do" reputation for nothing. John's electrical engineering expertise met this problem head-on and within a half-hour's "tinkering" the range finder was in ready-to-go condition.

The camera that we intended to use was a standard German Leica M-3, fitted with a Questar lens, a lens normally used for photographing the stars and planets but easily adapted to the Leica.

We wanted to be certain that the photographs needed for our survey would be sharp and that the necessary distances would not pose a problem.

Thus equipped, John and I headed for Lutfabad. We explained to the in-charge Iranian colonel that we had some work to do at night and asked him to dismiss the Iranian soldiers who normally would have patrolled our survey area. Because we could not rely on the Questar to take acceptable photographs at night, we took those photos in broad daylight, hiding behind whatever cover we could find to avoid the attention of the so-near Soviet watch-tower guards.

Late that same night, probably about two a.m. and, as I remember, under a moonless sky, John and I proceeded to do our survey. We spent the next several hours on our knees, quite literally, crawling from one mark to the next, taking accurate compass and range readings as we went along. Each "mark" consisted of a very-normal thin-steel barbeque skewer, about eighteen inches long, with a small piece of white cloth tied to its handle, thrust into the ground, then moved to the next mark; visible enough to us but, we hoped, invisible to those watch-tower guards.

The most difficult part of this exercise, John and I later decided, was taking notes as we went along, without the help of a flashlight. We felt quite exposed and a flashlight beam, even so small, was out of the question.

From the station we sent all of our survey data to Headquarters. Many months later I saw the resultant three-dimensional Plaster-of-Paris model, in living color, even showing sage-brush clumps, the Iranian and Soviet guard posts, the fence, the watch towers, the railroad, everything.

Not a bad night, I thought.

On a subsequent visit to Lutfabad, and emboldened by our night-time survey, John and I asked the in-charge colonel if there were some way we could safely look back at our "hut," the building that housed the railroad-surveillance camera. Up to that time we had not risked a walk around to the side of the building that faced the railroad and through which the camera took its pictures: We wanted to see what the Soviets saw with their binoculars from their watch towers.

Much to my surprise the colonel said, "Sure, we'll just hop into my jeep and have a look. But you two guys first have to put on fatigues and try to look like Iranians."

So we put on fatigues, olive-drab caps and sun glasses and off we went. The colonel drove up to the gate in the fence, used routinely to go after stray sheep and goats, spoke with its Soviet guard and off we went, along a dirt track about ten meters inside the Soviet Union. After taking a good look at our building, we turned around, re-entered Iranian territory, and that was that.

Needless to say, John and I never mentioned this escapade to anyone at the station and certainly not at Headquarters. It may have been the only time during the Cold War that two CIA officers entered and exited the USSR, illegally, with no one knowing about it. And to have done so without "permission" made the event all the more satisfying. It's that "can-do" attitude.

Our Beaver

Iran-Soviet Border at Lutfabad

Soviet Watch Tower

Chapter 7

Moon Over Mashhad

The city of Mashhad, in northeastern Iran, is easily the most "metropolitan" population center in that far-off part of the nation. It is also home to a walled Islamic worship center, including a beautiful golden-domed mosque that is one of the holiest places on Earth for Shi-a Muslims, who make up nearly all of Iran's population.

It also happens to lie barely forty miles from the border with the then-Soviet Union and for that reason Mashhad (Meshed, in those days, to the CIA) was a place of great interest and importance to our Soviet Operations section within the CIA station in Tehran.

Our repeated trips to Lutfabad, to service the railroad surveillance camera, always were routed through Mashhad. The Station's Beaver aircraft took me to the city's airport, then we flew to a small airstrip near the town of Quchan, about 75 miles to the northwest. From there, an Iranian military jeep took me to Lutfabad, where, on my first visit, I quickly befriended a family who were friends of my Iranian military escorts. The camera required servicing once a month, so my visits to that small village and its hospitable family, with whom I spent at least one night on each visit, became rather routine.

The Station's purchase of a Beaver aircraft—a small, single-engine airplane built for short runway takeoffs and heavy cargo transport—was a logical choice. Also known as the L-20, the aircraft had been produced in large numbers by the deHavilland Corporation in Canada and the Iranian Air Force, in 1946, had been one of deHavilland's first customers. Thus, a few of its pilots were familiar with the airplane although their first purchase was no longer in service.

All of this is to say that I developed a knowledge and understanding of that scene which was unique within the CIA station. If for any reason Lutfabad and its surroundings became of interest for reasons other than the photo-surveillance operation, I would be able to help.

And so it was.

Readers can be forgiven for not remembering, or being aware of, the fact that Soviet communism's grand experiment began on November 7, 1917, the day that saw an end to the long-smoldering Great Patriotic Soviet Revolution, as the Communist Party leaders so proudly referred to it. For most of the rest of us it was known, simply, as the Bolshevik Revolution.

In my later years of service at the American embassy in Moscow, November 7 was *the* day. Soviet military forces put on hugely-impressive displays of their considerable power. Parades with tanks, guided missiles, marching infantry troops, aircraft fly-bys, all proudly observed by the Politburo's big shots from atop Lenin's tomb in Red Square.

Readers may also be forgiven for having forgotten, or being too young to remember, that on October 4, 1957 the Soviet Union launched into orbit the world's first earth satellite, called "Sputnik." (Most English speakers pronounce this word "SPUTnik," which always bothers me just a bit because, in Russian, it is SPOOTnik.) The word means "little traveler," and indeed it was small, a round metal ball less than 12 inches in diameter, as I recall, but its beeping was heard around the world and thus began the Space Race.

Now this story takes on a dimension that I find hard to believe 55 years later, even though I was very much a part of it.

The CIA can never be accused of lacking *imagination*. That's what its leaders get paid to do, among many other things: imagine what threats, enemy capabilities, etc., lie just over the horizon that America's policy makers should know about.

Well, within a few days of learning, with the rest of the world, about Sputnik, our Soviet Operations section at the Tehran station received a lengthy cabled message from Headquarters outlining the following scenario:

November 7, 1957 will mark the fortieth anniversary of the Bolshevik Revolution and we all know how proud is the Soviet leadership of this event and how they love to show off on anniversaries. Forty years is likely to be very important to them.

And with Sputnik now an established fact, there just might be an even more spectacular event in the Soviet "works," something that the entire world could see for itself, far more impressive than Sputnik. If this were to happen, the Soviet propaganda victory would be beyond measure. There was not much the Americans could do to prevent it, but if it should happen, the CIA had better know about it, ASAP!

The "thinkers" at Headquarters also pointed out in this lengthy message something we all might have missed were it not for their sagacity: The upcoming November 7 would see a total eclipse of the moon and, owing to the celestial gods, this eclipse would be visible from Earth and from somewhere where *the CIA has access*, in northeast Iran, i.e. Lutfabad or somewhere close by. (Afghanistan would have been another likely place but the Agency did not have the required capabilities there.)

So, a lunar eclipse on November 7, so what?

Again, we must never discount the imagination thing. Now that we know about Soviet rocketry's capability, so recently demonstrated by Sputnik, it is just possible that the Soviets will launch another rocket, this one to impact on the lunar surface with a huge phosphorescent explosion that, during the eclipse, will be visible to the naked eye of every man, woman and child who can see the moon. *That*, were it to happen, is the propaganda triumph which the CIA must know of the moment it happens in order to tell the world that we were not surprised, in other words, the American president will be among the very first to know.

(I was never persuaded that this line of reasoning made a whole lot of sense, but, Hey, I was just a foot soldier about to follow orders.)

And orders they were. With this enormous opportunity out in front of us, Headquarters *ordered* us (along with the required bureaucratic politeness "if feasible") to organize an operation that would put a specialist, coming from Washington solely for this purpose, in position to "monitor" the eclipse and watch for that phosphorescent flash. And one or two of us from our section would of course accompany him to add more eyes to do the watching.

But more than that. The specialist, a hybrid officer from TSD and the CIA's office of Communications, would bring with him a portable and specially-built radio receiver capable of monitoring the electronic emissions (ELINT) from the Soviet rocket, on its way moon-ward.

Now our small Soviet Operations section has some hurried decisions to make. We have just 30 days to get our team into position to watch the eclipse. Who will lead this group, how many of us can be spared from our other work, can we get the needed logistics support from our Iranian military helpers, will our Beaver be available, how about security at the Mashhad airport, security in Lutfabad, how to make this caper look "normal" to the Iranians who will be involved?

I look back on this whole affair and have to admit I was pleased to be chosen as the team leader. I had just observed my 28th birthday a few days earlier on October 3, not exactly an old, seasoned pro.

So the next day I scurried off for a meeting with one of our Iranian military helpers and we planned the operation. I can't remember, for certain, if I was allowed to tell the Iranian officers the real reason for the mission, but probably so. And I'm sure they rolled their eyes, out of my seeing of course, as I already had done, more than once.

The planning required some important specifics. Headquarters wanted us to choose an observation post that was as high above sea level as we could find, to approach as nearly as possible a line-of-sight radio path to the Soviet launch facility at TyuraTam-Baikonur, some 500 miles to the northeast. That would allow our ELINT radio receiver to pick up the Soviet telemetry emissions very soon after the rocket's launch. To do this, we had to rely on Iranian local knowledge to find a peak, or ridge, that we could reach on horses, to carry our team and its gear. And none of this could be arranged by telephone from Tehran, as we had to assume that the Soviet embassy in Tehran was tapping into Iranian telephone conversations. (So far as we knew, the Iranian military had no secure communications links to that part of the country and we would not have trusted them with our plan even if they did.)

This meant we had to fly to Quchan-Lutfabad, in the Station's Beaver aircraft, to make the arrangements face to face with our trusted contact in Lutfabad, and to be sure, ahead of time, that they would work. So, off I went on my familiar milk-run, but this time with a very different kind of mission in mind.

Our specialist from Headquarters' TSD/Commo Division arrived on schedule and I met him at Mehrabad Airport. I took him to his hotel, briefed him on our progress to date, and arranged to pick him up the next morning for the first leg of our journey. He had with him the Agency's one-of-a-kind ELINT receiver, a black metal box about the size of a volley ball with rounded corners and some knobs and dials. He told me Headquarters had a project name for it, as expensive and unique as it was: The Thunder Mug. "Do you think it will work?" I asked him. His response was not reassuring: "Nobody knows."

I explained to him that receiving and recording good ELINT telemetry was only part of our mission. Watching that lunar eclipse and the (maybe) phosphorescent blast on the lunar surface was the other part. And his would be an extra pair of eyes.

So, at the appointed time, our team piled into our Beaver at Tehran's military airfield. The team, in addition to myself and the tech from Headquarters, included a young Iranian from the Shah's intelligence service with whom our Soviet section had been in close liaison for several years, his sergeant-helper—a tough but pleasant guy who could get things done about as well as any Persian I ever worked with—and the aircraft crew, two Iranian Air Force pilots, assigned to us by the Shah himself.

We used the same home to overnight as I had been "visiting" on my surveillance camera visits. They were very close to our Iranian military hosts and we had no choice but to trust them, even though they lived within a few kilometers of the Soviet border and, in theory at least, could have been leaking the things they learned about our activities to relatives or friends on the other side of that "fence." It was a similar situation to that in Iranian Astara, on the other side of the Caspian Sea.

The next morning we were driven in an Iranian military jeep to a pre-arranged spot where our horses were waiting for us, along with their driver, another person who would soon enough see what we were doing on the top of the ridge to which he had been directed to take us. So by now I'm beginning to worry—that's what a young operations officer does, worry about things that somehow have moved beyond his control—about the extra people who are learning of our activity, which would appear very strange to anyone, anywhere, at just about any time.

We reached our ridge top well before dark and pitched the one tent we brought with us to protect us from whatever weather might come along. The locals told us that snow might be headed our way; this was early November, after all, and our ridge top was somewhere between 3,000 and 4,000 feet above sea level.

The Iranians had brought their own shelters and food for the whole group. They were very good at improvising small camp fires and preparing shish kebab, usually with tomatoes and onions and, of course, the kebabs came from Iranian sheep, some of the tastiest meat I have ever eaten.

(I digress here to mention something I've learned only recently, about the origins of the word "shish kebab." Traditionally, on the shish kebab skewer, there are *six* pieces of meat, alternating with tomatoes, onions, peppers, mushrooms, whatever. The Farsi word "shish,"—pronounced sheesh—which of course I knew, means "six," six pieces of meat. So now you know, if you didn't before.)

November 7 arrived, on schedule, the next morning. Darkness was hours away and our big moment would arrive on time. While waiting, we used our little RS-6 agent radio to let the Tehran station know that we were in place and ready to go. They, in turn, notified Headquarters, which quickly returned a message, relayed to us on our ridge top, "Good Hunting." No one cheered.

What I remember most about that all-day waiting was that it was becoming progressively colder and we all knew that, if it became cloudy, our watching game would be in the tank before we had a chance to see our long-anticipated eclipse. But as often happens, the cold ensured a clear night sky. Eventually it darkened, the moon came up over Afghanistan to the east and, sure enough, the crescent sliver of a dark shadow began to creep across the lunar surface. I don't recall how long we had to wait for the moon to go completely dark, and if the Soviets had done what our thinkers back home thought they might do, that high-powered rocket was already well on its way and its Baikonur launch pad already in its cool-down mode.

So we waited and watched and waited and watched. The full eclipse began to fade, as all eclipses must, and we saw nothing to write home about, quite literally. Disappointed or relieved, probably a little of each.

We reported our "findings" to the Station in Tehran, they relayed the same to Headquarters. For reasons I've long forgotten, we were asked to stay another night, which seemed even more bizarre than the original rationale for the mission. But by now, the morning of November 8, it had clouded and a light snow began to fall. This, too, we reported to the Station and, mercifully, there was some pity among our superiors and they told us to come on home.

A good thing, too, as the snow thickened and seemed determined to make our retreat even more difficult than had been our arrival.

With a half-century of hind-sight to help, I no longer think of this operation as a fiasco. No doubt those were serious people who conceived the plan after considering the suppositions that led to it. It was the CIA's job, after all, to do what it could to protect us all from whatever the Soviet Union's warped leadership had in mind. The Agency's response to the (likely?) rocket to the Moon over Mashhad was just another on the long list of its efforts to do just that.

Our Moon-Watch Outpost

Land Rover

Chapter 8

A Summer to Remember

When I arrived back in the States with my family, all four of us were more tired than we realized. Living abroad had had its downside, especially for me. Like most of the officers who served in the Middle East, I had had many bouts with diarrhea, simply because it was impossible to be sure of drinking good water and eating clean food when I was traveling. At home, good sanitation was not a problem; out in the boondocks anything could happen. A few unlucky men came down with amoebic dysentery, an ailment that can stay with a person for many years and, occasionally, is fatal.

So our home leave was to be a much-needed time for re-charging our batteries.

We flew to Frankfurt, Germany and picked up a brand new Volkswagen Beetle which I had ordered before leaving. Our two sons, then six and three, at first loved to ride in the VW's "boot," located just behind the back seat. But that became boring for them after awhile, so my wife and I told them that one had to stay in the boot while the other sat in the back seat. This was long before seat-belts, of course, so the boys spent most of our driving time tormenting each other. By the time we reached Seattle, we were more tired than when we had left our overseas post, thanks to the "boys-will-be-boys" behavior of Scott and Mike.

I left my wife and the boys with their grandparents and returned to Washington. Before leaving for home, I had asked Headquarters to enroll me in a Russian-language brush-up program. I had used my Russian abroad mainly with our household help, all of them Russian speakers who had escaped to Iran from the Soviet Union. But that kind of language "practice" wasn't enough and I knew that the Russian language program at Headquarters was staffed by former Soviet citizens, themselves escapees from the USSR.

I had arranged to live for two months with a young couple, Agency employees, who also had escaped from the Soviet Union during the final year of World War II. So this was a "total immersion" experience. I even rode to and from work with Alex and practiced my Russian with him. He would point out all kinds of things as we drove along the streets and highways, insisting that I name, in Russian, everything to which he pointed. It was very good practice.

One summer Sunday, Armed Forces Day, we decided to drive out to Andrews Air Force Base, in Maryland and east of Washington, to watch the air show. We would use my car, which I had purchased years before and left with a friend/colleague, who lived in downtown Washington, DC, while I was in Tehran.

After the air show, we walked back to where I had parked my car, only to find it missing. It was a 1950 Ford and, as I soon learned, this car was easy to "hot wire" and steal. So now Alex, his wife and I had to hire a taxi to get back to his home. I filed the necessary "stolen car" report with the Maryland state police and for the next three or four weeks I rode back and forth to work with Alex, wondering if I'd ever see my car again.

One day, as we were returning from work, we stopped at a red light and there, off to our right in a convenience store parking lot, I spotted my car. Alex pulled into the parking lot and I flagged down a motorcycle policeman and explained what had happened. At first he seemed skeptical, but as I was carrying my set of keys to the car and could explain to him what I expected to find in the car's trunk, he accepted my story. He asked me if I had reported the theft to my insurance company, which I had. Then he told me that the car was no longer mine, if the insurance company already had agreed to "buy" the car from me. He further explained that he would notify the insurance company, they would come for the car, and whatever was in the trunk was no longer mine.

I returned with Alex to his home and nearly forgot the incident. The insurance company already had agreed to pay me as much or more than I could have received in a private sale. But then one day Alex's phone rang and at the other end was an FBI agent. The car carried Virginia license plates because I had lived in Virginia before going abroad. In the glove compartment the FBI agent had found papers belonging to my friend who was garaging the car for me and he lived in the District of Columbia. The car had been stolen in Maryland. So there were now three jurisdictions involved in the theft of a car worth no more than eight hundred dollars, an "interstate crime" with which the FBI had to bother itself.

The few times I've thought about this fiasco, I've told myself how fortunate I am to have worked for the CIA, another bureaucracy to be sure, but one in a much different line of work.

Chapter 9

Early Challenges

Judging by our contemporary understanding of the CIA's successes, most dramatically revealed by the killing of Osama bin Laden, one would have to assume that a lot of very successful people are doing a lot of effective work, behind the scenes and out of the public's view. That's the way it should be and occasionally I have been irked by former CIA officers who write books about their marvelous achievements or beat up on their former employer for what they consider to have been major screw-ups or gross failures of one kind or another.

I suppose I could be accused of the same temptations, when writing this autobiography. My rationale is that what's in my memory is so old that no one cares any more, no extant operations are being discussed, no living former "helpers" are at risk, or the descendants of same, owing to what I have to say.

One needs to recall that in the early 1950s, when I went to work for the Agency, the Soviet Union was America's perceived Number One enemy, the Cold War was raging, Stalin recently had detonated his first hydrogen bomb, and trying to collect useful intelligence on that nation of one-third the world's landmass was probably the most difficult thing ever undertaken by any bureaucracy of the United States government.

One of the reasons for this maddening problem was that the Soviet Union was a hermetically sealed empire. No one, but no one, was allowed to cross its borders unless previously approved by its paranoid Communist leadership. That meant that only foreign government officials and a very few other folks were allowed to enter the country and to stay there for more than a few days.

These foreigners were watched by the hawk-eyed KGB's internal security service whenever they so much as walked out of their embassy buildings to go shopping or for a walk in one of Moscow's many parks. So, as collectors of good intelligence, they were virtually useless.

Of course the CIA was very much aware of these realities, and soon after its establishment by the National Security Act of 1947 it began to devise ways to "insert" people (agents, spies, by whatever name), illegally, into the country.

Dropping a man out of an airplane, at night and by parachute, was the operational flavor of the year, but the method was far from fool-proof. For one, to reach the Soviet Union the airplane had to cross the unfriendly East European land mass, and those countries' radar systems were, ultimately, under control of the very same KGB. And, even if that barrier could be skirted, the Soviets had a radar fence around their 15,000-mile perimeter. So, what to do?

We learned some time later that the CIA had managed to dig a tunnel, through East Germany and to Berlin, known, naturally enough, as the Berlin Tunnel operation. This unlikely project went on for a long time and collected an enormous amount of useful intelligence as its operators were able to tap into telephone and telegraph lines without the Germans catching on. But this was Germany, after all, not the USSR, the CIA's primary target. No one ever considered digging a tunnel all the way to Moscow, from anywhere. So, still, what to do?

Well, if one looks at a good map, it is apparent that the Soviet Union has a lot of water around its edges. The Baltic Sea for one, the Caspian Sea for another, and many miles of Pacific Ocean on the eastern edge of that huge country.

So, *boats* might have come to mind. And indeed they had. That same map will reveal that, in addition to its thousand-mile common land frontier, Iran's border with the Soviet Union includes the Caspian Sea, the world's largest inland sea that, in those days, just happened to produce the world's finest caviar. But, again, I digress. (More about Iranian caviar, later.)

A closer inspection of our map will show us that on the Caspian Sea's western shore are two small towns, each named Astara, one on the Soviet side of a small river, the Aras, and the other on the Iranian side.

So, why not put our agent in a boat on the Iranian side and have him motor his way, at night, around the mouth of that same river, to the Soviet side? In principle, pretty easy. In practice, not so.

For one thing, the residents of those two Astaras were/are Azeris, a closely-knit Turkic-speaking ethnic group, at least some of them probably kinfolk, and Soviet border controls notwithstanding, these people know how to communicate with each other; they've been doing it for generations.

So this rules out, in our operational planning, any notion of launching our agent-in-the-boat from Iranian Astara. As those World War II posters reminded us, "Loose lips sink ships."

In our next chapter we'll see how the CIA tried to take advantage of this geographic teaser.

Chapter 10

The Boat

One of the more intriguing sub-parts of CIA's Headquarters in Langley, Virginia was a unit of the Clandestine Service known as "TSD," the Technical Services Division. This unit was populated by an amazing array of men and women who could do almost anything that an "illegal" operation might require. Fortunately, all of them were on *our* side.

If you wanted a forged document, say, to prove your (phony) identity to a foreign journalist, you got it from TSD. If you needed a driver's license to drive to your agent meeting in a foreign capital, you got it from TSD.

The agents who were prepared to jump out of airplanes into the Soviet night skies had to have absolutely fool-proof identity documents that would "work" within hours of their hitting the ground. Any stranger showing up in a village or small town would be suspect in that fearful society. Soviet militia men were constantly checking the identity papers of the local citizens. So our just-arrived-by-parachute agent had better have the real stuff in his pockets, or the game's up before he even gets started.

TSD knew all about these risks and their associated demands and they employed the best forgers outside America's prison walls. They had to simulate Soviet paper stocks, the exact kind used in Soviet internal passports, work permits, the document authorizing a Soviet citizen to live where he lived, the document he needed for permission to travel, and many others. "Pocket litter," the kind of "stuff" that one would be expected to carry around—an unused bus ticket, half a candy wrapper from a local shop, an IOU from a friend—whatever it was, these folks fabricated it and made it look as real as the real thing.

But they did a lot more than that. When a CIA operation required some kind of "unusual" equipment, if TSD couldn't provide it, probably no one else could either.

Which leads back to our thinking about using a boat to get our agent from Iran into the Soviet Union, in darkness and undetected. What kind of boat might do the trick?

We've mentioned the working principle within the CIA: "compartmentalization." How much do we tell, in this case TSD, about what we need and how we intend to use it? As it happened, each branch within TSD had a chief, natural enough, but that one man was the one with whom the operational plan was discussed, in all its risk-laden details.

I wasn't in Headquarters when our need for a boat came to light. I was in Tehran, thinking about how to get that agent from the Iranian shore to the Soviet shore, just a few miles away, so close and yet so far. So we turned to TSD, in Langley.

What they came up with was the RB Nine-point-five (RB-9.5), and would you believe, this is CIA-speak for "Rubber Boat, 9 1/2 feet long," no kidding. Even TSD had its limitations when it came to imaginative labeling of its products. Furthermore, the boat was *not* made of rubber. Rather, a World-War II–developed synthetic material which withstood sunlight and the other ravages of Nature that usually cause real rubber to deteriorate.

So, TSD's creation eventually arrived at the Tehran station and I unpacked it. What to do now? Well, as I've said, I lived in a beautiful home with a swimming pool out front, so why not see if the thing at least floats in my own swimming pool? No one is going to see what's going on in the privacy of my own home—within four compound walls—and if the boat doesn't do what we know it must do, we'll send it back to TSD.

Not to worry. The boat, in my swimming pool, at least, was okay. But that's only the boat. What about the motor that is going to push it around the river mouth and onward to the Soviet shore beyond?

Here, the story gets more complicated and a lot more interesting.

Outboard motors, as any boater will tell you, make a lot of noise, especially when the throttle is wide open. Our boat, to successfully insert our agent onto Soviet soil, had to be quiet, *real* quiet, else the motor's noise might alert those ever-present KGB border guards to what's going on, in the dark, and our agent will be in hand-cuffs minutes after he lands. That's not an option, and TSD knows it.

So, anticipating this need, the TSD engineers brainstorm this question: How can we take an off-the-shelf Johnson 25 HP outboard motor and make it silent?

I've long forgotten how they did this, but when that outboard motor arrived at the Tehran Station, it indeed was virtually silent. My partner John Aalto and I tested it in my front-yard swimming pool and I have at least one picture of this unlikely scene to prove it.

But testing this boat in a swimming pool is one thing, and no one would expect that kind of "testing" to be enough to risk the life of a CIA agent who is going to depend on that boat to get him safely to that Soviet beach. So, again, what to do?

Well, John and I already had been in Iran long enough to know that the Caspian Sea, many miles to the north, was *the* place to make more tests of our RB-9.5. This was the same water body, after all, that our agent would, some day, traverse on his way to that tempting Soviet beach a bit north of the Aras River's mouth.

So John and I loaded the folded-up RB 9.5 into my Land Rover, and off we go, north through the Elburz mountains to the Caspian Sea shore. We needed a "cover" for this trip, something to explain to the locals our being there: Why would a couple of young Americans come to this out-of-the-way place?

We had researched this question ahead of time and discovered, to our joy, that this part of the Caspian Sea littoral almost always sees large flocks of ducks, flying south from the Soviet Union.

That meant that John and I were now "hunters," armed with shotguns and lots of shells, and we're going hunting out on the waters of the Caspian Sea. Who would doubt us? If we just happen to be testing our RB 9.5, who would notice?

This scene became even more troublesome when we discovered that the motor did *not* function as it was supposed to: It was not *always* silent and it was sometimes hard to start.

JA and I had booked ourselves into a small hotel in the resort town of Chalus, right on the Caspian Sea coast. Two floors up, as I recall and, naturally, no elevator. So after determining the motor's deficiencies, John determined to fix it, right on the floor of our hotel room, before we bedded down for the night. As I've said, JA was an electrical engineer and a genius at fixing just about anything. He took the motor apart, right on top of a beautiful Persian rug. We worried about grease and oil besmirching that beautiful carpet but decided that it was a risk we had to take.

Within an hour John had repaired and reassembled the motor and we were ready to go early the next morning. Very early, as we wanted to be out on the water before too many of the locals were aware of our presence.

Earlier in this story I've mentioned Iranian (Persian) caviar. In those days Iran produced the best caviar in the world because the shallow waters of the Caspian Sea littoral, within a stone's throw of our hotel, were perfectly suited to shelter and grow the Beluga sturgeons that produce this marvelous delicacy. We had been in Tehran long enough to have had opportunity to buy caviar, sometimes from unlicensed peddlers, and at prices unheard of elsewhere: ten, fifteen dollars per kilogram.

One brief event that John and I will never forget. We had just come back from eating dinner at a local restaurant and were about to ascend the steps to our hotel room (looking forward to fixing the motor), and out of the shadows stepped a boy no more than ten years old. He held in his grimy hands a can of caviar, mixed with weeds and grass from the scene of the butchering process. He realized he was about to try to sell his product to a couple of foreigners and he correctly guessed that we were Americans: "Caviar, mister, cheap?" We could hardly believe our good fortune and were in no mood to dicker with the youngster. The can weighed about one kilogram, a little more than two pounds, and the boy was happy to part with it for the grand sum of 200 *rials*, less than three dollars, American money. That, still today, is the best "deal" I ever made.

The next morning it was still dark when we hauled our folded RB-9.5 to the water's edge, inflated it and, after parking the Land Rover in a safe place, edged out onto the Caspian's surface. It was getting light and we could see and hear commercial fishermen moving their boats out into deeper water. They were tending the nets they had put out the day before, we assumed to capture sturgeon. When they saw our boat—something completely new to them—they called to us, in Farsi of course. We raised our shotguns, pointed seaward and laughed. They responded in like fashion. John had deliberately removed the silencing cover so as not to show the Iranians that there was something unusual about the boat's motor. He gunned it and we roared off, leaving the fishermen behind.

The water we were moving over was not deep, probably no more than six feet, with extensive beds of tall reeds that rose up to ten feet above the surface: just the kind of cover the sturgeon needs to raise its young. It was also perfect cover for these two "hunters" to wait for the anticipated Russian ducks to come their way. By the time it was full daylight we had maneuvered the boat, now moving silently, making sure it was stable in sharp turns and at various speeds. The silenced motor performed perfectly, just as we had hoped it would. Now we could relax and wait for those ducks.

Over the next hour or so, John and I probably fired our shotguns a hundred times. There were ducks everywhere, so many that we hardly had to aim, just point and shoot. Using a duck hunt as cover for an intelligence operation is not something one gets to do more than once in a career. John and I still laugh about it, more than fifty years later.

Testing the RB 9.5

Duck Hunting Cover

That duck-hunting caper on the Caspian Sea was not the only time I went hunting with JA.

The American embassy employed a number of local workers, not all of them Persians. One of these was a man we called "Pop," an Assyrian and a Christian. He was one of the embassy's most versatile and useful workers. Pop could fix just about anything mechanical or electrical and his skills were needed.

Pop also was a hunter. He had connections all over the country, and after we had been working in Iran for several months and had become good friends, he asked JA and me if we would like to go hunting with him into Iran's western mountains. He explained that this was Kurdish country and that the locals there considered themselves part of Greater Kurdistan, a self-proclaimed "homeland" that had for centuries extended westward into Iraq and north into Turkey. The Kurds had little use for the government in Tehran but enjoyed a kind of "unspoken" truce: "You leave us alone and we'll leave you alone."

Pop also explained that because of the generations-old tensions that prevailed in the region, just about every Kurdish family owned at least one weapon and many of the tribal men were good hunters.

The area was home to at least two types of mountain animals, a mountain sheep (Mouflon) which the Persians called "Gooch," and a mountain goat, or Ibex, the East Caucasian Tur. Neither of these animals, we learned, is quite as large as its similar cousins found in North America but they are every bit as sure-footed and hard to hunt because they prefer to live in the highest reaches of their mountain range. We would soon learn just how "high" that meant.

We drove into Kurdistan in my Land Rover, a long drive over very rough roads, coming to within 50 miles of Iran's border with Iraq. We spent the night in a village near the city of Sanadaj and soon learned why the Iranians, Pop included, consider the Kurds among the "dirtiest" people on the planet. Whether this was local prejudice didn't matter. There were flies everywhere in our village "hotel," which wasn't really a hotel but a wayfarer stop for people passing through, a sort of caravanserai without animals. Fortunately, JA and

I had brought our own sleeping bags and mosquito netting and we made it though the night without more than a few insect bites.

The next morning, early, Pop woke us and said it was time to get going. We wolfed down the usual Persian breakfast of flatbread and tea, JA and I sneaking out a Hershey bar that we had secreted in our ruck sacks. We found a petrol station, gassed up the Rover, and headed up into the mountains. We would meet our "guides" about 20 miles up the road, where it ended at a trail head. That trail would take us into the mountains and when the trail petered out we would go cross-country.

How Pop arranged all of this has always puzzled me. Apparently even in this remote part of Iran the telephone system worked well enough, and JA and I already had learned that tribal peoples have an uncanny way of keeping in touch.

Our "guides" turned out to be a couple of villagers, men probably in their late thirties. They spoke Kurdish, not Farsi, but Pop knew enough Kurdish to tell them what we wanted. They had never guided Americans before and asked Pop if we knew how to fire a rifle. He assured them that we had hunted in the United States and were looking forward to hunting in Iran, something very few Americans are able to do.

Pop explained to us that these guys had spent most of their lives in these mountains, sometimes hunting, sometimes smuggling back and forth across the Iraqi border. They had part-time jobs in their home village and would expect some "baksheesh" for their labors. At this point they got into a heated argument with Pop, apparently over the amount of money we would pay them for their guiding services. Pop told them we would give them 100 tomans (1,000 rials, or about $13, American money) for two days' work. JA and I thought this was a pretty cheap price for two guys for two days but Pop assured us it was more money than they would normally make in two weeks, so not to worry.

With the usual Persian haggling behind us, we set off on the trail, leaving the Rover behind. Pop assured me it would be safe, that very few Kurds would come this way, knowing that our small group already was working up the mountainside, looking for game.

Pop was about 10 years older than JA and I, the two "guides" about the same age. They set off at a pretty brisk pace, JA and I could barely keep up with them, and we worried that Pop would soon be far behind. To our surprise, he held his own, after giving his rifle to one of the guides to carry.

(I should digress at this point to explain that JA was a very good shot with a rifle or a pistol. His father had been a member of the U.S. Olympic rifle team many years earlier and JA had learned at his father's knee. I had watched him fire his 30-06 rifle, out in the desert a few miles east of Tehran, while we were doing the obligatory sighting-in. He could hit a soup can at 100 yards and think nothing of it.)

The climb up the mountainside was about as tough as anything I had ever done. I was carrying my rifle and a small ruck sack, but my breathing became so heavy that I wondered if I'd be able to handle the rifle if we should see game. We knew that the Ibex we were pursuing have excellent eyesight and that the instant they saw (or smelled) us they would be long gone. We'd be lucky to get off one shot.

After about an hour of walking we came to the rim of a deep, boulder-strewn canyon. The canyon headed about 1,000 yards to our left and quickly dropped to several hundred feet below us. Our guides had spotted several Ibex on the opposite side of the canyon, about 300 yards away. We decided to stop moving and watch them, to see if they had spotted us. One of them moved across JA's field of vision, then turned to face us, as if to decide if he was in danger. That gave JA a target of about four square inches, a head-on shot, at 300 yards. He squeezed the trigger, his 30-06 barked, echoing up and down the canyon, and the Ibex disappeared.

The two guides howled their disapproval: Why would anyone take a shot like that, scaring off the animals who would now be even more difficult to find?

At that moment, JA told Pop and me he was pretty sure he had hit the Ibex, even though we couldn't see it. When Pop relayed this to the guides they, laughed: No one could make a shot like that. Let's go and find other game.

JA was insistent. I told him to stay put, to keep his eyes on the spot where he had seen the Ibex disappear. We agreed that the guides would be no help in finding the animal because they were convinced that JA had missed. I decided to walk around to the canyon's other side but, as it was getting dark, JA would have to guide me. So off I went, clambering over rocks, up to the head of the canyon and back along the other side. JA was shouting instructions across the canyon and when I had reached the spot where he had last seen the Ibex he told me to look closely, just behind a large boulder. And sure enough, there was the animal, stone dead with a bullet hole just below its throat.

The guides could hardly believe it, but to earn their money they would have to come to the other side of the canyon, load the Ibex and bring it back. And hurry, as it was getting quite dark.

We found a fairly level spot on the mountainside and while JA and I rolled out our sleeping bags, the guides quickly built a fire and dressed out the Ibex. We had brought along some food and water in our ruck sacks but we quickly learned that, if you are a Kurdish mountain man, fresh Ibex liver is a delicacy, especially when roasted on an open fire. While our guides were enjoying their roasted Ibex liver, JA discovered that the guides, while dressing out the animal, had ruined its cape (the animal's shoulder, neck and head) and any kind of mount would be able to show only the animal's 14-inch spikes. So much for "professional" guides.

(Later, John discovered three growth rings on the spikes, showing the animal was three years old, not huge, but big enough.)

There would be another day of hunting, for me a real adventure. But I digress to note that those Ibex spikes, today, occupy a special place on one of the walls of JA's summer home in Western Montana. When I visit him there, those spikes bring back memories of a hunting adventure like few others.

Ibex Country

JA and I rolled out of our sleeping bags the next morning and found that a light snow had fallen during the night. Our guides were already up, had made a fire and were heating water for tea. Pop had been up awhile and told us that the weather was looking "iffy" and we had better get back to the Land Rover; it wouldn't be a good idea to be caught out in these mountains with an early snowfall on the way.

The hike back to the Rover was mostly downhill and we made good time. When we reached the vehicle the skies already had started to clear and we wondered if we could have another day of hunting before going back to the village. We had brought along enough food and wanted to keep going. Tehran was a long way off and we probably wouldn't get a chance like this again. Besides, we had hired the guides for two days, not one.

Pop knew what we were thinking and he pulled the guides aside and got into a discussion, mostly in Farsi and Kurdish, so we had no idea what they were talking about. When they had finished, Pop explained that the guides were pretty certain we could find the

Persian mountain sheep, or Mouflon, if we were willing to drive another 50 or so miles. The terrain they had in mind was less rugged than the Ibex country we were about to leave, but as we could expect at least a half-foot of snow to cover the ground, the walking would be easier and if we found sheep we might be able to track them in the snow.

This was one of those times when my Land Rover proved its worth. In four-wheel drive and with its "all-weather" tires, it could go just about anywhere, snow or no snow. JA and I sat in the two front seats and Pop and the two guides were comfortable enough in the jump-seats behind. Most of our drive was down off the mountain, then across a flat plain, then back into some higher terrain. Eventually, we reached a river and, like many Iranian rivers, there was no bridge. This situation came as a surprise to JA and me but for Pop and the guides it was a no-brainer: We would wade across the river, do our hunting and come back to the Land Rover before nightfall.

Fortunately, the river was no more than knee-deep and flowing at a rate that the five of us could negotiate without fear of getting dumped. Keeping our rifles and food out of the water seemed the most important worry at that moment. Once on the other side, we climbed into higher terrain, walked another half-hour or so, giving our wet socks and boots time to dry out. Blisters were always a concern and JA and I had planned ahead to bring dry socks, just in case.

There was about a half-foot of snow covering the ground, as we had expected, but the sun was shining and things were looking better. We stopped long enough for the guides to build a small fire, boil some water for tea. Then we were ready to make a serious search for the Mouflon.

Pop explained that with just five of us, it would be best to stick together as a group until we spotted game, then be prepared to split up should that become necessary in order to track any animals we might see. The Mouflon, or "Gooch," as the Iranians referred to them, preferred to move in small groups, usually no more than three or four, and always with one of that group the designated "scout," the animal responsible to look for trouble. For the Mouflon, this "trouble" usually was from somewhere below, because of the high terrain they preferred. The animals had some of the best vision in the animal kingdom and sneaking up on them, sight unseen, was the hunter's most challenging task.

Our guides had eyes almost as good as those of the Mouflon. They had been living in these mountains all their lives and could spot any movement at a much greater distance than could JA or I, or even Pop, for that matter. After we had walked another half-mile from our tea-stop, one of the guides motioned for us to take cover behind a large boulder. He had spotted something but wasn't certain what it was. He crawled a few yards to another boulder, took a look, and motioned us to come closer. He had a pair of Mouflon in view.

I didn't know about JA, but at this point my heart rate had elevated enough that I could feel it pounding in my chest. Because JA had had a successful hunt the day before, the guides wanted me to get off the first shot. I was able to use a small boulder as a rest for my 30-06, lined up the Mouflon in my telescopic sight and squeezed the trigger. The animal, probably 150 yards away, dropped but then got up again and began a slow, wobbling walk away from us, obviously trying to escape even though badly wounded.

The five of us had to make a quick decision: whether to keep going, looking for more sheep, or follow the wounded animal. Pop thought it best if he, JA and one of the guides moved on and around the edge of the slope where the guides were certain there were more sheep, although they would be on the move after hearing my rifle shot.

So we parted company, one of the guides coming with me, the other three moving off and around the mountainside.

The wounded animal chose a long, downhill slope, an easier escape route than going back up into the mountains and it was leaving a trail of blood spots in the white snow, easy enough to follow. After following the blood trail for a quarter-mile or so, my guide became quite agitated. I couldn't understand what he was saying but it was clear enough that he wanted no part of tracking one mountain sheep. I argued with him, as best I could with my few words of Farsi, but he would have none of it. He turned around began a half-trot to catch up with the others.

So now I was alone, "my" wounded Gooch several hundred yards ahead of me. And I became aware of the fact that I had left my ruck sack and hat in the Land Rover, leaving me without any protection from the bright sun, and no drinking water. Well, I thought, I can do with melted snow, so long as there *is* snow. But as I followed the animal downhill, the snow began to disappear and after another quarter-mile I was walking on bare earth.

By now, the Mouflan had collapsed, it could no longer walk. I approached, feeling bad about the animal's suffering. I had two rounds left in my 30-06, walked up to animal and put it out of its misery.

What to do now? I had never gutted an animal but I was determined to bring this creature back to camp, if nothing else to show my guide that I had been right to follow the animal.

I had a pocket knife and a short length of twine in one of my pockets. The "gutting" process nearly made me ill but I managed to finish it, tied the animal's four legs together and hoisted it onto my shoulders. I had no idea where I was or how far away were my hunting companions but I sensed that continuing to move downhill was the best thing to do. After another half-hour I saw a small stream, another 500 yards below, running from my right to left. There might be a village or at least a few people living along this stream, such was the reality of life in the vast wilds of Iran. When I reached the stream's edge, I realized that the animal on my shoulders was too heavy to carry any farther, as dehydrated and tired as I was. I found three large boulders, a few yards from the stream's edge, and carefully dropped the animal to the ground, covering it with the boulders so that the local hyenas could not reach it. I would come back to retrieve "my" Mouflon, although I had no idea how this might be possible.

After another half-mile walking down the river's edge I heard a loud growl, off to my left. It was a large Iranian sheep dog, the type of dog I had seen before but had never encountered. Persians treat dogs very badly, considering them to be "dirty" animals, and many of them run wild. But the sheep dogs, although treated badly, are necessary for controlling the flocks of sheep upon which many Persians depend for their livelihood. (Unlike the sheep dogs I later saw in New Zealand, this one was quite large, probably 30 inches at the shoulder, maybe 100 pounds.)

This dog was, obviously, very protective and his growls let me know that I had better stay clear. He was large enough, if he decided to attack, to do a lot of damage and I was not about to succumb to a dog after all I had been through. I thought about it, knowing I had but one shell left in my 30-06. If I kill this dog, I'm safe from the dog, but what about the people who own him? Likely they are not far off: Not a good choice.

I'll never know why, but that dog decided to leave the scene. He turned around and trotted down the river's edge and out of sight, around a bend.

I had but little choice but to follow him, but at a safe distance. The wind was blowing upstream so I didn't worry about the dog's catching my scent and deciding to come back to attack.

By now I was stumbling along the river's edge, dehydrated and exhausted. I knew better than to drink from the stream, as many Persian villages are situated close to streams and use them for washing clothes, among other things, and I had long since learned to consider any flowing water to be polluted.

I rounded another bend in the river and ahead of me, not more than 200 yards, was a very small village. The dog apparently had alerted his owners to the presence of a human, somewhere upstream. Within a few moments two small children came running up to meet me. They were smiling, and in their child-like Farsi asked me "Are you in trouble?" I tried to return their smiles, admitting that I was indeed in trouble: An American hunter, lost, thirsty and very tired.

Then a few of the village elders appeared, they, too, curious about this stranger who had wandered into their midst. I explained that I was an American, working in Tehran, on a hunting trip, and lost.

My companions, four of them, were "somewhere" in the mountains above this village. (That much I could explain in Farsi.)

They insisted that I come in to one of their adobe huts. They put down a reed mat on the earthen floor, asked me to lie down and sleep. But first, they insisted, I drink tea, a lot of tea, with as much sugar as I could handle. These were wise people: They recognized my dehydrated condition and knew how to fix it.

I lay down on the mat, gulped as much of the sweetened tea as I could handle, pulled a piece of mosquito netting over my head and shoulders and almost immediately fell into a deep sleep.

At least an hour later I was awakened by a man shouting, *Bali, Amerikani hastam*—roughly translated, "Yes, we have your American with us." I could barely hear, a long way off, more shouts, all in Farsi and unintelligible to me. My hosts came running into the hut, all smiles, to tell me that my hunting companions were not far off, just above the village and descending a ridge to come get me.

Needless to say, it was a happy meeting. They wanted to get going. Evening was approaching and we had that river to cross before getting back to the Land Rover. By now I was awake enough to remember "my" sheep, still hidden under those boulders a few hundred yards upstream. I explained to Pop where it was and he told one of the guides to fetch it. While we waited for the guide to retrieve the animal, I asked Pop if he thought the villagers would accept a "thank-you" gift from me; I had several one toman notes in my wallet and would be glad to part with them. Pop said it would be best if he gave them the money. I already had learned that Persian villagers can be very hospitable people, especially to friendly strangers, but they usually had a certain sense of pride about accepting "thank-you" gifts.

We bid our good-byes and thank-yous and headed downhill. The small stream I had been following would eventually take us to the river we had waded across earlier that day. When we found the crossing point it became obvious that the warm sun had melted much of the snow and the river had risen a few inches. We made it across, barely, and no one got drenched. The Land Rover was waiting for us, untouched and just where we had left it, and we began the long trip back to Sanandaj. We dropped off the two guides, paid them there well-earned money and headed for "home."

As a footnote to this story, I might add that I have never again gone hunting with a rifle. Something about that wounded "Gooch" sticks in my memory.

JS With Two Guides

Chapter 11

Aerial Photography

Thinking back on it, I'm pretty sure that my involvement with an aerial photography operation, while I was in Tehran, had to be one of the most satisfying things I ever did for the Agency. It was not often, after all, that an ops officer was able to actually see, even *feel,* the hard intelligence that "his" operation had produced, knowing too, that the intelligence was important, new, and never before collected in a like manner. And even more than this, eventually to learn something about how that intelligence was used at the other end of the "information chain."

This will take some explaining.

As I have said, when describing our "moon watching" activity on November 7, 1957, the Tehran Station's Soviet Operations section had established a close, working relationship with several hand-picked Iranian intelligence officers. This official liaison relationship had the Shah's personal approval, so it was a partnership of great importance and one to be nurtured carefully.

I was one of the few officers who met regularly with these Iranian intelligence officials, at a secure facility on the outskirts of Tehran. We drove to this place separately, being careful that few, or no, others saw us getting together. We talked about many things and the Iranians kept us informed about whatever developments they thought would be of interest to us.

At one of these meetings, probably in early Fall of 1958, I learned that the Iranian military attaché group, at their embassy in Moscow, had received permission from the Soviet government to begin flying supplies and personnel to and from Iran's embassy in Moscow. For the Iranians, this was simply a cost-cutting measure, as it was much easier and cheaper to fly their own aircraft north from Tehran to Moscow than to fly commercial aircraft west, north through Europe, and then east to Moscow. And, as I recall, this "milk run" was already in effect and had been for several months. The Iranian air force had an American-built DC-3 twin-engine "Gooney Bird," which did the job nicely.

Providentially, as it turned out, the DC-3's range was limited and it could not fly non-stop from Tehran to Moscow, having instead to make a re-fueling stop at the airfield in Tbilisi, the capital of the Georgian Soviet Republic, some 600 miles to the northwest.

The Iranian pilots of this aircraft, two of them, were aware of the Station's liaison relationship with their Army intelligence colleagues and they passed on to me, via one of the intelligence officers with whom I met regularly, a very interesting piece of "news."

On their most recent approach to the Tbilisi airport, flying north to Moscow, they saw on the ground off to their left, while they were on final approach and no more than 500 feet off the ground, what appeared to them to be Soviet military aircraft, delta-wing jet fighters, something they had never seen before.

Needless to say, I reported this finding immediately to Headquarters and within a day of so our Soviet Operations section received a reply that, clearly, shared our enthusiasm for the obvious collection opportunities. The message included some important research: The Soviet facility that undoubtedly had produced these aircraft was known to be the "Mikoyan-Guryevich Aircraft Factory No. 31," and, sure enough, it was located right alongside the same airport being used by "our" Iranian flight crew.

The potential for taking pictures of these aircraft, assuming they remained outside and on the airport's tarmac, was obvious, but no one could know how long they might remain where the Iranian crew had seen them. So this put some pressure on Headquarters to send the Station an aerial camera, film, and some instructions on how to use it. No one in the Station had had experience of this kind so we decided I might as well be the one to learn how, and quickly!

I've described my early training as a new CIA officer, and it included a lot of the "basics" about photography, so that when the camera arrived it didn't take long for me to feel confident and comfortable loading film into it and handling it as if I were really taking pictures from an aircraft. It was a hand-held instrument, as I recall, box-shaped, perhaps seven inches on a side. The film format was a large one, as would have to be the case for this kind of photography. The settings for aperture and shutter speed were straightforward, all in all a pretty simple piece of equipment.

Now it remained for me to teach the Iranian DC-3 crew how to do this. They were smart guys but had never before been asked to undertake this kind of mission. There was also the not-so-insignificant problem of what to do with the camera while the aircraft was on the ground in Moscow, at least for one night, while the crew collected its cargo from the Iranian embassy for the return trip to Tehran.

As soon as my Iranian military contact arranged for me to meet with the DC-3 crew, I went through the procedures for using the camera. As I say, they were bright people and caught on quickly. I told them not to worry about the film, there was enough on the camera's large spool to do what was expected of them. Then, on a separate visit to the DC-3, parked at Tehran's military airfield, I constructed a concealment device for the camera in the very rear of the DC-3's cargo-configured cabin, deliberately choosing a place where any Soviet "inspection" would be hard-put to reach.

I remember this part of the operation quite clearly as it was a sweltering day and the interior of that DC-3 must have been at least 120 degrees.

So, now, the waiting game began. We could hardly wait for "our"

DC-3 to make another run to Moscow, holding our breath about what would happen to the aircraft while on the ground there: Would the Soviets find the camera, confiscate and develop the film, detain the crew, accuse them of espionage? A few unpleasant possibilities, to be sure.

I've forgotten how long we had to wait but, eventually, we got a call from our contact: The crew was safely back, the camera had not been compromised, and as far as they knew there were pictures on that film.

We had a rather extensive photo shop at the Tehran station, manned by an officer from, yes, TSD, and he helped me develop the film in his darkroom. The negatives were startling: Two delta-wing jet fighter aircraft, side by side with enough spacing between them for the photo analysts at Headquarters to make comparisons and all the other miraculous things these specialists do. We sent the negatives to Headquarters and waited, probably anxiously, to learn what the film showed.

What it showed was the first-ever pictures, of any kind, of the prototype MIG-21 super-sonic jet fighter, the first super-sonic fighter to enter the Soviet Air Force. Headquarters was ecstatic, if that's the right word for a large bureaucracy, and the station received some atta-boys that were well received. As I remember, we were able to repeat the operation only once, about a month later, because after that the MIG-21s had been moved out of sight.

Sometime later this aircraft was given the NATO codename "Fishbed." Eventually the Soviets sold it to many of their Socialist allies, and for many years it was the fighter plane of choice for those countries. It had entered service in the Soviet air force in 1959, just a few months after the CIA knew a lot more about it than anyone might have supposed, owing to those photographs.

As I said earlier in this report, I was pleased to learn, eventually, about how this intelligence, in part, was used in the United States. I am writing this book from my Covenant Shores retirement community on Mercer Island, Washington. A few years ago I became a good friend of Guy Townsend, also a resident at Covenant Shores, and a

U.S. Air Force Brigadier General at his retirement. Guy had been a test pilot for the Air Force and later a Boeing Company official. He test-flew every heavy bomber built by the Boeing Company before it was accepted by the Air Force.

When I shared my story with Guy, a year or so before his death in 2010, he told me that at the time of "my" aerial photography operation in Tehran, he was test flying the American F-100 series jet fighters (four of them) at Edwards Air Force Base in California. He was certain that the intelligence gleaned by the photo interpreters, of the film brought back by that Iranian DC-3, had been an important part of the "mix" with which he and others worked when test flying those prototype American jet fighters. The analysts were able to make useful estimates of the MIG-21's capabilities and limitations, information of great interest to Guy and his fellow test pilots.

I found Guy's assessment to be even more satisfying than the success of the operation in Tehran. We really made a contribution, however small, perhaps, to the safety of our own country. That's a satisfaction that not every intelligence officer can have and it ranks among my fondest memories of the "usefulness" of my career.

Chapter 12

Mount Ararat

When I first arrived in Tehran, in April 1955, I learned that nearly every official American working there used an Iranian-driven automobile for routine transportation. The reason for this was a practical one: Automobile traffic in Tehran could charitably be described as "wild," and it was impossible to find an insurance company that would stand behind a liability claim against an American driver should he or she be involved in an accident in which an Iranian citizen was injured. With Iranian drivers behind the wheel, an injured citizen wouldn't bother to sue because the driver had little or no money to go after.

I understood all this once it had been explained to me by our administrative officer. But I needed something other than a typical American four-door sedan to do the kind of traveling I knew my CIA job would require.

So I bought a Land Rover, at that time the British version of our American Jeep. It was an uncomfortable vehicle in which to make a long trip, its canvas cover leaked air and it was noisy. But it had four-wheel drive and could go almost anywhere, on road or off. I did accede to the requirement that I use a driver, although it seemed to me to appear ludicrous for an Iranian to be chauffeuring me around in my Land Rover.

Naturally, when I needed my Land Rover for operational work, outside Tehran, I would drive myself, almost always with someone else from the Station because we all knew the value of having a partner alongside in case of trouble.

I made many trips in that Land Rover, sometimes driving all the way to Mashhad, a distance of more than 450 miles, over some of the roughest road I had seen, then and since.

One of my "milk runs" took me, in my Land Rover, to Iran's northwest regional capital of Tabriz where I would meet with a CIA officer. The drive from Tehran to Tabriz was about 350 miles, a very long one-day trip but worth the effort to avoid overnighting in the marginal hotels that one might find along the way.

There was only one road that lay in that direction and it eventually crossed into Turkey, near the town of Maku and not far from where the frontiers of Turkey, Iran, and Soviet Armenia intersect. I knew there was some risk in making this drive because the road was approaching a kind of no-man's land and I would be driving within five to ten miles to the west of the Soviet Azerbaijan frontier. But I was curious to see what kind of "security" I might encounter in the area and I thought that if an Iranian border guard should flag me down I could tell him I was on my way to photograph Mount Ararat. An Iranian border guard would understand my interest in Mount Ararat, the resting place of Noah's ark. Even in Muslim Iran, the locals in this region would know the biblical story of the mountain they could easily see on a clear day.

I admit to growing increasingly apprehensive as I approached Maku but by then I had decided that I really would take a picture of Mount Ararat. The sky was clear and, sure enough, the 17,000 foot peak appeared right in front of me, through my Land Rover's dirty windshield. I stopped, got out, took a couple of pictures and headed back to Tabriz and Tehran.

Just six years later, on an airplane flight from Moscow to Yerevan, the capital of Soviet Armenia, I had the good fortune to look out my window and see Mount Ararat again, not that far away. I photographed it and like to think I may be the only living person who has two pictures of that legendary mountain, taken from two such unlikely places.

Chapter 13

Betrayal

As I have reported earlier, the Tehran Station's Soviet Operations group, of which I was one, enjoyed a close and helpful liaison relationship with the Iranian intelligence service. There were three of these men, two officers, plus their driver, with whom we met regularly, at least once a week, in a secure facility located to the north and west of downtown Tehran.

Some of our officers were under deep cover. We held regular meetings with them, too, at one of several safe houses that we maintained for that purpose.

Each of these men, of course, spoke fluent Russian and, when needed, they could handle one or two Turkic languages.

Their work for our Soviet operations group was specialized, nearly all of it devoted to the interrogation of Soviet-citizen agents who had been dispatched across the Soviet-Iran border with various missions, but in all cases to penetrate some part of Iranian society and then, after building their covers, to report to their Soviet intelligence handlers at the Soviet embassy in Tehran.

That embassy, incidentally, during the 1950s, employed more "diplomats" (many of them, of course were intelligence officers employed by either the KGB or the GRU, the Soviet military intelligence service), than any other Soviet embassy, anywhere in the world, and that simple fact was a constant reminder to us of how important the Soviet leadership considered Iran as an intelligence target.

In the back of our minds we understood that we Americans in Tehran also were targets of the Soviet intelligence services, not just the thousands of Iranians living and working there.

Our deep cover interrogation team produced some interesting intelligence, learning much about how the Soviet internal intelligence services recruited and then handled their agents. Each one of them, of course, was groomed to cross into Iran and then use whatever skills he brought to his mission. Most of these cross-boarder agents were native to those Soviet republics bordering Iran, Azeris, Armenians or men from one of the Central Asian republics. The Iranian population was sprinkled with a mix of these nationalities so that an agent, dispatched by the KGB or GRU, would not stand out simply because of his appearance or language.

What our interrogators learned, among many other things, was the lackadaisical attitude that these agents' handlers had toward the Iranian border controls that the agents would have to negotiate to enter Iran, illegally of course, and undetected. One of our interrogators told us that the man he was talking to told him that his Soviet handler had assured him he could "walk right through" the border, without even being stopped.

We knew that Iranian military personnel, especially those at the bottom of the pecking order, were not well motivated to do their jobs, but border guards, working for any government, usually have a higher sense of responsibility than many of their compatriots who are given less responsible duties. Even so, we wondered how the Soviet agent handlers could make such wild promises.

In fact, our interrogators came to believe, after working with these captured Soviet agents for a period of time, that, probably, most or all of them were caught trying to sneak into the country so that it was unlikely that there were many, or any, of them "out there" doing their spying. We passed this impression along to our Iranian military contacts and heard, later, that the Iranian border guard commanders were pleased to learn that their work seemed to be paying off.

Among all the CIA officers working in Tehran, our Soviet Operations section was quite small. We were outnumbered by others in the station, about five to one. These officers had, for years, been collecting intelligence from within Iran, unrelated to the Soviet Union. Many of them spoke usable Farsi and had developed good networks of informants within various parts of Iranian society.

Much of this work was done "unilaterally," without the knowledge or approval of the Iranian government. Some of it, as with our Soviet section's liaison contacts with the Iranian military, was well known to the Iranian authorities, some of it even with the Shah's personal approval.

So it was only mildly surprising when word came from CIA Headquarters in Washington that an agreement had been reached between the Shah and very senior officials in Washington that the Tehran station would undertake a massive program devoted to the organization and training of a new Iranian intelligence service, which came to be known as SAVAK (Sazeman-e-Ettelaat), the Organization of Intelligence and National Security.

(*SAVAK eventually—over the next fifteen years or so—became the Shah's personal spy system, illegally imprisoning, interrogating and even torturing thousands of Iranian citizens who were suspected of opposing the Shah's increasingly dictatorial rule. The organization ran its own prisons and earned a deserved reputation for its brutality toward its own people. That, however, was not what the Station anticipated at the time it was directed to midwife this new intelligence service. But SAVAK's activities, so feared among the Iranian population, were a significant contributor to the eventual downfall of the Shah, in 1979, the hostile takeover of the American Embassy in November of that year, and the establishment of the Iranian Islamic Republic under the leadership of Ayatollah Ruhollah Khomeini.*)

When the Station received this directive its top leaders huddled to determine how to divide up the workload, which would be a substantial addition to those activities already in play. And it made sense that our Soviet Operations section would be able to contribute. After all, we had the expertise that would help teach the new SAVAK officers how to run intelligence operations against their giant neighbor to the north.

My role in this new environment was to meet with a middle-grade Iranian military officer who had been suborned to SAVAK's own "Soviet Section," that part of the new organization that would focus on the Soviet Union and its presumed efforts to penetrate its Iranian targets. The man was in his late 40s and he could speak and read Russian. Although he had served in Moscow some time earlier, he knew nothing about the work he would be expected to do. That meant that I would have to teach him the fine points of *counter-intelligence*, how to protect his own (new) security service from Soviet efforts to infiltrate its ranks. He also needed to be taught the fundamentals of intelligence operations, much as I had been taught in my first year on the job with the CIA.

I met regularly with the man. His English was good enough that I was able to do my teaching in that language and I developed an extensive written curriculum, reviewing with him all the things I could remember from my own training, now some seven years earlier. He was sufficiently interested in the curriculum that he asked me if I could have it translated into Farsi, so that he could share it with others on his small team.

I turned that chore over to one of our Iranian liaison officers who were aware of the relationship that the station had recently developed with the new SAVAK. Within a week or two, the translated-to-Farsi curriculum came back to me and I gave it to my "student." We continued to meet for many weeks, going over all the materials until I decided I had done all I could.

As it happened, this activity ended when I reached the end of my second tour in Tehran, in the summer of 1960. I took my family back to our home in the Pacific Northwest for a well-deserved home leave. A month or so later I returned for duty in my home branch, the one I had left five-plus years earlier, at CIA Headquarters in Langley, Virginia.

What awaited me there was very unpleasant news. "My" Iranian student had been arrested by the very SAVAK of which he was a new member, and jailed without a trial. He had been found to have been recruited by the KGB while he was serving in Moscow. The KGB had used one of the oldest tricks in the books, putting him in touch with an attractive younger woman. He and she had bedded down one evening, were photographed "in the act" and the officer, a Muslim with a wife and family, could not risk the scandal of exposure; it would have ended his career. So he had no choice but to agree to do the KGB's bidding. I was told that he had turned over to his KGB handlers in Tehran the curriculum that I had prepared, plus the notes that he had taken during each of our meetings. Furthermore, it had to be assumed that he had identified me (I had worked with him using an alias, of course) to his KGB handlers from available photographs of Americans working in Tehran.

As I thought about this disquieting news, I could not help but imagine what that man must have gone through at the hands of his SAVAK interlocutors as they forced him to tell them everything he knew about his relationship with the American CIA officer. The last I heard of him he was still in prison, in Tehran, and unlikely to become a free man any time soon.

A careful reader of this story might well ask what we had done at the beginning of this relationship to vet the young officer, to "run name traces" on him, as I had learned to do very early in my CIA career. We had done all of the things possible, that was always a routine process. But we knew so little about individual Iranians, especially persons too young to have yet built a paper trail, that we simply were unable to be careful enough.

Looking back, I've concluded that the damage was not all that bad. What the KGB learned about the CIA's training methods, its security practices and all the rest, was all very standard stuff and should have been of no surprise to the KGB debriefers in Tehran. That they identified me, as a CIA officer, was a risk we all take when we become involved in operations that require that kind of exposure.

But to this day I wonder about that man's life, many years of it spent in a squalid Iranian jail cell, probably involving torture, and where he had so much time to think about his betrayal.

Part Four – Home
and Out Again

Chapter 14

The Watershed

Almost immediately after my return to Headquarters from Tehran in 1960, I learned there was a certain buzz going around: Things were going to be "different."

Frances Gary Powers, in his U-2 spy plane, had been shot down in May 1960 and Powers was then subjected to a show trial in Moscow, with the world watching on television. We were learning, too fast, perhaps, that the United States and the Soviet Union were on a collision course, one that might bring the world to nuclear war. Scarcely two years later, in October 1962, the United States and the Soviet Union again squared off in what became known as the Cuban Missile Crisis. Fortunately, it was Nikita Khrushchev who "blinked," and that crisis passed.

But within the CIA, the watershed had already happened. That was because, eight years after Joseph Stalin died in 1953, the Soviet Union finally had decided to open its borders, ever so slightly, and it was now possible for foreigners to enter the Soviet Union, legally.

The ice-breaker had occurred a few months earlier, in July 1959, when Vice President Richard Nixon and Soviet leader Nikita Khrushchev held their famous "kitchen debate" at the American

Exhibition, held in Moscow's Sokol'niki Park. The exhibition displayed many examples of modern American technology and know-how and, for the long lines of Muscovites who waited hours to see the exhibit, it was an eye-popping experience.

The events that soon followed were much more modest, a few "cultural exchanges," which saw American musicians and other artists coming to Moscow to perform before Soviet audiences. Soviet performers were given permission by their government to come to the United States, or to European countries, to show their talents. It was the beginning of an attempt by the Soviet leaders to promote a "feel good" atmosphere. The Politburo apparently had decided that its hermetically sealed nation was ready to allow its citizens a peek at the outside world and this important fact had been demonstrated, dramatically, at that American exhibit in Moscow.

What this all meant for the SR Division of the Agency's Clandestine Service: It was no longer necessary to plan, and to try to execute, those so-difficult illegal "insertion" operations of agents into the Soviet Union, by parachute drops from aircraft, from boats-in-the night, whatever.

Now, it would be possible for the CIA to "piggyback" some of those Western travelers who could enter the Soviet Union legally, and return safely.

It is hard to appreciate what an enormous impact this change had on the CIA's modus operandi. Since its inception in 1947, the Agency had been required to insert agents into the Soviet Union illegally, by the methods I have described. A whole generation of operations officers, myself included, now had to refocus its thinking about how to exploit these new opportunities.

And exploit them we did. The Division quickly tooled up, both at Headquarters and at its overseas posts, to find individuals who would be traveling, legally, into the Soviet Union. Most of these visits, at first, were to Moscow, less often to Leningrad. But over time, they expanded into other cities: Kiev, Odessa, Minsk, wherever local Soviet organizations wanted to invite foreigners to visit. Most of these early visits were artists of one kind or another, usually musicians, opera performers, well-known foreign conductors who occasionally would lead Soviet performing groups. Eventually, businessmen and women began to make these "exchange" visits, scientists too.

It became obvious that Soviet leaders, especially in the cultural world, were starving for a look at the West, denied them for decades by their paranoid Communist Party rulers.

One by-product of this "new world" had a particularly demanding impact on America's FBI, the Federal Bureau of Investigation. As I've said, this opening to the West required, in most cases, an exchange. If an American group of musicians performed in Moscow, for example, a Soviet group would appear in New York. The FBI, of course, assumed that among these artists would be several who had been tasked by the KGB to learn—and to report back—what they could, depending on their access. Occasionally, the FBI learned, one of these Soviet performing groups would include a professional KGB official, posing as, perhaps, a trumpet player.

So the cat and mouse game continued, but with many more nuances than had been in play in the bad old days of illegal agent insertions.

I should add that these new ground rules had an immediate impact on all the work I had done in Iran. The facilities and the ready-to-go plans no longer were needed. It was natural enough that I felt some disappointment about this turn of events, but I realized that if the Agency was to do the job it was meant to do, it would take advantage of the opportunities now opening up. And I intended to be part of that.

Speaking of "illegal," I mentioned earlier the ill-fated U-2 flight of Francis Gary Powers. Powers was jailed after his televised show trial in Moscow, but not for long. Some time earlier, the FBI had finally apprehended Rudolph Abel, the Soviet spy who had worked in New York City for many years and, from all accounts, rather successfully. Abel was one of those deep-cover agents, an "illegal," in espionage parlance, and the Soviet authorities wanted him back. He could tell them much more of interest, about his experiences in the United States, than Powers was worth to them as a source who had already told them everything he knew. So the two governments worked out an exchange and the two men returned to their homelands. I have sometimes wondered if they considered their experiences to have been worth all that they went through. It's a question that many in the espionage business eventually must answer.

Chapter 15

SR-9

It's not often that a guy remembers a conversation over a urinal in a men's room; but I do.

In those "temporary" buildings from World War I, strung along Washington, DC's Reflecting Pool, to the east of the Lincoln Memorial, were "I," "J," "K" and "L" buildings. To the unaware, these letters meant nothing, just right for housing most of the CIA's Clandestine Service.

I believe it was "J" Building that housed the Moscow Station branch of SR (Soviet Russia) Division. This branch, as all the others in the Division, had a number, SR-1, SR-2, and so forth, and SR-9 was the least well-understood of them all. Most of the intelligence officers who worked in the Division understood that "SR-9" was something special, with super-secret things going on that everyone else was expected to only guess about.

So, I'm standing there at one of the men's room urinals and a friend of mine walks up to do what guys do at a urinal and he asks me "How'd you like to come to work with me, in SR-9?"

I could hardly believe what I had just heard, realizing that I had just been offered at least a chance to learn a little bit about what was going on in SR-9.

I said something stupid like "Sure, when do we start?" My friend told me to come by any time and he would introduce me to his branch chief.

That conversation at the urinal probably changed the trajectory of my career from that moment forward.

The SR-9 branch chief had been in a senior position at Headquarters while I was in Tehran. He was in the Division's information loop and able to follow what was going on at the Tehran Station. He liked what I had done there and, apparently, thought I could contribute to the mission for which his branch was responsible: supporting the CIA's station in Moscow.

At that time, the very existence of a CIA station in Moscow was unknown to all but a few senior officials within the CIA, so sensitive did the CIA consider its presence in the Soviet capital. The station's cable traffic received special handling, ensuring the most restricted distribution possible.

My interview with the SR-9 branch chief was brief and pleasant. I had known him from earlier times, but had never worked for him. He assigned me to a couple of operational files, operations currently on-going in Moscow, and I quickly settled in to what became the most interesting and challenging assignment of my Headquarters experiences.

I quickly learned that the Agency's officers in Moscow—it was a small group—were working under very difficult restrictions, imposed by our own embassy. The State Department had yet to accept the notion that American espionage, within the Soviet Union, was part and parcel of United States policy toward the USSR, endorsed by the White House. I soon came to realize that most career State Department Foreign Service Officers, especially in the higher ranks, were persuaded that "diplomacy" could only be successful, especially in the Soviet Union, in the absence of the sullying influence of intelligence operations, which of course would have to be supported by our American embassy in Moscow.

This tension between the State Department and the CIA, over this issue, was to be a long-term problem for our operations planning, the staffing of our Station and even the execution of our operations in Moscow.

I should explain that my "conversation at the urinal" happened in March or April 1962. What I did not know, at that time, was that one of CIA's most successful and important operations, within the Soviet Union, had come under a cloud of suspicion and uncertainty.

Colonel Oleg Penkovsky, an officer in the Soviet Military Intelligence service (the GRU), had been working for the CIA for about two years. His officer rank had given him access to the GRU's top-secret library, and for months he had been photographing highly-classified documents and passing his Minox camera film to his CIA contacts in Moscow. Now, suddenly, the Moscow station had not heard from him.

Penkovsky had been able to travel abroad on official business and the branch always managed to have one or two of its officers meet with him, face to face. At the most recent of these meetings Penkovsky had told his handlers that he was planning to go to the Seattle World's Fair, to begin in the summer of 1962, as part of a Soviet delegation. His travel already was approved, it would be his first visit to the United States and, he correctly believed, that visit would provide good opportunity for his handlers to meet with him in more secure and relaxed circumstances than had been possible up to that time in European venues.

My friend-colleague, the one who had paved the way for my assignment to SR-9, knew that I had grown up in the Seattle area, had attended its University of Washington and he thought that my local knowledge would be useful for what had become an urgent task: to go to Seattle and set up a safe-house arrangement so that Penkovsky's handlers would have a place to meet him whenever he could get away from the Soviet delegation with which he would be traveling.

So the two of us flew to Seattle, found a suitable apartment in a building not far from the World's Fair grounds, put down a deposit (all of this in aliases, not revealing the Agency's hand) and returned to Headquarters.

Soon thereafter, from Moscow, our station reported what we had all dreaded might happen. One of the station's officers had been arrested by the KGB. He was attempting to service a dead drop, in downtown Moscow, expecting to retrieve a message from Penkovsky. As we learned later, two KGB "goons" were waiting for him, hustled him into a waiting car, and took him to the Lubyanka, the KGB's notorious Headquarters in Moscow. Our officer had diplomatic immunity, so the KGB could not hold him for very long.

His attempt to service that dead drop had been triggered by a signal, part of Penkovsky's communications plan with our Moscow station. It was a piece of white tape, placed on a certain lamp post, which one of our station officers could check at least daily. When that piece of tape appeared it meant that there was a message waiting to be picked up at the dead drop.

We later learned that when Penkovsky had been arrested by the KGB, he was forced to reveal these details and it was then a simple matter for the KGB to set up the arrest of our officer. Penkovsky had been given the telephone number of one of the Station's officers, to be used only in the most extreme emergency, and that information also was now in the hands of the KGB.

The KGB decided to make this event a *cause célèbre* and the world soon learned about Penkovsky's "perfidy." He was put on trial in Moscow, the trial was televised, he was convicted of high treason and, later, executed by a firing squad. (Some stories about his execution, from former Soviets who claimed to know, said Penkovsky was strapped to a stretcher and put into a crematorium, alive. The grizzly scene was photographed and then displayed to others as a warning about what happens to traitors.)

As one might imagine, the fallout from this disaster produced reverberations that rippled through the Agency like a small tsunami. What had happened, where were the security leaks, who "screwed up"?

The answer to those questions is a story about which I know little or nothing. What I do know is how the Penkovsky roll-up affected my own career.

The "fallout" included the sudden departure from Moscow of two of our station's officers, each of them being declared *persona non grata* by the Soviet Ministry of Foreign Affairs. They had been identified by Penkovsky during what must have been a brutal interrogation by his KGB captors.

One of the two had been our Deputy Chief of Station and the Division had to find replacements for these officers, and quickly. I had already been tabbed to replace the DCOS when his tour was up but now that whole process, which normally would have taken another year or more, was put on a fast track.

Our DCOS had been working at the Moscow embassy as its counter-intelligence specialist. The KGB was constantly probing to learn about our embassy's personnel, especially to identify the CIA officers they knew had to be there. So that whenever an embassy official became aware that he or she had come under the KGB's scrutiny, our officer was the one in whom that official would confide, and as appropriate, seek advice as to what to do about it.

In order to qualify as the replacement for our Deputy Chief of Station, I would need several months of preparation, training, on-the-job experience before I could assume that job at our Moscow embassy.

Chapter 16

Cairo

And that is what happened. I was assigned to an agency in Washington whose officers specialized in counter-intelligence. I spent about a month there, learning the ropes. Then, by prior arrangement, I was sent, with my family, to Cairo where I would spend the next few months learning how a counter-intelligence officer does his work in the field. That experience would prepare me for the job in Moscow.

Some time later, when I believed I had learned enough about my new job, I told Headquarters that I was ready to move on to Moscow.

Here, I should offer readers a glimpse of my duties while I served in Cairo. The work included some of the most interesting travel I've ever done.

One of the things a traveling counter-intelligence specialist does, as one might expect, is to cover his region of responsibility. The Cairo embassy's region included countries I had never seen before: Yemen, Ethiopia and Sudan, to name the three that I visited. These visits, I soon learned, were not particularly welcomed by the ambassadors in charge of these embassies. My job was to inspect each embassy's security procedures and this covered a lot of "stuff" that might not be popular with the embassy's workers: How does the embassy protect its classified documents, do the locks on the doors work as they're supposed to, what about precautions against fire, fire drills for the staff, and on and on. In my heart of hearts I didn't have much enthusiasm for these "inspections," but they were required and I did my best.

The most onerous part of this job, I soon learned, was my responsibility to interview any American employee who might be "in trouble," for whatever reason. Almost always this "trouble" was linked to the suspicion that the employee was gay. In those days being gay was the kiss of death for any American who was working overseas and whose gay-ness became known. And, probably, for good reason.

The KGB had long been known to use sexual deviancy, if discovered in an American working abroad, as an effective blackmail tool. The KGB would arrange to have an attractive male cross paths with the target, they would be photographed doing their thing. The American would then be approached by a KGB official who would usually have photographs of the American's "indiscretions," and if he (this never happened to women, as far as I know) failed to cooperate he would be exposed and his career, most likely, would be finished.

My security inspection trip to Yemen was probably the most memorable of those travels. In those days Yemen was divided in half, the northern half under loose control of a Communist government, the southern half not so. South Yemen's capital was in Ta'izz, its northern capital, as now, Sanaa. The State Department, owing to the relatively low priority if afforded Yemen, had a consulate in Tai'zz, but no embassy. The Consul General was a very pleasant guy and he took me in his private car to the sea coast, not far from the ancient village of Mocha, whence the famous Mocha coffee beans that, years earlier, had been a major export crop for that impoverished nation.

What I remember most about that visit to the Red Sea shoreline was a bathing area that had been staked out, into the warm ocean waters, probably the size of several large swimming pools. Sharks were known to roam these waters and so a protective "cage" had been constructed of re-bar steel rods, to keep the sharks out of the swimming area. I couldn't help but notice that the spacing between these re-bar rods was at least twelve inches and that said a lot about the size of those sharks. No doubt one had to be wild about swimming to risk the experience.

That evening, back in Ta'izz, I decided to go for a stroll. The CG had told me, jokingly, that Yemen was slowly modernizing, as he put it "plunging headlong into the 14th century." And so it seemed as I wandered through the city's bazaar. There were any number of young men (no women, of course, in this fiercely Muslim society) sitting on their haunches, chewing ghat, the mild narcotic so favored in that part of the world. Each of them wore a wide belt over his shoulder and one around his waist. The shoulder strap held a Kalashnikov semi-automatic rifle, the imported weapon of choice from the Soviet Union, and in the waist band a dagger, in its sheath about fourteen inches long.

The next morning I told my CG host about my stroll the evening before and he told me I really shouldn't have done that. And that mild scolding reminded me that I had been the object of many curious (hostile?) stares as a walked through that bazaar.

Even so, I was determined to buy one of those daggers and take it home with me as a souvenir. I did that and that same dagger hangs on the wall of my apartment, not 40 feet from where I am writing this story.

I recall flying on to my next inspection visit, leaving the airport at Tai'zz in a small propeller-driven twin engine airplane, on what seemed a too-short runway, getting airborne just in time to avoid a serious accident. The English-speaking passenger sitting next me remarked that this was typical of commercial flying in this part of the world. Allah (God) was really in charge and what the pilots did really didn't matter.

We flew over the southern end of the Red Sea and landed to re-fuel at Asmara, the capital of Eritrea, then on to Addis Ababa,

Haile Selassie's capital of the ancient kingdom of Ethiopia. My security inspection of our embassy there was uneventful but I recall being impressed by the extremes of opulence and poverty in that city. A taxi-ride of no more than 15 minutes took me from palaces and mansions to dirt-floored huts, rag-clothed little kids and unbelievable filth, separated by no more than two or three city streets. I had never seen real slums before and that brief taxi ride taught me a lot about how the rest of the world, much of it, really is. And what an enormous task the United States had taken on, after World War II, to try to make a difference in these far-away places.

From "Addis," as it was referred to by my Foreign Service colleagues, I flew to Khartoum, Sudan's troubled capital. Our embassy was located, roughly, in the city's center and as I drove there from the airport it was obvious that Khartoum was on some kind of "high alert" status. There were armed militiamen at every street corner, some of them were stopping and inspecting ordinary vehicles. I tried to get an explanation for what I was seeing from my taxi driver, but he shrugged his shoulders as though this were "normal."

As usual, my security inspection required me to do a walk-through of all the building's rooms, hallways, its basement, its outside perimeter. The American Ambassador was not pleased that "his" embassy required a security inspection, but he also knew that the Department's Office of Security, to which I reported, was a bureaucracy not to be trifled with. He reluctantly acquiesced to my standard interview and then directed a subordinate to escort me through those parts of the building I had not already visited.

The tail end of my inspection took me to the embassy building's flat roof top and from there, to the northwest, I could see the confluence of the Blue and White Nile rivers. There was something almost magical about that "picture," knowing what I had learned about the significance of these two mighty rivers in the history of the African continent.

Now, my on-the-job training was finished. It was time to move on to Moscow, where *real* adventure awaited.

Egypt's Pyramids

The Sphinx

Part Five – Moscow

Chapter 17

A National Tragedy

There are moments in every person's life when he/she remembers exactly what they were doing at the moment of the event: When you first heard about the Japanese attack on Pearl Harbor, or President Roosevelt's death or, in my case, when the news of Joseph Stalin's death reached my ears from a loud speaker at a Washington, DC tram stop, March 5, 1953.

So it was as I was about to fly to Moscow, with my family, to begin my tour of duty there, the most demanding of my career.

One of the last-remaining parts of preparation for my assignment in the Soviet capital was a two-day briefing session, in Frankfurt, Germany. Part of this preparation included an informal dinner gathering at the home of the man who would become my European supervisor.

We were sitting in his living room, having a pre-dinner cocktail, when his phone rang. He went to the phone, listened briefly, and returned to us guests, his face already ashen white. "The president has just been shot," he told us. John F. Kennedy had been mortally wounded that day in Dallas, November 23, 1963. We sat in stunned silence, dinner forgotten. Some time later the phone rang again and we learned that Kennedy was dead.

I returned to my hotel and my waiting family and we continued our preparations to board a flight the next morning, Frankfurt to Moscow.

By the time my family and I arrived in Moscow and were driven to the embassy and our new living quarters, all of its officers were wearing black ties, the official expression of mourning, something for which my training had not prepared me. The Soviet Union's head of state, Nikita Khrushchev, and foreign minister Andrei Gromyko already had visited the American ambassador's residence at Spaso House and signed the book of mourning. Many other foreign representatives in Moscow were to follow that somber tradition.

So the introduction to the most exciting and challenging assignment of my career got off to a worrisome start: Every American official working abroad would wonder, over the next few weeks, how this tragic event would affect America's relationship with the Soviet Union. After all, the Cuban missile crisis was just thirteen months behind us and the Soviet leadership was still smarting from that embarrassing debacle.

There was even some speculation within the CIA, some of it rather vigorous, that the KGB had engineered Kennedy's death. Its Sixth Chief Directorate was known to have a ready-to-go assassination squad and it was no secret that Khrushchev himself was in trouble with his Politburo comrades over his failure to withstand Kennedy's firm resistance to the Soviet nuclear bluff in Cuba. But the American investigation of the Kennedy assassination, and its eventual Warren Report, seemed to satisfy those leaders who mattered that Lee Harvey Oswald had indeed acted alone.

As compelling as had been Kennedy's assassination, my work at the embassy soon settled down to a number of routine, daily "musts." One of these was to check, each morning, with the embassy's code room, to learn what had come from CIA Headquarters during the night. In those days the Agency was so concerned about the security of its communications with Moscow that it declined to use the

State Department's communications coding system for its classified messages. We had not yet arranged to have our own communicator in the code room so it fell to me to use the specially-developed one-time-pad to decode incoming messages and to write and encode our responses to Headquarters. It was an onerous and time-consuming job but one that had to be done.

Another of my routine duties was to make sure that the officers in our Station had access to the embassy's secure room, or "bubble," as it was known. The bubble was a room within a room, its floor, ceiling and walls constructed of tough, clear plastic, easily inspected (by me, weekly) for the presence of microphones. The KGB had successfully bugged other embassies in Moscow, of that we were certain, and this relatively new "bubble" provided a reliably-secure place for conversations, not just for our CIA officers but for everyone else in the embassy who had sensitive things to say to one another. The embassy had an iron-clad rule: No one speaks a word, outside the bubble, that he/she would not want the KGB to hear.

Chapter 18

Agent Communications

The reader might ask, "Just what did you CIA guys DO in Moscow?"

Not surprisingly, much of our work was devoted to preparing and maintaining those support facilities that are needed when an agent returned to Moscow from an overseas posting or when we were able to recruit a new one in Moscow.

These support facilities consisted mostly of communication "tools," the means by which the Station could pass to the agent instructions, equipment, funds and whatever else the agent might need for his maintenance; and means by which the agent could send messages back to the Station.

In those days it was unsafe to meet face to face with an agent and such meetings were never even considered, so thorough was the surveillance by the KGB. In fact, the KGB used an entire sub-division of its Moscow Headquarters, including a motor pool which was located a block north of the embassy building, just to follow the American officers.

Of course we were acutely aware of this activity and each of us learned, by personal observation, that we were not followed every time we left the building, or at least that seemed to be the case. And therein lay a real problem: Some KGB surveillance teams were very good and were able to do their following without us (their "rabbit") being certain that we were, in fact, being followed.

At other times, the surveillance was very obvious, and we assumed that the "goons" just wanted to let us know that they were there.

The fundamental principle in agent communications, naturally enough, was that the agent must *never* be seen in close proximity to a CIA officer, especially seen in the act of exchanging something, else the KGB surveillance would quickly identify the citizen, perhaps even detain him immediately, for a thorough search.

To deal with this, we developed a method for passing messages to an agent which we called the "brush pass." It was effective when executed with precision but required careful planning and training. Of course the agent would receive this training while he was outside the Soviet Union and able to meet with one of our officers; a sufficient amount of on-the-street practice was absolutely essential.

As the name suggests, the message to be passed was transferred from a CIA officer to the agent in a brush-by meeting, on foot, where the two men could be seen near each other for no more than a second or two. This required split-second timing and, as I've said, a sufficient amount of on-the-street practice.

A variant of this method was employed in the Penkovsky operation, described elsewhere. The wife of one of the British Embassy officers, an MI-6 official who was part of the operational team that supported Penkovsky, made it a habit of taking her infant child for a stroll in a baby carriage, a common enough scene on the streets of Moscow. With the needed pre-arranging in place, Penkovsky would walk toward the baby carriage and in one deft motion drop his "package" (usually a small can of microfilm) into the baby carriage. The mother would take a few more steps, then stop to "adjust" the blankets covering the infant and, depending on her sense of her surroundings either cover the film can with the blankets or move it to her purse.

This particular brush-pass "routine," incidentally, provided the

CIA with some of the most useful intelligence it had ever collected, up to that time. But more of that elsewhere.

There were several other types of agent communications, each one necessary to maintain the connection so important to the maintenance of the Agency's agents in Moscow.

"Signals" were crucial in any communications package: How to let the agent know that the Station had something to give him, or he to let the Station know that he had something for it.

These "gimmicks" are well-known to any movie-goer who watches spy-thriller films: the potted flower on the apartment building's balcony, either there or not there; three candles in a street level apartment window, instead of two. The list is as long as one's imagination.

In the Penkovsky operation, for example, the officers supporting Penkovsky used white plastic tape, affixed to a certain street lamp pole. Because the tape was visible to anyone who happened to look, and did not "belong" there, it was put in place at night, the agent would look for it the next morning, and the tape was removed the following night, after dark. In this instance, the person placing the tape on the lamp post was not an intelligence officer but rather someone suborned for this purpose, who was not likely to be of enough interest to the KGB to be under constant surveillance.

Then there was the "safety/danger" signal. This signal would alert the Station that the agent was in some kind of serious difficulty and, depending on circumstances, that he would be out of touch for awhile. This kind of signal required more ingenious planning than the others because if the agent were in the kind of trouble that would prevent him from putting out the signal, it had to be already in place. In other words, the "safety signal" required an action of some kind, by the agent, the "danger signal" did not. So if, for example, he had been arrested or was unable to perform for some other reason, he had nothing more to do in order to alert the Station.

An example of this would be a lamp post located near the agent's home or work place, or both. The lamp post, like most lamp posts, would show a certain amount of graffiti. The agent, as he comes and goes to work or his home, quickly places a chalk mark on a designated part of the lamp post. If he is unable to do this, the absence of the chalk mark indicates some kind of trouble. For the system to work reliably, the lamp post must be observed frequently by someone in the Station's "loop."

So it is apparent that whenever an active agent was working in Moscow, the Station had plenty on its mind to make sure he was okay and being cared for as well as possible.

The other most-often used communication device was the "dead drop." I have explained in an earlier chapter how this worked in Washington, D. C., an envelope taped to the underside of a wash basin in a public restroom. The principle is always the same: The "package" should be in its hidden location no longer than absolutely necessary, and the timing of its retrieval must be convenient to either the agent or the officer, depending on who is retrieving the package.

These dead drops were of vital importance to our agent operations in Moscow and each of the Station's officers was tasked to find new ones, report their locations and provide instructions on how to use them.

I remember being tasked to locate a new dead drop in a city I knew to be populated by several large and attractive pre-revolutionary churches. These were popular tourist destinations and my wife and I could visit them without attracting attention from the tails we had to assume would be watching us.

As I had expected, one of these churches was crowded with tourists milling about, gawking, thus making it difficult for our presumed tails to know what we were really up to. After about 15 minutes in the church I found a "niche" in its structure, easy to describe later to any agent who might need to use it. I whispered to my wife to have a look and she later helped me write up a description of *the* spot. It would have been helpful to have been able to photograph the drop site with my tourist camera but if a surveillant were to see that it would render the whole exercise futile.

So these were the sorts of routine, mundane things that officers of the Moscow Station had to do if we were to be ready to provide an agent with a communications package, vitally necessary to the care and feeding of those few Soviet citizens who were willing to risk their lives to help us.

Finally, I should recall a "live" exchange of information via a dead drop, in which a Soviet agent delivered to the Station some very important information. This action had happened some time before I arrived in Moscow, but its successful execution was still the subject of excited conversation, as these events were not all that frequent.

The Station's officer, accompanied by his wife and visiting mother-in-law, went for a stroll in one of Moscow's large parks, a common enough thing in the eyes of his (presumed) surveillance. The three of them sat on *the* park bench, the locus of the dead drop. They chatted long enough to look about and be reasonably certain there were no tails in view. The mother-in-law got up off the bench to adjust her garments (a pre-planned distraction) and the officer swiftly reached under the bench and retrieved the agent's package, which had been held there by a magnetic limpet. It sounds simple and easy but the tension involved in one of these actions is at a high level; after all, the agent's life is at stake, if anything goes wrong. The worst that can happen to the officer is his being ordered by the Soviet Foreign Office to leave the country. For the agent, if the officer's activities have compromised him, the penalty would be far worse.

As I look back on this account I realize that the masculine gender is just about always in play. Were there not a few *women*? Truth be told, in the 1960s the Agency had not yet "matured" to the point that women were accepted as operations officers, at least not at its Iron Curtain posts. I was very fortunate to have had a top-notch administrative assistant helping me in my office, a single woman. She was the only female assigned to the Station. Throughout the embassy, I recall no women who had jobs other than "secretarial," so this was also State Department practice at that time, not unique to the Agency. Some time later, after I had left Moscow, women were being accepted, and trained, into the operations of the Clandestine Service and I believe they served admirably. However, it probably was a very long time, if ever, before women were assigned to handle male agents, for obvious reasons.

Chapter 19

The "Signal"

For several years the embassy's security people had been aware of a strong electronic "bath" that flooded the building's west wall. This radio energy was known to emanate from a small building just outside the embassy's walled perimeter. This radio energy "bath" soon became known as The Signal and, maddeningly, no one had been able to learn its purpose. The situation appeared to pose such a threat to the workings of the embassy that the Department assigned one of its technicians full-time to determine the purpose of The Signal and then, if possible, to defeat it. This officer came from the State Department's Office of Security. He kept me informed of his activities but they appeared to me to be so arcane that I had to trust his abilities and his judgment, both top-notch.

The presence of The Signal was a constant reminder, to those of us who knew about it—and most of the embassy staff did not—that our Soviet hosts would continue their relentless efforts to learn what we were doing. The Signal, we had to assume, was some kind of electronic surveillance or "masking," so that traditional bugging, microphones in the walls, were only one part of a larger picture.

Was The Signal intended to mask radio transmissions from

the near-by KGB motor pool, which we knew was being used for automobile surveillance of our embassy's vehicles? Was it used to jam our own electronic equipment, with which the embassy's military attaché section tried to intercept Soviet telephone traffic? Was it intended to irradiate some kind of special listening device already planted in the embassy's walls?

Quite simply, we just didn't know.

After we had analyzed The Signal for more than a year, and still did not understand its purpose, the ambassador decided to file an official protest with the Soviet Foreign Office, complaining, truthfully, that the radiated energy which penetrated the embassy's west wall was a health hazard to people working in the embassy's offices. His Foreign Office contact promised "to look into it," and, eventually, the Foreign Office responded that the ambassador must have been mistaken, as the Soviets knew nothing about such a thing. Still, The Signal continued to blast away at the embassy's west wall!

This potential health issue had already become a concern to the medical experts at State Department Headquarters in Washington and they requested the embassy to install an energy-absorbing material (something resembling Styrofoam) in all of the west wall's windows. My office was one of those affected, as were many others. The view out of my two office windows had been nothing to write home about but now I had none at all.

An interesting post-script to this story about The Signal. When my wife and I returned from Moscow to the States, we were required to submit to a very thorough physical examination, because of our exposure to The Signal. I never understood why my wife was required to undergo this rather invasive examination, as she had never been in the part of the embassy building that was exposed. I, of course, had been sitting in my embassy office desk chair, my back no more than two feet from the window. Some years later I learned that one of the embassy's U.S. Marine guards, after returning home, reported that his young wife had suffered a miscarriage and he filed suit against the State Department, claiming that, had he been aware of The Signal's danger—he claimed that the radiation energy had damaged his "reproductive capacity"—he would have left the post. I knew little about the details of the lawsuit but it seemed to me an unwarranted assertion. Nevertheless, the State Department rewarded him with an out-of-court cash settlement, just to avoid the unwanted publicity.

Sometime later, I read in the *New York Times* that the well-known columnist Jack Anderson had published an account of the work of our military attaché operation. He told the world that our attaches had tapped into Soviet radio-electronic security and had succeeded in listening to, and recording, not only the KGB's mundane Moscow auto-surveillance activity but the Soviet military's electronic commands to its strategic nuclear bomber fleet, its missile guidance systems and much more.

Anderson was called to the carpet in a Washington, DC dust-up and, of course, he claimed that everything he had written about was "common knowledge" and of no consequence to the security of the United States. There are a few of us, still alive today, who remember and resent that episode of journalistic opportunism.

Chapter 20

Bugs

I have mentioned the ambassador's residence, Spaso House. This home, located in the Arbat district of Moscow, not far from the embassy building, was a pre-revolutionary mansion, its construction completed in 1914, just before the beginning of World War I. It had been the residence of the very first United States ambassador to the USSR, William C. Bullitt, who came to Moscow when the United States first extended diplomatic recognition to the USSR in 1933. The home was perhaps the most opulent in Moscow and for years served as the guest house for the many American presidents who came to Moscow.

In 1952 Spaso house made news when the world learned that a listening device, or "bug," had been discovered in the ambassador's Spaso House study, allowing the KGB to overhear every conversation taking place in that room. The microphone had been planted in a wooden carving of the Great Seal of the United States, presented by a delegation of Young Pioneers to Ambassador Averill Harriman in 1945, as a "gesture of friendship" to the USSR's World War II ally.

That event passed out of mind rather quickly, as the Cold War deepened and relations between the two countries became more tense.

However, the significance of the Spaso House "bugging" had not been lost on the Department of State's security specialists, nor on those CIA officials whose job it was to think about the security of the Agency's station in the Moscow embassy: If the KGB had been willing to risk the fallout from discovery of its one microphone in the ambassador's residential study, then bugging the embassy building, where dozens of officers worked every day, would be a much more attractive target.

During the early years of America's diplomatic relations with the Soviet Union, the staff working in Moscow was quite small and its embassy building was located in downtown Moscow, not far from the Kremlin. Soon after the war ended, it became clear that the Americans had outgrown their downtown embassy and that a much larger building would be needed. After a lengthy search, the State Department decided to lease a large, 11-story building located on Chaikovsky Street, part of Moscow's "ring road," a broad boulevard that encircled the entire city. This building would become the new American embassy and would serve that function for the next half-century.

The building needed extensive renovation before the Americans could move in and detailed plans were developed to include office locations and residential apartments, all under one roof.

Floors two through seven were rebuilt as resident apartment units, varying in size to accommodate the families of Foreign Service personnel. The ground floor was to be reserved for the embassy's administrative and consular offices, considered to be less sensitive and therefore requiring a much lower level of security protection. It would be on this floor that a small group of Soviet citizens would work, to help the American staff with the many social and recreational activities that were more difficult to arrange through the down-town offices of Moscow's many cultural outlets: theaters, travel agencies, music halls, opera and sports venues. The parent organization of this group of Soviet helpers was called the Department of Assistance to the Diplomatic Corps (in Russian, UPDK) and it supplied the staffs for similar groups in most of Moscow's other embassies.

It was obvious that this arrangement allowed the KGB to track the movements of every foreign diplomat in Moscow. Travel arrangements, especially, were booked through this office. Even music and language lessons, held within the embassy building, were arranged in this manner. So that an American working in that building had a very difficult time arranging any activity beyond the knowledge of the Soviet authorities. This fact would, much later in my tour of Moscow, have consequences that might impact the future of my career.

During the renovation of the building, a huge undertaking for the Soviet workers employed for the task, the construction crews draped the entire building with a huge canvas "envelope," ostensibly to reduce dust and noise and to protect the ground below from falling objects and other debris normally associated with such a large job.

As we were to learn later, that "envelope" allowed those Soviet workmen all the time they needed to install a massive bugging of the entire building, many microphones that would, by comparison, make the earlier Spaso House bugging appear as child's play. I would eventually have an important role in the discovery and dismantling of this "system."

Part of my routine duties required me to meet regularly with the Chief of Station, in the bubble, and with other station officers. My office was located directly adjacent to the Marine Guard desk. That desk, manned around the clock every day of the week, controlled all the comings and goings of everyone who had security-clearance access to the embassy's restricted areas. The Marine guards had their own living quarters in the embassy building's north wing and, in a security emergency, the push of a button would bring at least eight of them rushing to their duty station.

Sometime early in 1964 the station received a cabled message from Headquarters that was the beginning, probably, of the most memorable few months of my Moscow tour.

The message, classified Top Secret and labeled "Immediate" to show its importance, informed us that a reliable source had told his CIA handlers that there was a "bug" in the office of the ambassador's deputy and that this bug had been providing the KGB with detailed transcripts of everything spoken in that office. (*This source, later identified as Yuri Nosenko, and his relationship with the Agency, has been the subject of several books, including* Wilderness of Mirrors, *by David C. Martin.*)

I took this message to the deputy chief of mission (the ambassador happened to be away at the time), told him that CIA stood behind what the message said, and asked him "what to do next?" The DCM clearly was upset at the news but, as a many-year Foreign Service professional, he told me that I should begin a thorough search for this "bug," to confirm whether the CIA's source was right. However, he reasoned, correctly as it turned out, that if there was a bug in his office there more than likely would be microphones in other offices. Rather than destroying his office, searching for this bug, I should find another office and begin my search there.

So the hunt began in one of the military attaché offices. After weeks of searching, the search team found nothing. By now this search, and the CIA sourcing of the report, had reached the attention of the Department's Security Office and they decided that the issue was important enough to dispatch a team of U.S. Navy Sea Bees (Construction Battalion engineers) to do the rest of the searching.

The Sea Bee team arrived within a couple of weeks. By that time, the senior military attaché had had enough disruption of his offices that he asked me to find another office space in which to search. Like the DCM, he thought that if there were microphones in the embassy's walls, there would be more of them, in other offices, and so it mattered little *which* office space was searched.

The embassy was extremely crowded for available office space, every section fully occupied. But adjacent to my office and the Marine Guard desk, was the embassy's "waiting room," a small room rarely used because people who came to visit the ambassador or others in the restricted area rarely, or never, had to "wait." So the waiting room became the place where an all-out, "final" search would be made for the alleged microphone that already had done so much damage.

The embassy routinely employed a team of Soviet workers, men with the mundane skills required for maintaining any large building and its occupants: auto mechanics, electricians, a plumber or two, and so on. Two of these men were assigned to the Sea Bee team to help dismantle that waiting room. At the time I thought it ironic that if a microphone were ever found, these same Soviet workmen, who surely reported regularly to the KGB, would be helping the Americans find, finally, a listening system that had been in place for more than a decade.

The waiting room, quite literally, was demolished. Each of the four walls, the ceiling and floor were torn off their supporting joists and studs, exposing everything behind, above and beneath.

A very old hot water radiator system provided heat for the entire building. Each room had at least one radiator, located beneath a window in an outside wall. Up to this point, the two radiators in the military attaché office had not been removed, owing to the extra difficulty of shutting down the water and the possibility for small flooding in the affected room. But as the waiting room was our last chance, the radiator had to come out.

As my office was right next door to the waiting room I was aware of what was going on during this demolition process. About three o'clock one afternoon, the technical security officer came to my office and gave me the "shhhh" sign, his finger over his lips, and motioned me to come have a look.

With the radiator now removed it was possible to see what had been behind it. The room had been painted, several times during the ten years since the building was first occupied, and the radiator's sections had allowed the paint brushes to apply paint only to the spaces behind and between those segments, leaving untouched bare plaster vertical strips. The technical security officer pointed to a spot on one of these bare strips and there, behold, was a hole in the plaster, no larger than the diameter of a pin.

The two of us looked at each other, broad grins of satisfaction spreading over our faces. We had found what we had been looking for.

The rest of this job would be done by the Sea Bees, the Soviet workmen were asked to leave. It was unclear, at that moment, if they were aware of our discovery but it really didn't matter because within the next few days the microphone system would be shut down, something the Soviet "listeners," wherever they were, could hardly miss.

What we found next, I had to admit, was a tribute to Soviet ingenuity. That nearly invisible pinhole in the plaster wall, purposely located behind the radiator so that paint would never plug it, led to a hollowed-out, wooden tube, probably twelve inches long. The tube, about the diameter of a drinking straw, was connected to the microphone, a round, heavy object about three inches in diameter and two inches deep. The tube was long enough to permit the microphone to have been embedded in the building's outside brick wall at the time of the building's remodeling. The microphone's wires were enclosed in a lead sheath, or cable, and, as we soon learned, there were 52 of them in the building's walls, all connected via these lead cables to a "trunk" cable that passed through the concrete floor underneath the building's north wing and from there, outside the building and underground, to the Soviet listening post.

I mentioned "Soviet ingenuity." It became clear to us, the moment we understood the microphone system's design, why the Soviets had installed it the way they did. They were aware, in 1952-53, that any modern intelligence service knew how to "sweep" a room for the presence of microphones. The sweeping process was a metal-detection system, nothing more. The embassy's microphone system had evaded detection by sweeping because the metallic components (the microphone itself and the lead sheathing) were at least twelve inches from the inside walls and, at that time, available metal detectors were not that sensitive. Further, the Soviets rightly calculated, the Americans would not think to "sweep" the outside walls of the building, many floors above street level.

I mentioned that there were 52 microphones in the system. It was not necessary to remove 51 more radiators to arrive at this number. Our technical security officer simply applied a noise generator to the discovered pin hole and then each apartment and office dweller heard a soft, high-pitched "howl," showing that that particular living or office space had, indeed, been bugged for the past decade.

Needless to say it was impossible, and unnecessary, to avoid telling everyone in the embassy what had happened. It soon became a kind of joke among the Foreign Service families, who lived in the building, to share experiences: "Why wasn't *my* apartment bugged? Maybe we're not important enough?"

As soon as the trunk cables had been cut, and the microphone system forever disabled, our ambassador, by now returned to Moscow, asked for a meeting with the Soviet Foreign Minister. At that meeting he lodged a formal, written complaint about the bugging. The Foreign Minister, in response, claimed that he had no knowledge of the matter (probably not true) but promised to look into it. To my knowledge, the ambassador never did receive a response.

The story made international news. Time Magazine ran an article about the bugging, and I believe this was the only "intelligence story," in my many years of service for the Agency, in which I was directly involved.

I've always thought back on this episode as an example of how "diplomacy" worked during the Cold War. The United States and the Soviet Union wanted to avoid war with each other, but each side did whatever it could, short of real hostilities, to learn what the other side was doing.

A recent foot-note to this story appeared in the September 2012 issue of Air Force Magazine. *Written by Peter Grier, Washington, DC editor for the Christian Science Monitor, the article details the long history of*

Soviet—and, later, Russian—attempts to conceal listening devices in the structures of the American embassy buildings in Moscow. Grier explains how Russian workmen were able to build twenty-first century technology into these listening devices, especially in the newly-constructed building that eventually, in May 2000, replaced the building in which I worked in the 1960s. The Russians, as they had done in the 1950s, focused their efforts on what they knew would be the embassy's secure areas, the upper floors of the building. Their tactics were similar but the technology much superior!

American Embassy, Moscow, 1965

Chapter 21

The Flight of the Sparrows

The Russian word for "sparrow," **воробей** = "voro**byay**," has an interesting colloquial meaning: a young, attractive woman who is out to put something over on the man she's with. "Bimbo" might be the nearest thing in English.

It was an important part of my job to provide an unclassified security briefing for every new arrival to Moscow, including adult dependents. I made sure that no classified material slipped into these briefings because the dependents did not have security clearances.

These briefings were held inside the bubble, usually with a dozen or so newcomers seated around the conference table. Some of the men, with previous "denied area" experience at other posts, had heard most of this stuff before and it was a challenge for me to get through all the things I wanted to cover without putting them to sleep.

But invariably everyone paid close attention when I began speaking about "entrapment." This was a term in common use wherever the KGB was free to roam in its never-ceasing efforts to trap Westerners, especially Americans, who would be living and working in Moscow for the next two years. The KGB considered every American adult to be a potential target, someone whose work or social life might provide an opening for them to exploit. The KGB's goal, of course, was to ensnare the target and force him or her to cooperate with them.

The embassy's security briefing book—it, too was unclassified so that anyone could read it—contained too many stories, to recite at one sitting, about KGB entrapment operations against Americans and other Westerners, in Moscow and elsewhere in the Soviet Union. But, as experience had accumulated over the years since the Americans set up shop in Moscow, it had become obvious that the use of "sparrows" was one of the KGB's favorite ploys, because they worked.

And I had to be worried about the fifteen-man Marine Corps security guard staff. Most of these men were corporals or sergeants, single and young, far from home and sometimes lonely. Their social life was far more restricted in Moscow than it had been at any of their previous posts. They were free to come and go. Their living quarters were in the Embassy's north wing but there was a loosely organized club located some distance from the embassy, known as "The American Club." By an arrangement with Moscow city officials, the Club catered only to Americans and other Western embassy staff. Its customers were mostly young single adults from the English-speaking diplomatic community.

It didn't take long for me to realize, after arriving at my Moscow post, that this American Club was a natural target for the KGB. If one of these Marines could somehow be compromised, entrapped, and then recruited, just imagine what that would mean to the security structure at the embassy. These Marine guards were the only people allowed in the building's secure area during non-working hours, they walked their patrols, throughout the building, all through the wee hours of the night. A Marine in the clutches of the KGB could do a lot of damage.

Not all of these young Marines were single. One of them, a Lance Corporal, was married and had a wife and small child living in the States. Somehow the KGB learned of this and, sure enough, one of its sparrows went to work on this young man.

She met him at the entrance to the American Club, struck up a conversation in her good-enough English and persuaded him to meet her at a nearby restaurant the next evening.

This in itself was against the rules, because every Marine guard on the post had been warned about just this kind of set-up. But loneliness and testosterone can be a fatal mix. The young Marine met with this woman several times, one thing led to another and, soon enough she invited him to "her" apartment in downtown Moscow. The apartment, of course, was a KGB safe house with a bedroom and camera facilities ready to go. The young couple did their thing, the KGB's camera worked perfectly and within a few days the young Marine was introduced to his new girl friend's "boss."

The "boss" was a young KGB officer who spoke good English. He told the Marine that he sympathized with his predicament, but that the photos in his possession would probably reach the Marine's wife back home if he refused to cooperate.

Needless to say, the Marine was terribly frightened, thoroughly ashamed of himself. He asked his interlocutor for a day or two to think it over and returned to the embassy.

Then, and this story could not be told but for what follows: The Marine went to his Gunnery Sergeant, the senior Marine NCO on post, and told him what had happened. The "Gunny" told his boss, a Marine colonel in the attaché office, who then told me the story. We all agreed: It's tough to watch a Marine in tears.

This event occurred fairly early in my assignment to Moscow and became one of the most effective parts of future security briefings for newcomers. It was a sharp reminder that, yes, it *can* happen here.

As a post script to this rather sad tale, I can say that the U.S. Marine Corps, when the circumstances are right, can be a forgiving organization. That was the case here. The young Lance Corporal, who was only a few months from rotation out of Moscow, was reassigned to another American embassy, outside the Soviet Bloc. Probably the Soviets did not bother him again. I had wondered, in fact, why they chose him for his sparrow experience, knowing he would soon be leaving Moscow. He had not yet received his orders at the time of the event so I believe they had hoped he would be assigned to another Soviet Bloc post, where their reach was long enough to threaten him again. In this case, however, "all's well that ends well."

I had wondered from time to time, as I anticipated traveling away from Moscow, if a "sparrow" might come across my own path. I would find out, for sure.

My first trip came about six months after I had arrived at the station. It was late Spring in 1964 and I anticipated decent weather throughout the Caucasus region. My traveling companion would be the chief of the consular section and we were to visit Tbilisi, Yerevan and Baku, capitals of the Georgian, Armenian and Azerbaijani republics.

Each of us was a happily married man, insofar as the KGB could know, so I imagined the odds that a sparrow would fly my way were pretty slim.

Wrong.

The first leg of our trip took us to Tbilisi, years earlier home to Joseph Stalin. I found it interesting that, despite Nikita Khrushchev's fierce denunciation of Stalin, in 1956 before a secret meeting of a Communist Party Congress, there were several flattering statues of the ruthless dictator prominently displayed on Tbilisi's streets. Khrushchev's "de-Stalinization" policy had required the removal of these monuments in most cities, his body had been removed from the Lenin mausoleum in Moscow, and most public references to him purged from view. But not in Tbilisi. I decided that the fiercely independent Georgians—who were known to despise their Russian masters—were not to be trifled with, in the minds of the big shots in Moscow.

One of the few tourist attractions in Tbilisi was its Natural History museum. I had not paid much attention to museums in the United States but this exhibit seemed to me to be well done and an inspiring glimpse into the past of the Caucasus region, something I knew nothing about. This three-hour visit was a good example of why the embassy wanted its officers to get out of Moscow.

Our Soviet helpers back at the embassy had purchased tickets for the two of us, to attend a dance performance at Tbilisi's ballet theater. We arrived early and found our seats to be good ones. However, we noticed, as the theater began to fill, that the one seat on each side of us remained unoccupied. The seats were reserved and I began to wonder who might eventually occupy them. I whispered to my companion, with a wink, to "get ready."

Sure enough, just a few minutes before curtain time, two very attractive women, probably a few years younger than we, slid into the two seats on either side of us. We smiled, said "Hello, nice to see you," in our best Russian and waited for the curtain to go up. During the intermission our two sparrows insisted on getting us some refreshments, the typically luke-warm Soviet version of Pepsi-Cola. While they were out of hearing I asked my companion what he thought we should do after the performance, as it was pretty obvious that the two women had something in mind other than just leaving the theater and going our separate ways. We agreed we'd just walk back to our hotel, let them tag along if they wanted to, but no way would they come into the hotel with us.

After the show finished, we got up to leave and the two sparrows asked, did we mind if they walked with us for awhile? Of course not, no problem.

The walk back to the hotel, maybe three city blocks, must have been embarrassing for these two women. They didn't seem to be experienced hookers and they behaved as though they were following orders from someone else, as no doubt was the case. Their attempts to be pleasantly flirtatious seemed forced and unnatural and my companion and I later agreed that they were more uncomfortable than we were. When we reached the hotel's entrance they wanted to walk "a little bit more," but we said we were tired (true) and wanted to go to bed. And that was that.

My companion and I were almost disappointed that it seemed

the KGB had trotted out its "B" team. Maybe they thought we weren't worth their "A" team or, more likely, this was the best pair of sparrows they had.

So it was a kind of "non-event," but the object lesson was a good one: However inept some KGB "approaches" may appear to be, we had to remember that they would never stop trying, because they believe that if they try often enough, they will succeed. Any foreigner traveling in the Soviet Union who forgets this does so at his peril.

Chapter 22

The Cherepanov Papers

"The Cherepanov Papers" was a name given to an event unlike any I had ever heard of in all my years in Soviet operations. Cherepanov (and I don't recall his first name) claimed to be an officer in that part of the KGB's "internal affairs" department that kept tabs on everything—and everyone—in Moscow's American embassy.

One day, in Moscow, he—or someone he trusted—approached an American visitor on a down-town sidewalk. The American spoke Russian, something that Cherepanov may have learned prior to approaching the visitor. He seemed to be agitated and frightened and he thrust into the hands of the very-surprised visitor a packet of documents, bound in brown twine, and unmarked. He asked the visitor to take the packet to the American Embassy, saying that they would know what to do with it. The man then disappeared into a nearby alleyway and was never seen again.

The visitor brought the packet to the American Embassy and delivered it to one of the embassy's consular officers, located on the street level of the embassy building. He told the consular officer what little he knew, as described above.

It needs explaining here that most, if not all, State Department officers coming on duty to the Moscow embassy had been briefed in Washington to be aware of "provocations," actions by any Soviet citizen, and usually at the behest of the KGB, that would put the American official at risk. An example might be a Soviet stranger asking an American embassy officer, who is walking toward the embassy, to deliver a book for him, to a friend at the embassy, someone he considers it dangerous to be seen with because of the Soviet militiamen who were constantly on guard duty at the embassy's entrances. In this example, the American officer obligingly accepts the book and continues to walk toward the embassy. He suddenly is apprehended by the ubiquitous "goons," the book is seized and found to contain within its pages a coded message, revealing Soviet "state secrets." The whole charade has been arranged to embarrass the American and his embassy. The next morning's issue of Izvestia *probably carries an article about the incident, again reminding Soviet citizenry to be wary of the Americans.*

Back to Cherepanov's "packet." The consular officer sensed that whatever was in the packet would be of interest to someone "upstairs where the spooks work," a reference to the embassy's secure area, known to house the CIA station's personnel. But because the consular officer did not know who these people were—and even if he had guessed he had no "official" connection with them—he took the packet to the ambassador's deputy, believing that he would know what to do with it.

What happened next is still the subject of a "How-could-this-have-happened?" legend within the archives of the CIA's Soviet operations records.

The ambassador was away and his deputy or DCM—Deputy Chief of Mission—notified the Chief of Station, asked him to come to his office and explained what little he knew about the packet, just what the consular officer had told him. But the DCM already had made up his mind to return the packet *to the Soviet authorities.* The Chief of Station pleaded with him to change his mind, to no avail. As a compromise the DCM agreed to allow the packet's contents to be photographed before it was returned.

The DCM then reached his contact in the Soviet Foreign

Ministry, explained what had happened, and sent the packet back to the Foreign Office.

When the station reported this event to Headquarters, it created a huge stink, to say the least. For years "The Cherepanov Incident" put a damper on the already-cool relationships between CIA's Soviet Division and its State Department counterpart.

And well it might have. Cherepanov's packet contained information about the KGB's in-Moscow surveillance techniques and limitations. He no doubt wanted to demonstrate his access to more information, in anticipation of further contact with the CIA station.

And, most revealing of all, Cherepanov's *name* was included in the packet's papers. By including his name—he probably believed that the CIA would know at least some of the names of the KGB officers in the unit for which he worked—he was taking another risk to demonstrate his access and his trust.

After the station reviewed the photographed documents it was clear that Cherepanov had wanted to connect with the CIA and that he was willing to take significant risks to prove his willingness to help.

Sadly, the Agency later learned that the KGB, after reading Cherepanov's "packet," tracked him down (in Siberia) and shot him.

There have been a few other examples of a Soviet "walk-in," someone who takes the initiative to contact the CIA because he has something to offer and is willing to take the risk. All of these walk-ins took that risk because they were fed up with the Soviet way of doing things and wanted to help. But this is the only event of which I am aware wherein the U.S. Government not only turned down the offer of help but demonstrably wrote the death sentence for the man making the offer.

Kremlin, Moscow River

Chapter 23

Travel

The embassy made it a practice to encourage its officers to travel throughout the Soviet Union, as much as their workloads would allow. It was helpful in a number of important ways: get to know what people outside Moscow were like (they were *much* different), improve one's conversational ability in Russian, soak up some typical Russian culture, which was somewhat different from the lavish productions put on in Moscow's great theaters and concert halls.

It was a "must" that this travel be done in pairs, two officers together. The reasons for this *a duo* policy made sense. If one of the team had a problem, illness, an accident, he had help right at his side, no need to rely on Soviet assistance that might or, more likely, might not be adequate. Just as important, but unspoken, if the officer got into trouble with the authorities (the "entrapment" idea, again) his sidekick would be expected to be a witness, to remind those around him of his and his partner's diplomatic status, and to call the embassy for help if it was needed.

Despite these built-in safeguards, travel had its risks of a different kind.

About half-way through my tour, probably sometime in 1965,

our Chief of Station went on a trip that eventually took him into the heart of Siberia, more than 2,000 miles east of Moscow. His companion was the embassy's agricultural attaché, a man who knew more about Soviet crop abundance and failures than did the Russians themselves. (Officials from the various state agricultural administrations, in Moscow, sometimes asked him to come to their offices to compare notes!)

Unbeknownst to our Chief of Station, who was enjoying himself while on this "free" trip, the FBI in New York City had just arrested a KGB officer who had been caught with his hand in the cookie jar. The Bureau asked the State Department to declare the Soviet official *persona non grata*, which the Department obligingly did, probably with no thought to what might then happen in the Soviet Union.

Even if the Department had considered it, it might not have mattered. It was important in those days to let the Soviet authorities know that when one of their "officials" was caught spying in the United States he would be sent home, asap, no questions asked.

The other side of this coin was something known as "reciprocity." If the Americans sent a Soviet official packing, for whatever reason, the Soviets would do the same to an American serving in Russia, whether or not he had done anything wrong.

The Soviets apparently had learned that our Chief of Station was just that, the head of the Agency's group in Moscow, and they chose him to give the boot, perhaps figuring that his departure would put a crimp in whatever we were doing. They had absolutely no evidence that he was doing anything illegal, while on his Siberian trip or at any time before.

Among intelligence officers assigned to all the Iron Curtain countries, this practice was, with a grimace, referred to as "career management." Most of us had invested years of experience in our work and in learning the appropriate language(s). But after an officer had had the "PNG" badge pinned to his lapel, he could no longer serve in any country under the control of the Soviets. So it was a serious matter to be asked to leave the country and in this case the station could do nothing about it.

What that meant to me was a sudden and unintended elevation to the role of Acting Chief of Station. Headquarters scrambled to find a replacement for our departed COS, but it took several months and during that time I found myself, so to speak, right under the ambassador's nose, and with a lot more work to do.

On a lighter note, I recall a trip that I made in the summer of 1964, far into the Soviet interior, to Irkutsk and Lake Baikal, nearly 3,000 miles east of Moscow. My traveling companion was the embassy's senior economics officer and he knew of my Agency affiliation. So both of us expected to be followed by the usual "goons." I had always wanted to fish in Lake Baikal because it is known to have a particular species of trout, the *Omul*, found nowhere else. I packed a small spinning rod and off we went.

The airplane flight was one I'll never forget. We were aboard the standard Ilyushin T-104, a two-engine jet aircraft that flew about 450 miles per hour. I remember looking down at the vast Russian taiga (forest) below us and I think it was at least two hours before I saw a gap in that vast expanse of green, some 900 miles of forest without a break! We landed at Omsk to refuel but had to wait on the ground much longer than scheduled so that when we finally arrived in Irkutsk, we were quite late. The "goons" apparently had given up on us and when we got off the airplane, very early in the morning, it was obvious that we were absolutely free of any surveillance. We were also very tired from the long flight but managed to find our way to the water taxi that would take us up the Angara River to the lake.

Lake Baikal is the world's largest and deepest fresh-water body, nearly 400 miles long. To drain that lake, the Angara River also is huge. It drains the lake at its southern end and flows generally northward until it joins the even larger Yenisey River which flows all the way to the Arctic Ocean, just north of the Arctic Circle.

The water taxi from Irkutsk to the lake plowed southeastward and upstream at a rather slow pace, so my companion and I, sleepy as we were, decided to take a nap. We had put our luggage in an overhead rack, my spinning rod alongside.

We must have really conked out because suddenly the water taxi's steward was shaking us and urging us to get off, we were at our designated stop and the next one was miles up the lake. So off we hurried, half-awake, grabbing our luggage and jumping onto the dock. Just as the water taxi left the dock I realized my spinning rod was still on that luggage rack. So ended my long-held hope of catching one of those unique trout.

But my disappointment was brief because we again realized that we were without the usual "tails." We were free to wander about the village of Baikal and visit its unusual maritime museum. And my companion wanted to visit the "mayor" of the village, just to say hello from the American embassy in Moscow. These "courtesy calls" were always well-received, especially in the smaller cities and villages so far from Moscow, where the locals rarely saw a foreigner, and even less often an American.

We had been chatting for ten minutes or so with the mayor and he obviously was enjoying himself, "hosting" two American visitors who had traveled nearly 3,000 miles just to visit "his" village. Suddenly his phone rang and he picked up the receiver. After listening for a moment, his face visibly blanched and he spoke in to the handset, "Да, они здесь,"—Yes, they're here.

So the "goons" finally had caught up with us, but only by telephone. They were still in Irkutsk and we were some distance from their "control." The mayor was embarrassed by all this, he probably had an even lower opinion of the KGB's surveillance tactics than we did. But he had no choice, he had been instructed to ask us to wait in his office until "transportation" could be arranged to bring us back to Irkutsk. We could have made an issue of this because, before leaving Moscow, we had stated our intention, in writing, to visit Lake Baikal. But being the polite visitors that we were we decided to go along with the mayor's difficult situation. Besides, it was a pleasant August afternoon, so we decided to wait for our transport outside the mayor's office and enjoy the view of the lake.

As luck would have it, a group of local youngsters was passing by and we called to them, in Russian, and asked if we could take their picture, that we were Americans and would appreciate a photograph of them as a souvenir. I doubt these youngsters had seen many Americans and they were more than happy to pose for us, with Lake Baikal just behind them.

After thirty minutes or so, a harried taxi driver arrived at the mayor's office, apparently having just been ordered by telephone to bring the two Americans back to Irkutsk. It was a long and bumpy ride, over a road with many potholes and much less comfortable than had been the water-taxi trip up the river, but at least we didn't have to pay for it. Apparently the KGB had a "fund" with which to cover such unexpected expenses.

Back in Irkutsk, we moved into the hotel which had been waiting for us. We were again under the watchful eyes of the Soviet "system" which always was ready to take the fun out of life, in order to protect the Great Motherland from its enemies.

Siberian Pre-Teens at Lake Baikal

May Day Parade, Surface to Air Missiles

May Day Parade, Three Stage ICBM

Red Square, St. Basil's Cathedral, Kremlin Clock Tower

Chapter 24

Checking Out

My tour in Moscow lasted longer than the usual two-year stint that most embassy officers put in. The State Department and the Agency both believed, correctly, that two years in the Soviet capital was enough, especially for the families of its officers who had to endure a relatively restricted lifestyle. As I had arrived in November of 1963, stretching my tour into summer of 1966 meant that I had served closer to three years than to two. But the timing made sense, as the summer months were when most of the rotations occurred throughout all of the foreign service agencies.

Leaving any foreign-capital post requires some planning. What to do with one's automobile, how much furniture to ship onward (sometimes it was possible to sell or give a few pieces to a neighbor), what about schools for the kids next Fall, giving notice to the occupants of one's home in the States, etc. And in the case of leaving Moscow, many families chose to spend some time in Western Europe, a little "R&R" (rest and rehab) on the way home.

And there was another bit of "planning" that went on inside the heads of the station's officers.

I should digress a bit here to mention that every officer at the

Moscow Station, at least once during his tour, would fly to one of the major West European cities to be met by an officer from Headquarters' Soviet Russia division. These meetings were essential to keep the station officers up to date on the happenings at Headquarters, or anywhere else that might impact their assignments in Moscow, stuff that could not easily by transmitted to the station by cablegrams or written dispatches. These meetings usually lasted two days and provided ample opportunity for a breath of fresh air, in addition to the update briefings.

One of the most interesting things we learned was that several officers serving in East European capitals had been approached, just as they were preparing to leave their posts, by local citizens claiming to have "hot" information for the United States government. These approaches always included the kind of information that would say something about the person's access, his place of work, and an appeal for a meeting prior to the officer's departure from the country. And, naturally, the officer would have to make a snap decision as to whether the approach was one with some real intelligence-collection potential or, just as likely, another provocation by the local intelligence service which, if accepted by the officer, might result in his expulsion, i.e. more "career management."

I had had the good sense to file this briefing somewhere in the back of my head. As it turned out, it was a smart thing to do.

Part of my checking out process included a trip to Moscow's American Express office where I would pick up the airplane tickets for myself and my family. This visit to the AE office had been arranged by our Soviet helpers at the embassy, so both they and AE office knew I was coming. The office was close enough to the embassy that I chose to walk.

I concluded my business with American Express, pocketed my tickets and headed back toward the embassy. When I was no more than ten or twenty meters away from the AE's entry way, a young man popped out of an alley way, grabbed my elbow and introduced himself. He said he knew I was an American and on my way to my embassy, a man he could trust, and would I *please* take with me what he had in his right hand, a fat paper envelope.

This was one of those supremely pregnant moments that no intelligence officer can ever forget: "What the heck do I do now?"

That briefing in the back of my head rapidly came forward: Obviously this could be a provocation, depending on what's in that envelope. A PNG possible? I sure don't want to be the victim of the KGB's "career management" program. My replacement is ready to come to the post. I have my tickets. And if this guy is real, he can try to contact the embassy another day.

I told the young man, after getting his name straight, to keep his envelope but that I might be able to meet him in Gorky Park, near its main entrance. He should sit on the nearest available bench and I would walk through that entrance at ten o'clock in the morning, three days hence. If I don't show up he'll know that I can't come. Fair enough? He had no choice but to say Yes and he quickly disappeared into the crowded sidewalk, the envelope still in his right hand. The whole exchange had lasted no more than a minute or two.

I would be fibbing to say that at that moment my heart rate was not elevated. I scooted back to the embassy and immediately asked the COS to meet me in the bubble. When he heard the story, he asked the ambassador to join us. The ambassador was skeptical, who could blame him, but he did agree that we should inform CIA Headquarters and get its reaction to the situation.

Headquarters returned its decision within a few hours: A trace of the man's name failed to turn up anything and without knowing what was in the envelope, which they agreed I should not have accepted in those circumstances, my going to Gorky Park was an unnecessary risk because if the KGB was behind the event it would surely open a new can of worms that no one, either the embassy or the station, wanted.

As I have said elsewhere, I don't remember ever going to work without looking forward to the day. I sometimes do, however, look "backward" to the day I checked out of Moscow.

Part Six – Home to Stay

Chapter 25

The Spike

When I returned to Headquarters from Moscow in early Fall 1966, I was promoted to become the chief of the Soviet Division's Moscow branch and if things went well it would be a two-year assignment. John Aalto, with whom I had served in Moscow for two years, was named my deputy. We had a good working relationship, having already known and served with each other for ten years. The branch was large enough that my new job would be a good measure of my managing abilities, heretofore untested. I had always thought of myself as a "field man," a guy who operated pretty much on his own—after being told what to do—and one not especially fond of the sometimes-petty infighting and politicking that can always be found in any bureaucracy. I soon learned that there were too many things going on for me to be closely involved with each one. I had to learn how to delegate responsibility and then trust my staff to do the work and do it well.

The branch already was dealing with a piece of "unfinished business," left over from an operation at the Moscow Station which had been dormant most of the time I served there, sort of out-of-sight-out-of-mind. Shortly before I arrived in Moscow in November

1963, the station had learned about a Soviet "walk-in," a citizen who claimed to have access to information about Moscow's air-defense system and its Table of Organization. If true, this would be a source well worth learning more about. The information he had provided was tantalizing but needed verification before we would risk establishing an agent relationship with him. He had provided a means of getting back to him, telling us we should leave written contact instructions for him in a package to be buried at the base of a specific kilometer post alongside the main highway between Moscow and Leningrad. He said he would check the location once a month until we were able to provide him with further instructions.

The station passed along to Headquarters as much as it knew and the branch decided it was worth trying to set up a communications plan with the man, else we would never learn if he was for real or not. The plan, written in Russian and on thin, water-repellant paper, was to be concealed in a metal "spike," a hollow aluminum cylinder about six inches long and an inch and a half in diameter and painted black. It was pointed at one end and had a sealed screw-top at the other. The design—it had been fabricated by TSD—was intended to make it easy for anyone to push the spike into the dirt at the base of the kilometer post, quickly and unobtrusively.

At that time, it was impossible for a station officer to plant the spike. The Penkovsky roll-up had reduced its staff sufficiently that those left were under constant KGB surveillance.

The branch knew about the Agency's in-place liaison relationships with several foreign countries and decided we could ask one of their representatives in Moscow to do the spike planting for us. The assumption was that such a representative would be of much less interest to the KGB than was his American counterpart and that a surveillance of the spike-planting activity was unlikely.

At a social function at Spaso House sometime later, our Chief or Station passed the loaded spike to the designated liaison contact. His superiors at home had briefed him on what to expect and what to do.

Two weeks later he returned the spike to our COS, telling him that he considered the planting to be too dangerous because he could not be sure he was not under surveillance.

After considering the available alternatives, our COS decided to return the spike to Headquarters. It contained a ready-to-go communications plan, written in Russian, that might have use somewhere else at another time.

The spike arrived in Headquarters, by classified mail, and was delivered to my branch. As it had been crafted by the Technical Services Division and was really their property, John Aalto and I decided he would return it to them on his next visit to their office, some distance from ours. He put the spike in his office desk safe drawer, along with his other sensitive files and, for awhile, forgot about it.

Like everyone in the branch, John was a busy guy and it was several months later that he found time to take the spike back to TSD. One day he phoned ahead to be sure the appropriate TSD officer was at his desk and told him he was about to bring TSD's spike back where it belonged.

As it happened, that TSD office was crammed with various monitoring devices, used in routine testing of TSD's many operational "gadgets." Among these was an active Geiger Counter and when John walked into the office, the instrument immediately began screaming its "live radiation" signal. Within moments the TSD officer traced the source of the radiation to the spike.

This event set off alarm bells throughout TSD and the SR division. What had happened?!

Within the next 24 hours the TSD technicians determined that the spike's contents had been heavily laced with the highly radioactive element Strontium-90.

It did not take long to recount the events in the life of the spike: It had been kept in the locked office safe of our liaison contact for no more than two weeks, the time it took him to decide not to plant it at the kilometer post on the Moscow-Leningrad highway. During the hours of darkness of that period, Soviet specialists entered the office, broke into the safe and, probably to their surprise, found the spike. They determined what it was for but could not know for whom it was intended or where it would be retrieved. So to follow it, they laced it with the radioactive material. TSD's examination concluded that with available monitoring equipment the spike could be followed from a distance of several hundred feet, making it possible for the KGB to locate the spike after it had been planted, put it under permanent surveillance, and wait for it to be retrieved.

An interesting sidelight to the investigation led to one of the accounts that the KGB defector Yuriy Nosenko had provided his CIA handlers. He told them that the KGB had a special group of men whose principle function was to break into the many embassies in Moscow, open their safes, photograph their contents and leave the scene with no one being the wiser. They used various kinds of radioactive materials to do their work and became known as the *bezubniys*, "the toothless ones." Their constant exposure to radiation caused their teeth to fall out, a grim reminder of the "dedication" of some of our KGB adversaries.

Now that we knew what had happened, and had a pretty good idea of how it happened, it was time to see what damage, if any, the irradiated spike might have inflicted on its way from Moscow to that TSD office.

The liaison contact had had it in his possession for no more than a week, the same for our Chief of Station. The Soviets no doubt followed it all the way to the airport, from the American embassy, as it traveled inside the station's mail system all the way to Washington, DC From there it was handled briefly by the internal mail system. But then it rested in John Aalto's safe for several months, not two feet away from John when he was seated at his desk.

The branch arranged for a thorough physical examination for John and he passed with flying colors, having worried for a few days about his "reproductive prowess" and how it might have been affected.

An unusual story, but its conclusion could have been worse.

Chapter 26

Trouble at Home

I would like to think that many autobiographers omit or downplay events or situations that have been uncomfortable issues in their personal lives.

So it is with my account of the break-up of my first marriage, after 20 years.

After concluding my two-year tour as the Moscow branch chief in Headquarters, I was promoted to a new assignment as deputy chief of an Agency facility in downtown Washington.

This job gave me opportunity to meet and befriend diplomats who were working in the nation's capital as representatives of their Eastern Europe countries: Czechoslovakia, Bulgaria, Poland, Romania. The Agency knew that some of these diplomats were in fact working for their intelligence services and it would be up to me to try to get to know one or more of these officials and, over time, determine if they might be susceptible to recruitment by the Agency. Not an easy task, to be sure, but worth trying.

I was able to invite several of these men, with their wives, to my home and to get to know them. Of course my wife, Colleen, was an important part of this effort, the essential at-home hostess. After several of these gatherings, she concluded that this kind of "social" activity would be a dead end for me, professionally, that the odds of success were so small that I would spend two years trying and come up empty-handed.

Needless to say, this kind of spousal interference presents the husband, me, with a dilemma. How to explain to Headquarters my shutting down a program that I had agreed to undertake? Her insistence was so strong—we fought over this for months—that I concluded it was either my career or my marriage.

In Virginia, in the 1960s, divorce was possible only if the aggrieved party could prove abandonment or adultery and neither of these would apply. What to do?

At that time I had not yet come to know Jesus and so guardian angels were something I knew nothing about. But probably every one of us, believer or not, has one of these helpful beings hovering out there, somewhere. That might explain what happened next.

The way one meets foreign diplomats in our nation's capital depends on a number of things, the most important of which is one's "status" within that status-conscious city. I had returned—just two years earlier—from my posting to Moscow, and I knew something about how embassies work.

One day I noticed an announcement in *The Washington Post* that the Czechoslovak embassy would be hosting its national day reception Saturday evening of the following week. I telephoned the embassy, gave my name to the answering receptionist and told her I had served in Moscow. I thought there might be several Czech officials at the national day event whom I had known in Moscow, did I need an invitation to come to the gala celebration? She said no, she would put my name on the guest list.

So I attended the event, alone because my wife thought the whole exercise was a waste of time. Fortunately, she was wrong.

There was a receiving line of about ten people at the embassy's entrance, headed by the Czech ambassador, and about half-way through it I shook hands with a Czech diplomat who appeared to be about my age, a first secretary I guessed. I told him I thought I recognized him from somewhere in my past, could we talk after the reception line broke up? Of course, he said.

A little later I met him again, we chatted for awhile, we exchanged cards and I asked him if he would like to have lunch some time. That would be fine. Was he free the following Monday? Yes. We agreed that I would pick him up at his embassy and we'd go from there in my car.

The next day, a Sunday, I telephoned a well-known French restaurant on 14th Street in Washington. I learned they did not accept reservations for lunch, only dinner, but that I shouldn't have any trouble finding a table for two. What I failed to learn was that they were closed on Mondays.

The next day, after finding a parking place, my new Czech friend and I walked the several blocks to the restaurant, only to find it closed. "Not very good spook-work, John," I mumbled to myself. I told my friend I was pretty sure there would be another restaurant, not far down the street and, sure enough, we found one, a Mexican place that was open and busy.

I've long forgotten what I had for lunch that fateful Monday but whatever it was introduced into my GI system a wee little "bug," known as Hepatitis A.

That same Monday afternoon, back at the office, I asked Headquarters to run a name trace on the Czech diplomat and, yes, he was a first secretary but also a member the Czech intelligence service.

Bingo.

But, not so fast. By Thursday I was feeling too crummy to go to work. I telephoned my Czech friend, told him I was ill and that I'd get back to him as soon as I felt better. I got a hurry-up appointment with my family physician. It took a day or two for the obligatory blood work to reveal the Hepatitis A and after asking me some questions, during my follow-up visit, my doctor traced the problem to that Mexican restaurant, most likely someone in the kitchen who had failed to obey the sanitation rules. The doctor also told me that

I had better be prepared to spend a few days in the hospital. This was not something I could deal with at home.

And so to the hospital I went, into one of those rooms reserved for patients with highly-contagious diseases. The nurses came and went with masks over their faces, dressed in white paper gowns which they disposed of after each visit. My family decided it was too risky to visit me and so I spent a very lonely week in my private isolation room.

When I finally was able to go home, my doctor told me to expect a very slow recovery, probably at least six weeks. This news didn't surprise me because I remembered how Hepatitis had affected some of my colleagues at the Tehran station, ten years earlier.

The at-home recovery was boring and, as predicted, slow. But it gave me plenty of time to think about my future and the result was always the same: No way out of the impasse I had reached with my wife, no apparent solution.

That "solution" appeared within a few days after I was able to go back to work.

Part Seven – Moving West

Chapter 27

Seattle

About a week after I went back to work, having more or less recovered from my bout with Hepatitis, I drove to the Headquarters building to check in with my section chief and overheard him telling someone else, "We really need a man in Seattle."

For a guy who was born in Seattle and raised nearby, that remark got my attention.

I knew the man well enough to ask him, "What's going on here?"

He explained that the Division had just decided to get into the War on Terrorism (this was in 1971, when that idea was yet unheard of) and it was looking for three officers who were willing to go "Out West" to look for people who might be able to help the Agency in its newly-assigned task to "do something" about the Islamist threat.

The Agency's thinkers knew that, throughout the United States, there were many Muslim students, from nearly every Muslim country in the Middle East, who were already enrolled in graduate programs at many of America's universities. These students had been given permission to come to the United States to study at whatever university they chose. The idea was that if these future leaders of the countries from which they came were given an opportunity to live and study in the Unites States, they would return to their homelands with a positive impression of America and, as they achieved influence in their societies and/or governments, would bring with them positive pictures of the United States.

The program was both educational and propagandistic but its sponsors—and my Division was one of them—already were committed to making it work.

So in answer to my question, "What's going on here?," the branch chief explained what I have just written. I told him, "Hey, I grew up in Seattle, I know the place like the back of my hand, and I'm available."

It did not take him long to decide that I would be the officer to go to Seattle. He had already chosen two other officers, to send to Denver and Dallas. In that way, the Division would have three new officers to cover the United States, west of the Mississippi River.

This happenstance visit to my section chief's office was, I later concluded, a most generous gift. It made it possible for me to pack up my family, move to Seattle and begin another phase of my career with the CIA. I would be working in a familiar environment, doing something I never before could have imagined.

While all this was going on I was still wrestling with my personal problem, Colleen's intransigence. I had urged her that the two of us should be going to church. Our older son, Scott, had joined a Boy Scout troop which was sponsored by the Presbyterian church in nearby Annandale, Virginia and I had been helping its scoutmaster on weekend outings, hikes and the like. It seemed odd to me that I would be doing this without setting foot in that church. But Colleen wasn't interested and I didn't want to make that another "issue;" there were already enough of those going on in our lives.

After our move to Seattle and the divorce proceedings had cleared King County's legal system, I found myself a "free man;" the first time in many years that I would be coming home to an empty nest. And there was another problem, related to my work. I would be trying to meet foreign students, to "cultivate" them and get to know them as well as I could. It would be very helpful to have a "hostess" to help me with these things. As I thought about this I wondered briefly about Joan, so far as I knew she was a happily married woman, living with her husband and two children on Mercer Island. I had best not even let her know I had moved back to Seattle.

A week or so later I had lunch with an old high school classmate, a friend and a man I hadn't seen in years. He had become an attorney in Seattle and was working in one of the city's more prestigious law firms. We chatted about old times, mutual friends, a catching-up conversation. Among many other things, he told me that recently he had represented Betty Jean in a divorce proceeding; she was now "unattached," maybe I should look her up.

Within a few days of this conversation I found BJ in the phone book, called her and explained that I was back in Seattle, with a new job. Would she like to hear about it? We met for lunch and I was surprised to sense that the flames were still flickering. More dates followed and within a few months we decided to marry; it was a "conditional" decision.

What I learned during this time was that Betty Jean had become a very strong Christian believer. We talked about her faith and I had to admit to her that I was pretty skeptical about "this Jesus stuff." I had worked for years with a bunch of very bright guys who had persuaded me that the stories about Jesus had been made up by "little old men in brown robes," and that this was mostly what the Bible was made of. BJ just smiled as she listened to this but she made it very clear to me that if we were to marry, I would have to learn the truth about Jesus and then make up my mind about Him. Without Jesus, no wedding!

It was BJ's insistence that pushed me into my search for a new spiritual life. I began going with her to her Lutheran church and she introduced me to some of her close friends, also Lutheran believers. Two of these friends were men about my age and they sensed that I needed some "help" if I really wanted to learn about Jesus. I talked with these men over a period of weeks, and it was obvious to me that they knew what they were talking about: the history of Christianity, the many proofs that were out there showing that Jesus really did walk this earth, the facts of His crucifixion and resurrection. It was, for me, a new beginning—and I've never looked back.

Chapter 28

N7562

Moving one's family from Northern Virginia to Seattle, with no plans to return, is something of a challenge: finding a buyer for one's home, decisions about what to sell, take, choosing a moving company, choosing the right time so as not to disrupt the kids' schooling, and so on. Our family had an extra "problem," but a pleasant one. We had to reckon with a thirty-foot trailer, to haul to Seattle; I would never have considered entrusting this trailer to a commercial moving company.

Inside that trailer was a sailplane, its wings unattached and slung neatly on both sides of the aircraft's fuselage. Same for the horizontal stabilizer.

And therein lies a story within a story.

During our tour in Moscow, we were entitled each year to a couple of weeks of "R&R," rest and recuperation. The family decided to drive to Norway in our Chevy Corvair, and we passed through the beautiful stands of birch trees between Moscow and the Finnish border beyond Leningrad, then across the forested southern end of Finland, and by an ocean-going ferry, into Sweden. Somehow, in Sweden, we found ourselves on a rural highway and, in the sky above, we spotted two sailplanes, obviously descending to land at an airfield.

Some years earlier, on one of my business trips to Europe, I was waiting for a flight out of the airport in Munich, Germany and I could see well across the airport's runways to a large, flat grassy area beyond. That large grassy area was a glider port and I could see several sailplanes being launched by a winch. The winch would tow them to an altitude of about one thousand feet above the ground and they would then cut loose and try to remain aloft. I'd never seen anything like it but it appeared to be exciting and fun.

That sighting at the Munich airport had stuck with me and when I saw the two sailplanes in the Swedish sky, so close, I said to my family, "Let's go check this out."

We found the glider port without much trouble, drove as close as we dared to the launching/recovery area, got out of the car and asked, "Who's in charge, here?" The first man we spoke to was an American expatriate who had come to Sweden to look for work. Two of his friends, also Americans, came over to talk to us. They explained how they had formed a small club, most of its members young Swedish men, all of them die-hard glider pilots. They didn't have enough money to afford a small airplane with which to tow them, and like the operation in Munich, they were using a ground-based winch to get them into the air.

My older son, Scott, was 11 years old at the time but he paid close attention to what was going on, obviously just as excited as I was about what we were seeing and hearing.

Eventually, when we returned to our home in Northern Virginia, the memory of our visit to the Swedish glider port was one that stuck. Two years later it had germinated into a decision: Scott and I would begin taking lessons; we wanted to learn how to fly a glider. We already knew there was a training facility called the Capital Area Soaring School, located at the airport at nearby Leesburg, Virginia. It was owned by Arthur Godfrey.

Scott was just 14 years old when we began taking lessons at the school. His legs were not yet long enough to reach the rudder pedals, so his instructors fitted them with "booster blocks." Also, he didn't weigh enough to meet the center-of-gravity requirement, so he sat on top of a bag full of lead bird shot. But a boy this age can be taught quickly and he learned to fly without having to deal with the bad habits that many older power-plane pilots bring to learning about sailplanes.

We began our lessons on the same day, July 27, 1969 and just a month later, August 27, we both soloed.

Now that we were qualified to fly gliders, we had to make a decision: Most of the students at the Leesburg school, after qualifying, would go on to rent sailplanes from the school. None of them had their own glider. Did we want to do that, or should we buy our own sailplane and fly it whenever and wherever we wished?

So we held a "family conference." How to afford to buy our own sailplane? I had already looked into this and learned that the Schweizer Aircraft Company, in Elmira, New York, would sell me one of its newest sailplanes for an even $5,000, if I was willing to drive to their factory and take delivery there.

Colleen and I were still paying down the mortgage on our home so the family budget scarcely could afford five thousand dollars. It was Scott who provided the solution.

When Scott was born, his grandfather, my dad, gifted him with a number of shares of common stock in Delta Airlines, then a brand-new company operating out of Atlanta, Georgia. The stock was intended eventually to pay for Scott's college education. The stock had done very well and 11 years later, Scott's "college fund" was worth considerably more than $5,000. Scott knew all about this and right in the middle of our "family conference" he said, "We could use *my* money."

Colleen and I could hardly believe what he had just said but we knew he was serious. We thought about it and decided we could use part of Scott's college fund to purchase the sailplane and repay the money, a little each month.

So we placed the order with the Schweizer Company and they promised to have "our" sailplane ready for pick up before Christmas, 1969. The days seemed to drag before we were ready to drive to Elmira. We left home early, covering the 250 miles in time for a late-afternoon briefing by the Schweizer production people. They wanted us to understand how to handle this beautiful new blue-on-off-white Schweitzer 1-26D, serial N7562.

The sailplane came with a trailer, of course, and we hitched it to our Ford station wagon. We spent that night in an Elmira motel, wanting to get an early start for home the next morning. A light snowfall began about bedtime and during the night I was awakened several times by Scott's movements toward our motel room's window: He wanted to be certain that our new glider was okay, sitting in the motel's parking lot, at three in the morning!

The next day the snowfall turned heavier as we moved south. This added some excitement, and concern, as we very carefully returned to our Virginia home.

We now had a sailplane in our driveway, something the neighbors quickly became accustomed to, gawking as they drove buy. I didn't want the sailplane sitting out in the winter weather so I contrived a system of ropes and pulleys and was able to hang the wings above the two cars in the garage and squeeze the fuselage in alongside. With the sailplane out of the weather and out of sight, the family felt better about it. We bought insurance and waited for Spring.

Scott and I flew our new 1-26 as often as we could that spring, summer and fall of 1970. Eventually we were ready to leave the home airport and head out cross-country, a big step for any newly-minted glider pilot. Part of that experience was to learn just how far our sailplane could glide from any given altitude above the ground. Sailplanes can't "go around" as they approach a runway and "getting too low" was always a concern. There were no open, level and safe farmers' fields on which to land, so if one couldn't make it back to the airport he was likely to damage the sailplane, or worse. A 1-26 lands at about 40-45 mph, fast enough to cause plenty of damage in an off-field landing.

It wasn't long before Scott and I learned about the Soaring Society of America, the SSA. This is a national organization that publishes its own monthly magazine, *Soaring,* and keeps its members up to date on what's happening in the soaring fraternity, not just in the United States but world-wide. We learned about the badges that new sailplane pilots can try to achieve: A silver badge required the pilot to stay aloft for at least five hours, to achieve an altitude gain of 1,000 meters (3,200 feet) and to fly a distance of 50 kilometers (32 miles), from the moment he is cut loose from his tow plane until he lands.

The five-hour-aloft requirement was more difficult than one might imagine. Thermal lift can be sporadic and so most new pilots chose to use "ridge lift." This is a weather phenomenon caused by a steady wind flowing against a ridge, the ridge forces the wind to flow upward. If the wind is steady and the ridge long enough the pilot can fly in that lift, back and forth, for as long as the wind blows. It was a boring experience, but a necessary one if the pilot was serious about claiming that silver badge.

These "duration" flights were the stuff of which world records were made. Sailplane pilots from all over the world constantly out-did one another, logging hours and hours of flight time. New Zealand, with its Southern Alps' mountain range, was a favorite for pilots who sought to establish ever-longer times aloft. Eventually, a pilot flying "the ridge" in New Zealand fell asleep, having been aloft for too many hours, and crashed. From that time on, that competition no longer was part of the record books.

Whenever a sailplane pilot decided to fly "cross country," he needed the support of a crew, usually a family member who would follow him, on the ground below with the sailplane's trailer in tow, ready to retrieve him and his sailplane from wherever the pilot decided, or was forced, to land. Getting back to the same airport from which the flight had begun was to be preferred, because the crew had nothing to do and landing at one's home airport was always easier and safer than the alternative. All too often the pilot would "land out," usually in a farmer's field, sometimes at another airport, but always requiring his crew to be there to take him and his sailplane back to the home airport.

As I've mentioned, the Silver Badge required the pilot to fly a distance of at least 50 kilometers, about 32 miles. Scott had already achieved that leg of his silver badge, while we were still flying in Virginia. But now he wanted to break the then-existing distance record for sailplane pilots under 16 years of age. To do that he would have to fly a little more than 97 miles, the record to beat.

Scott was ready for this challenge and one day he left the Wenatchee, Washington airport (Fancher Field) in our 1-26. I was his crew that day and we were in touch by CB (citizens' band) radio. His goal was Davenport, Washington, a small farming community on the high-plateau country of eastern Washington state, almost due-east of Fancher Field and just 100 miles distant. The winds were west to east and the thermals that day were strong, perfect conditions. I quickly acquired Highway 2, the west-east highway that connects western Washington with Spokane, and chatted with Scott as he worked his way eastward. With the strong thermals he found himself flying at altitudes between 7,000 and 10,000 feet, so that reaching his goal turned out to be relatively easy. Still, he wasn't certain that he had covered the needed 100 miles, his on-board maps notwithstanding. He called me on the radio and asked, "Dad, are you *sure* that's Davenport down there?" I assured him he had done what he had set out to do. He landed without incident at Davenport and a proud father and his happy son motored back to their home airport.

As every licensed pilot knows, no matter what kind of airplane one flies, he/she is required to record every flight in a log book. I believe this to be a regulation of the Federal Aviation Administration, but whether or not that is so, looking back at one's log books provides some interesting information and, sometimes, can bring back memories of special flying experiences.

The log book published for sailplane pilots—by the Schweizer Aircraft Corporation—has columns for such entries as the date of the flight, the sequential number of the flight, the type of glider, its registered serial number (as N 7562), type of tow (by a tow plane or winch). There are two columns for "altitude," the tow-release altitude above ground level and the maximum altitude attained during the flight. Another column records the location of the airport from which the flight originates, the time aloft—both dual and solo—and a wider column for "remarks." The "dual" column anticipates two things: the dual flights required during the pilot's learning phase and those dual flights required, by FAA regulation, for an annual check ride with a certified flight instructor.

My own log books, just two of them, record that my last flight occurred on June 25, 1986, 17 years from the time of my first flight. The record also shows my last flight to have been number 289, for an average of only 17 flights per year. And that is why I gave up soaring, with some reluctance, in 1986: I was not flying often enough to consider myself to be "safe." The SSA's monthly magazine *Soaring,* every now and then would record a fatal crash, usually caused by a mid-air collision which happened now and then when too many glider pilots were circling in the same thermal. The other cause of fatalities, usually, was a sailplane entering—and being unable to recover from—a spin. Some of the newer sailplanes, with their narrow wings and high aspect ratios, were virtually impossible to exit a spin. The best solution, obviously, was to avoid getting into one, i.e., keep your speed up and never allow the sailplane to stall. But every time I was reminded of a fatality in our soaring fraternity, I wondered if the pilot had lost his edge, his ability to "stay safe."

Every annual check ride included spin-recovery maneuvers but these check rides always were in two-seat gliders, usually the Schweitzer 2-33 (in which Scott and I learned to fly) or the equally-docile Blanik. Both of these trainers were easy enough to haul back out of a spin. I never tried to spin either our 1-26 or my Standard Libelle, which I purchased from fellow glider pilot Nelson Funston in the spring of 1979.

The Libelle, which Nelson had registered as "Juliet November" (the letters "JN" painted on both the vertical stabilizer and on the underneath side of the starboard wing), was what was referred to as a "standard" racing sailplane. It had a 15-meter wingspan, was made of fiberglass, and had a best glide ratio of about 34 to 1, meaning that at its most efficient speed (about 50 mph) the glider would descend one foot for every 34 feet of forward progress. Another class of racing sailplane was referred to simply as "15 Meter." The major difference in these two gliders was the addition of movable wing flaps in the 15-meter version.

Then there was a third class, "Open," which meant that the competing sailplane pilot could fly any kind of glider he wanted to bring to the contest. These ships had longer wingspans and, in the hands of a skilled pilot, could fly faster and farther than those gliders with 15-meter wings.

The reason for the two-letter marker on each glider: In any sanctioned contest, each entrant, during the race, was referred to by his ship's two-letter "code," e.g., while aloft Nelson would be referred to simply as "Juliet November."

The 1-26, on the other hand, was made of metal and fabric, had a best glide ratio of about 23 to 1, at a speed of about 45 mph. So the Libelle was a large step up for me. It was a fun-to-fly sailplane. By the time I purchased it I had improved my radio system. In the 1-26, Scott and I stayed in touch via a CB (Citizens' Band) radio. Problem was that, at least in those days, there were a zillion truck drivers and others using the few available channels and it was often difficult to find a channel that was open long enough to use it. The Libelle was equipped with a standard aircraft-frequency radio, a much better arrangement.

Another improvement involved some of the Libelle's instrumentation. I installed a variometer with audio; that made it possible to judge my rate of climb (or descent) without having to look at the instrument itself. It sent out a constant sound which varied in pitch as the glider's rate of climb increased or decreased. In strong thermals, that audio-vario virtually "screamed" at the pilot, a beautiful sound!

I also installed an oxygen system, knowing that I might try to climb well above 10,000 feet, the altitude above which the brain doesn't work as well as it should unless gradually acclimated. My log book shows an altitude gain of 13,500 feet, the flight topping out at nearly 18,000 feet asl. The date was March 29, 1980, above Fancher Field in Wenatchee, Washington. My soaring group usually spent the month of March at Fancher Field because that was the time of year when we could expect upper-altitude wave formations caused by westerly winds being forced upward by the Cascade Mountains just to the west. Occasionally, these bands of wave lift are marked by lenticular cloud formations, making the lift area relatively easy to find. On the day of my flight, the upper air was dry enough that there were no clouds. But once the sailplane enters that wave lift, there's no mistaking it. It is the smoothest, most silent kind of lift the glider pilot can experience. And if the wind is blowing fast enough, sometimes in excess of 60 or 70 mph, the sailplane may actually move backward, relative to the ground below, another unusual experience known only to a relatively few people!

Not only was the altitude gain somewhat remarkable, but it was the first time I had flown since the previous July. I remember most about this flight how bitterly cold it was at that altitude. Sailplanes have no "heating system," space and weight considerations preclude such luxuries. The pilot wears fur-lined boots, long underwear under heavy pants, a wool shirt under a goose-down lined jacket and a wool cap. The other threat is an iced-over canopy. Gliders rarely are equipped with IFR (Instrument Flight Rules) instrumentation. If the pilot can't see out of the cockpit, a deadly spin is a virtual certainty.

Looking back on it, all this reads as though it might have been dangerous. Maybe it was, but those days in sailplanes were some of the most exhilarating of my 83 years, and I have two log books to prove it.

Glider Takeoff

Scott and N7562

N7562

Juliet November

Years later, after I had returned to Seattle, my two sons had transferred into the local school system. At the time I was pretty sure they would be ready for Washington State's school system. Virginia had a reputation for having excellent schools and Scott's high school, J.E.B. Stuart in Falls Church, Virginia, was reputed to be one of the best in the country.

Scott was two years ahead of Mike and already a high school senior. Like many kids at that age, he hadn't thought much about his future and, as a concerned parent, I had to wonder what I could do to "steer" him in a direction that would help him choose an interesting and rewarding career. My own father had been pretty much "hands off" about this, giving me plenty of room to make my own choices. But it seemed to me that with Scott's love of flying and his keen interest in sailplanes, he would do well to consider pursuing these interests—more than just an occasional flight in N7562.

I had done some research about the local chapter of the Civil Air Patrol, an organization with close ties to the United States Air Force. The Air Force supported the CAP, knowing that it was a reliable training ground for young men (now women, too) who had a love of airplanes, some of them already flying sailplanes or powered aircraft.

One afternoon, after Scott came home from school, I asked him if he had ever heard of the Civil Air Patrol. He said yes, he had, one of his friends at school was a member. How would he feel about joining? "Why not?" he responded.

I've forgotten what happened next but not too long after this conversation, Scott came home one afternoon wearing a CAP uniform, Air Force blue and shiny black boots. He began to attend CAP meetings and it was obvious that he was enjoying the experience.

That led me to some more research, this time about the U.S. Air Force Academy in Colorado Springs, Colorado. I learned about the Academy's entrance requirements, what kind of young men they were looking for, what their graduates could expect by way of a career.

Up to that time, Scott and I had not talked very much about his future: What did he want to do with his life? His answers were about what I expected, he really hadn't thought about it enough to have a firm opinion. I told him what I had learned about the Air Force Academy: It offered a Bachelor of Science degree in a number of fields, both technical and otherwise, but it required a commitment from its graduates to serve in the Air Force for at least five years, followed by three years in the Air Force Reserves. During the early years of that commitment, its graduates would be taught how to fly the Air Force's principal fighting machines, jet fighters, and its large long-range bombers and cargo-carrying aircraft.

Admission to the Academy required a nomination from the applicant's senator or congressman, but the process was not political. Scott did not have to know or have "pull" with his political representative.

So with some help from me, Scott wrote a letter to Senator Henry M. ("Scoop") Jackson, asking for an appointment. A few weeks letter he received a welcome reply: Scott was invited to take a competitive examination, along with other appointment applicants. That exam would determine his admission status.

When the results of this exam came back, Scott learned that his performance was not quite good enough for direct admission to the Academy. But, if he wished, he could go to the Academy's "prep school." This was a special, one-year program at the Academy for those applicants who had done well in their exams, but not well enough for admission as first-year cadets. The prep school program would focus on basic English, math and some science courses.

I talked to Scott about this. He wasn't disappointed that he had failed to "make the cut," and he believed he could do well at the prep school, even though it would mean five years at the Academy, instead of four. We both thought that his experience as a licensed glider pilot might make a difference.

And indeed it did. Not long after Scott enrolled in the prep school, his instructors learned that he was a competent sailplane pilot and it wasn't long before he was designated as one of the Academy's sailplane pilot-training instructors.

Five years later Scott graduated from the Academy, as Lieutenant Frederick Scott Sager. He had told me a few years earlier that he was dating a young woman who had come to the United States from Vietnam and that they would marry soon after his graduation.

Scott's post-graduation assignment took him and Kim to Lubbock Air Force Base in West Texas where Scott continued his flight training in the Air Force's C-141 cargo fleet. He remained with this program and eventually fulfilled his five-year commitment.

In those days America's commercial airline fleet depended heavily on Academy graduates as its essential "talent pool" from which to hire new pilots, nearly all of whom had accumulated hundreds of hours of flight time during their Air Force careers. Scott wrestled for a few months about *which* airline he should contact and decided that Northwest Airlines would be the way to go. It was headquartered in Seattle and working for Northwest would allow him to live nearby.

So Scott and Kim moved from Lubbock to Gig Harbor, Washington, bought a beautiful home overlooking Puget Sound and began raising their family. Eventually, I became the proud grandfather of three beautiful girls: Becky, Diana and Nicole. Today they are very much grown-up young ladies but I rarely see them because they live far away. Nicole and Becky live in Southern California, Diana in far-off Tennessee.

To update this story with a bit of irony: Northwest Airlines recently was purchased by Delta Airlines, the very company whose stock made it possible for Scott, many years earlier, to help his family buy N7562. Scott now wears the Delta uniform, flies a Boeing 757 from its left seat and is thinking seriously about getting back into soaring, perhaps even buying his own sailplane. As time flies by, he will be eligible to retire in just a few more years.

Chapter 29

Foreign Students

When I arrived in Seattle, as one of the three "singletons" that had come West to set up shop for the CIA, I already knew that there would be no "road map" to help me get started. No one had ever done this before. We were expected, somehow, to establish ourselves in the local academic community so that we would be able to meet and befriend those visiting Muslim students who would eventually become our targets for recruitment.

The CIA's official charter does not allow it to operate in the United States *unless* its activities are clearly linked to collecting intelligence on foreign countries. That part of our mission was clear enough and within the charter's limits. But as a courtesy we always let the local FBI representative know what we were doing, at least in general terms. So one of my first tasks was to contact the Seattle FBI chief and to let him know of my presence. He already had been alerted from Washington, DC that I would contact him as soon as I arrived in Seattle.

With that courtesy call behind me I was ready to go to work.

The University of Washington is Seattle's largest educational institution; at that time there were about 18,000 students on its campus. How would I identify the very few Muslim students among that large population?

Fortunately, there were several American citizens who already were in touch with Seattle's local CIA office. This office was part of the Agency's nation-wide network of overt collectors, offices which enlisted the cooperation of willing citizens who traveled abroad. These citizens were not trained agents, rather they were ordinary folks whose businesses or other professional pursuits took them to foreign countries. They brought back all manner of reporting, some of it very useful, some not.

I had been a pretty good student at the "U-Dub," a kind of affectionate abbreviation of the school's real name. So I went to the U-Dub registrar and put down my money and enrolled in a mathematics class, anything to appear as a "real" student. I would receive an ASUW card, go to my mathematics class and, at age 42 would be, very obviously, the oldest student in my class.

Unfortunately for me, this mathematics class was all about "sets," something I never did understand and after six or seven sessions I stopped going to class. No matter, my ASUW card entitled me entrance to the HUB, the Husky Union Building. The HUB was a place where students came to study, to read newspapers, drink coffee and, for a few minutes at least, get away from the pressures of campus study. So, naturally enough, it was there that I hoped to meet my "target" students.

Sure enough, after I had visited the HUB for a few days, I saw a student who appeared to me to be older, with black hair and brown eyes and, from what I saw of his reading, not very comfortable with the English language. He was alone and I guessed that he might be from an Arab country and so I moved over to where he was sitting and asked him where he was from.

He seemed surprised that another student, even an older one, would bother to notice him. He smiled and said he was from Damascus, Syria, and that his class in the English language was giving him trouble. I returned his smile and offered my few words of Arabic, showing him that I knew something of his part of the world.

At that time, in Syria, there was an on-going struggle for power among the country's competing political factions. I was aware of these daily news items and told him that I hoped that none of his countrymen would be harmed. I asked him if he had family back home and, if so, how were they coping with the situation. He said that his mother and sister were in Damascus and, according to the most recent letter he had received from them, they were okay.

This "chance" conversation with the Arab student was, in retrospect, typical of the kinds of lead-ins that I used to ingratiate myself with my target students. Probably not very noble, but nonetheless effective. We spooks are thick-skinned; we have to be, otherwise the CIA would not be the successful know-all that the United States Government expects it to be.

Within a few days I learned that there were at least two faculty members in the Pacific Northwest who had volunteered their services to help the Agency. These were young men who had escaped European communism or Middle East tyranny and they believed they owed it to their new country to help, however they could. One of them had escaped the Hungarian revolution of 1957. He was a political science assistant professor at a major Pacific Northwest university. Another was from Syria, a man who communicated regularly with his friends and family in Damascus. I telephoned each of these men, told them I was working for the CIA and could I come to meet them. They were pleased to hear from me and we agreed to meet. I wanted to be certain that our meetings would be discreet, and I arranged to meet them in local hotel rooms. It was important that they not know my real name, in the event that somehow the local media would learn about our meetings.

These meetings continued for several years. My Syrian source reported regularly on the goings-on in Damascus. His relatives were political people, as he was, and they were close to the Syrian leaders. More than once he gave me current, and important, information that our intelligence sources in Damascus were unaware of.

The Hungarian-turned-American told me about graduate students on his campus that he thought might be willing to help the CIA.

These connections were typical of the Agency's "spotting" network that had spread across the United States. We wanted to know about the young men and women who were being educated in the United States. We believed that after a year of two of graduate studies in America, they would return to their native lands with a positive impression of things American. In some cases, we hoped, they might be willing to accept an assignment from the CIA to report on events in their home countries. We never considered these recruitments to be "spying" or "espionage," rather the willingness of these young men and women to help America learn what it needed to know to make sure that our countries could live in peace and prosperity with each other.

One of my contacts was in touch with an Arabian graduate student from a Persian Gulf state whose father, at home, was the chief of staff for a high-level government official. I arranged to meet this student, posing as an investor in petroleum ventures who was hoping to develop business contacts throughout the region. Over several months, our business interests morphed into a personal friendship and I suggested that he might want to meet a colleague who knew even more about United States' business interests in his oil-rich homeland than I did.

This tactic was typical of the CIA's recruitment process, or the "hand-off," as we called it. It was important that the case officer (me) who had developed the potential source, would never be the one to "pop the question" (the recruitment pitch). That would be up to another officer who would appear, also in alias, as a friend or colleague. It would be up to him to secure the target's agreement to help the U.S. government.

And this is what happened. My "hand-off" colleague appeared in a local hotel room, I departed, and the Arab student agreed, after a long conversation with my "friend," to help the United States.

Within a few months of this recruitment and after our new source had returned home, an arch rival of his government's leadership planned to assassinate its president. The plot was short-lived, but such an event would have had serious implications in that oil-rich part of the Middle East: It was in the United States' interests to know what was going on.

Soon after the turmoil had subsided, our source and his father talked about the events of that tumultuous day. Forty-eight hours later a detailed report of what had happened—and the leader's plans for the future—was included in President Nixon's early-morning intelligence briefing.

Not every CIA recruitment operation enjoyed this degree of success but we knew that if we kept at it, our efforts would be more than rewarded.

Chapter 30

A Recruitment

By the time I had been involved in Soviet operations for nearly 25 years, from 1951 until the mid-1970s, it had become all too clear to me—and to every other operations officer doing this kind of work—that recruiting a Soviet citizen was one of the most difficult tasks the Agency had ever set out to do. A successful recruitment, after all, meant that we had found someone willing to betray his own country, a willingness that could easily cost him his life were he to be found out. I never knew the exact number of the Agency's successful recruitment operations but I understood it not to be large.

It should go without saying that trying to recruit a Soviet citizen would be much easier to do in one's "own back yard," rather than in an overseas location, certainly easier than trying to do it inside the Soviet Union.

That meant, of course, that the Agency was always on the lookout for opportunities to learn about Soviets who were visiting the United States and, where possible, to try to gauge their susceptibilities to a recruitment approach. Sometimes, this task was made easier when we already knew something about the Soviet before he came to this country. The Agency's data bank (RID, the Records Integration

Division) was enormous, as it kept track of interesting foreigners from all over the world.

So it was during my assignment to Seattle that the Agency learned about a Soviet citizen who had been invited to attend a conference to be held in a large western city.

It needs to be recalled that the Soviet Union, in the 1970s, had been "open" to foreigners for no more than 20 years. The Soviet Politburo decided in 1958—six years after Joseph Stalin's death—to allow itself some exposure to things Western, most dramatically demonstrated in the famous "kitchen debates" between Soviet Premier Nikita Khrushchev and then vice-president Richard Nixon, at the American Exhibit in Moscow.

The conference to which this Soviet citizen had been invited was typical of the kinds of events that the Soviet government was willing to allow its citizens to attend.

One day, in my office-at-home, I received a telephone call from the chief of the CIA's Seattle office. He had just received a cabled message, from CIA Headquarters in Langley, Virginia that would be important for me to see. I scooted into the chief's office to learn that Headquarters already had a list of the Soviets who would be coming to this same conference. There were three and we had to assume that two of them were the typical KGB "watchers" who always attended these events, to make sure that—in this case our "target"—did not do anything foolish.

Our "target," as I learned from the Headquarters cabled message, had already become of interest to the Agency, owing to a comment he had made some time earlier at a social function in one of the South American capitals. At that function he had told an American guest that his knowledge of the Soviet petroleum industry's failure to "keep up" had led him to admire America's superior technologies in that field. He hoped that someday he could connect with knowledgeable Americans but that to do so he would have to go to the United States.

A routine name trace on the individual, in the agency's Records

Integration Division, resulted in one of those rare "hits" that can make the operations officer's life more exciting than usual.

The American had the good sense to report this off-hand conversation to the nearby American embassy and that nugget soon found its way into the CIA's massive file system: the beauty of name tracing, again displayed.

After learning what little there was to know about the man, I asked Headquarters for permission to try to contact him and, if possible, to learn what he had in mind by wanting to talk to American petroleum specialists.

Headquarters quickly responded to my request with an encouraging "all clear" okay. It was now up to me to develop an operational plan that would be acceptable.

One of the first things a case officer looks for in this kind of situation: What kind of in-place assets are already available that can be put to use in this specific situation? A favorable answer to that question obviates the need to drum up something entirely new. In response to my queries at the local Seattle office, I learned that one of its regular, and trusted, American contacts was a woman who loved to entertain, especially when it was possible to include foreigners in her large parties. She had good contacts in the conference city and, we hoped, she could arrange for an event to which some of the attending Soviets would be invited.

I would be on her guest list and pass myself off as a businessman interested in overseas petroleum investment opportunities, a legend that I had used before. We knew our target had professed similar interests and, with a little luck, I should be able to meet him and establish a relationship that would support several meetings.

The scheme worked, even better than I had hoped. During our first meeting I told him that I had been around enough to know that Soviet visitors usually had to be aware of their watchers, the *stukatchi*. Was this a problem for him? I didn't want to cause him any grief just because we were seen together. He assured me that he knew who his watchers were, they seemed to trust him, and he wasn't concerned.

Our next two meetings were brief, no more than 10 or 15

minutes each, and we had become friendly enough that I thought it safe to invite him to go on a drive with me to see the surrounding area. He had shown an interest in seeing new places, especially now that he finally had an opportunity to see something of America. I suggested that we drive out into the countryside, where he could have a better view of our Western landscape. The drive would give him a chance to see some of America's richest agricultural lands as well as a few new oil-well pumpers.

The drive assured me of a "captive audience" for several hours. We talked about many things and he began to share his real feelings about his "Motherland." He had seen so much injustice and arbitrary cruelty, the stifling of technology inquiry if it did not "fit" with the Communist managers' ill-informed ideas. He hoped the United States could somehow exert its influence, short of war, to help the Soviet people find a better life.

I told him that, given his attitudes and apparent determination to help his people, he should be talking to someone other than myself. In my travels and experiences I had met American officials who would be interested in hearing what he had been telling me. Would he consent to an introduction to such a person?

He thought about this for a few moments and said he would be happy to do that. I told him it might take a few days to arrange such a meeting but as he was not due to return to Moscow for another ten days, there would be time. I dropped him off near his hotel and made a beeline for the nearest telephone.

Now it was time to arrange "the handoff." My operational supervisor was working out of San Francisco and I had kept him informed of my progress. One of his Soviet operations officers was ready to fly to meet me the moment I thought the time was right. He arrived two days later and together we planned our next steps.

We booked a local hotel room, I contacted my new "friend" and invited him to come and meet us. We had to wait for a time when he would be free to leave his conference center, and we wanted him to be careful not to draw attention to himself. He understood the need for these precautions and assured us "not to worry."

My "friend" was actually a CIA colleague with whom I had worked for many years, part of our Soviet operations "family." He had a naturally-friendly personality and hit if off with our target immediately on their first meeting. After the cordial introductions and some informal chit-chat, I excused myself, telling the man I knew he was in good hands.

The meeting in that hotel room was a classic and later I sometimes rued the fact that we had not secretly taped the conversation. My "friend" skillfully but in low-key explained that he represented the U.S. Government (not the CIA) and that the government already knew something about his attitudes, that we assumed from what we had learned that he was a friend of the United States and might be willing to help us better understand his country's motives and intentions. We were not asking him to become a "spy," just a friend, but one whose profession would give him access to information that would help.

He agreed to this "informal" relationship. At that point, my friend had to assume that he would not see the man again, at least for some time. How could he connect with the man in the future? He said that he probably would be traveling abroad again, perhaps within the year, because he occasionally participated in international conferences. He did not want to risk being contacted inside the Soviet Union, a precaution with which we readily agreed.

Recruitment operations of this kind usually require some pre-planning, and in this case that paid off, big-time. I had earlier visited a suburban post office about ten miles from my home and, using an alias, rented a post box. I would continue to pay rent for the box for as long as it took for our new "recruit" to use it. It was, in "spook talk," a dead-letter drop.

At the meeting my friend-colleague gave the man the post office box number and the name and address that went with it, telling him that the name on the box belonged to someone who really was in the petroleum-research business, someone he met at the conference. He should protect it but not worry about its being found by others. He would write to that box *only* when outside the Soviet Union and to announce his whereabouts. Someone would come to meet him within a few days of receiving his letter.

Of course we had no way of knowing where or when, if ever, our new recruit would appear. The waiting game began.

Some seven or eight months later, I retrieved a letter from our recruit. He was in Athens, attending an international conference. He would be there for two weeks. He gave us the name of his hotel and a phone number.

Good fortune smiled on this event because my friend-colleague in San Francisco had served in Athens and knew the city as well as could be expected. He boarded the next flight, found our new recruit, and met with him over a period of several days.

There must be a let-down with which I end this story. I have written about the CIA's insistence on compartmentalization. I do not know, nor have I asked, what happened after that meeting in Athens. Tragically, my friend-colleague in San Francisco died a few months after that meeting, before I could talk to him. Someone "out there" knows what happened next. I do not.

Chapter 31

Fresh Off the Boat

In 1974 the United States Congress unanimously passed an amendment to its trade laws, known as Jackson-Vanik, named after its co-sponsors Senator Henry M. "Scoop" Jackson of Washington state and Representative Charles Vanik of Ohio. Although the USSR was not named in the amendment—it affected all countries with non-market economies that limited emigration—it was aimed squarely at the Soviet Union's restrictive emigration policies which, up to that time, had made it virtually impossible for Soviet Jews to leave the Soviet Union. The amendment said, in effect, that the Soviet Union must allow Jews to leave the country if it wished to receive "most favored nation" treatment in its trade relations with the United States. The penalty for refusing to allow Jewish emigration would be much stiffer tariffs on Soviet export products destined for U.S. markets.

Given the dire economic conditions then prevailing in Soviet Russia, the Communist regime had little choice but to comply. Within a year or so the first Soviet Jews were awarded exit visas and began to leave. The Jackson-Vanik gambit was beginning to pay off and its results would add a new—and final—chapter to my career with the CIA.

The new law did not say anything about *where* the new émigrés were to go. Many of them wanted to go to Israel and did so. But each of them was required to go through a processing center in Rome. The processing interview determined what the émigré had done—his or her profession, trade, employment, etc.—in the Soviet Union.

It was assumed that many Jews in the Soviet Union were engaged in highly-classified fields—research, engineering, manufacturing, computer technology—all related to the Soviet military establishment. Soviet Jewry provided some of the best minds available and the Soviet leadership had every reason to be concerned about an upcoming brain drain. To forestall this, those Jews who were employed in the most sensitive jobs were denied permission to leave, the Soviet leadership correctly assuming that those Jews who did emigrate would satisfy the objectives of Jackson-Vanik.

Within two years of enacting the amendment, the first reports began arriving from the Rome processing center. These described the occupations of those émigrés who had decided to come to the United States rather than go to Israel. Most of these reports revealed that the émigré would have little or no intelligence value, owing to the work he/she had been doing. But every now and then a report would show that the émigré knew things that the CIA should know more about.

I learned about the program from an old friend/supervisor with whom I had served in Tehran and at Headquarters. One of his first tasks was to identify CIA officers—most of them, as I, retired—who knew the Russian language well enough to debrief these fresh-off-the boat émigrés. They could be expected to know little or no English.

He telephoned me one day, saying he had an opening that I might find interesting. Would I mind going to the Seattle office to take a secure telephone call from him? It was an opportunity too good to pass up and the next day we talked about it. It sounded challenging and, above all, a chance to become a real *collector* of useful intelligence.

Most of my career had been devoted to making it possible for *others* to do the collecting. Now I could do some of it myself.

I soon learned that I was among about a dozen retired CIA officers, many of whom I had worked with years earlier. It was like old home week and our new boss told us we would have periodic conferences so we could meet together and compare notes. It should be productive—and fun.

Each of us was given a simple set of marching orders: We would work in alias, never revealing our true identity to the émigré—just in case. After the initial meeting, we would send to Headquarters a "knowledgeability brief," or KB, and if Headquarters decided the émigré was likely to have useful information, we would phone him/her and ask for another meeting. One part of this drill was a bit different: We would identify ourselves, during the very first contact (almost always a telephone call), as representatives of the Agency so that the émigré knew exactly to whom he/she was speaking. This was important: Virtually every émigré I ever contacted was more than happy to tell me whatever he/she could, to help their new country.

One of my very first contacts was a man I'll call Peter. He knew a lot about Soviet microchip technology, in those days an important intelligence topic. I had to buy several English-to-Russian and Russian-to-English dictionaries because some of the technical terms that came up in our conversations were Greek to me. I met with Peter about once a month over a period of a year or more and his reporting was well received at Headquarters.

About a year into our relationship, a close friend of Peter's, a man he had known very well in the Soviet Union, arrived in Seattle. It was common for mutual friends to show up in the same cities because each of them had to be sponsored by an American citizen, to guarantee that the newly-arrived émigré would not soon require government assistance.

Peter's friend had worked in a Soviet research facility that equated roughly to America's IBM. His knowledge of that facility's organization, its research processes and accomplishments, told the CIA an important number of specifics about Soviet computer capabilities and, importantly, limitations, that heretofore had been unknown. His reporting was so well received at Headquarters that I was asked to arrange for him and his friend Peter to come back to CIA Headquarters for what we called a "community debrief," several days of meetings where analysts from different parts of the intelligence community could speak directly with the émigré.

I worked with this program until I retired in 1991, interviewing former Soviet citizens who told us about the Soviet petroleum industry, its military ship-building programs, metallurgical industry and a number of other important intelligence targets. It was a very satisfying way to close down my career, so many years after that long-ago EOD in 1951.

Chapter 32

The "Off Years"

My official retirement happened in 1977, 26 years after my EOD in 1951, but that was by no means the end of my service with the Agency. Within a few months of my "retirement" I went back to work on a contract and those contracts—several of them, over the years—extended my service until I was eligible to receive Social Security benefits, just after my 62nd birthday in 1991. It was during those "retirement" years that I was able to mix business with pleasure, working for many months at a time, then taking time off to do other things.

These "off years" gave Betty Jean and me a chance to do things that never would have been possible otherwise. For example, one of my working colleagues in San Francisco (whose role in a recruitment operation appears elsewhere in these pages) had recently visited New Zealand and he and his wife returned to the United States with glowing accounts of that far-away land, "down under."

Betty Jean and I were so impressed with his narrative that we decided to try it ourselves and it wasn't long before we flew to San Francisco, boarded an Air New Zealand 747, and some 14 hours later found ourselves in Auckland, New Zealand's North Island capital.

Driving out of our rental car station was a new challenge: Everyone was driving on the wrong side of the road!

We found the country to be charmingly reminiscent of the United States as it was before World War II: The pop-up toaster had yet to arrive in Kiwi-Land. The motel's radio was powered by tungsten tubes. The television set had all of two channels to watch and the voices, in Kiwi-talk, were nearly unintelligible. We learned to watch cricket, and eventually became fans of our own favorite players. We watched little kids barefoot and wearing shorts, playing rugby in weather that required heavy coats for us. It took a few days to master driving on the wrong side of the road, but once that hurdle was crossed we felt safe motoring through the countryside.

But the fishing was what appealed to me most. New Zealand was still an undiscovered fisherman's paradise, especially for a fly fisherman. I helped BJ learn to handle a fly rod and one day, on a North Island river, she caught her first-ever rainbow trout on a fly, something she considered one of her finest achievements.

We went to New Zealand three times over the next ten years. Our second visit took us to the country's South Island, home of the Southern Alps, with glaciers as magnificent as any in North America. The fishing there was as good as or better than on the North Island. We hiked the famous Milford Track, learning that Kiwi "trampers" spend their nights in huts, not in do-it-yourself campsites as we did in the Pacific Northwest. One day, while we were in Te Anu, I hired a guide and we flew in a float plane to a river rarely visited by anyone, so remote it was. It was in that river that I had probably the finest dry-fly fishing of my life. The fish, all wild rainbow trout, came to the fly as if it were their last meal and then put on marvelous displays of runs and jumps, before I released them back into the river.

While on North Island, we spent much of our time in the charming village of Turangi, at the mouth of the Tongariro River, the stream made famous throughout the world by the novels of Zane Grey. Grey visited New Zealand four times in the late 1920s and the trout fishing in the Tongariro was better than he had seen anywhere.

I spoke with a Kiwi fisheries manager, stationed near Turangi, and learned that it was from California's Russian River that steelhead eggs had been packed in salted barrels and transported by ocean-going sailing ships, in the 19th century, to be planted in New Zealand's rivers, one of them the Tongariro, creating the world-class rainbow trout fishery that already, in the 1980s, was attracting fly fishermen from all over the world.

Our third trip to New Zealand was more than just a vacation, it was a mini-migration. We stayed in New Zealand for six months and would have stayed longer but for a Kiwi regulation that required foreign visitors to leave the country after 180 days. At Christmas time, we were invited to share a traditional English Christmas dinner in the Turangi home of our favorite motel-keepers, an expatriate couple from London who had come to New Zealand many years earlier and never went back. That meal lasted for about three hours, with much caroling, more courses than we could count and, probably, too much English pub "refreshment."

Because we knew we would be staying in New Zealand for six months, we wanted to spend roughly half that time on each of New Zealand's north and south islands. The ocean-going ferry trip to South Island, we had learned during a previous visit, could be a difficult one. Cook Strait, where the Pacific Ocean and the Tasman Sea meet, separates the two islands and rough crossings are common.

After crossing to South Island, we spent a few days in Marlborough country, home to New Zealand's relatively new wine-making industry. The Kiwis at that time were new to viniculture but they were producing a decent Chardonnay and some of the other white varieties. Their "Marlborough" label sold well throughout the country and was slowly edging into the overseas export market.

From there we motored to the small town of Motueka, sited on the western edge of Tasman Bay. We knew that in a few more days Halley's Comet would be at its brightest, this in February 1986, when it approached Earth as close as it would come for another 76 years. We also understood that there would be better viewing in the Southern Hemisphere than back home in Seattle. Fortunately, the night skies were clear and Betty Jean and I stayed up until two a.m. to see this once-in-a-lifetime event.

One day in summer of 1978, Betty Jean and I were returning from a visit to friends who lived in eastern Washington state, on the other side of the Cascade Mountain range. At the summit of Washington's route 410, the highway crosses Chinook Pass, a break in the mountains about 5,000 feet above sea level. There was a turn-off in the highway and several nearby picnic tables, so we decided to stop, eat our sandwiches and enjoy the view. We noticed a sign, "Trail 1,000, The Pacific Crest Trail." After finishing the sandwiches we decided to find the trail and learn something about it.

We walked about a half-mile, to the north, and found ourselves in a vast expanse of huckleberry bushes. The berries were ripe and it appeared as though no one had been by to pick them. That suggested that the trail, even so close to a major highway, was not at all "crowded." We decided to come back again, soon, but next time we would have back packs, a small tent and enough food for several days on the trail.

For me, there was an interesting history to hiking. While serving in Iran, I usually carried with me a rifle or shotgun, sometimes for "cover" for my operational visits to regions near the Iran-Soviet border, at other times for real hunting. John Aalto and I had gone hunting together a number of times in the mountains of Iranian Kurdistan, looking for Iranian mountain sheep (Mouflan) or goats (Ibex). In those days both of us were still in our twenties and the hiking, although strenuous, was manageable.

After our return from Iran to the Unites States, John and I teamed up in 1961 for a memorable week-long fishing-hiking adventure into Wyoming's Jim Bridger Wilderness area, where the trails and lakes hovered between 9,000 and 10,000 feet above sea level. So I had a number of hiking "miles" under my belt, but as a much younger man.

Jim Bridger Wilderness

Years later, after BJ and I were married in August 1972, we decided that part of our honeymoon experience would be a hike into that same Jim Bridger Wilderness. I knew the trail and the lakes from my earlier experience with John. BJ surprised me as she carried a pack nearly as heavy as mine and never complained, even at 9,000 feet up!

So our first hike on the Pacific Crest Trail was something like "old home week." We hiked from Government Meadows—the route used by some of the Oregon Trail pioneers in the mid-1800s—to Chinook Pass, that part of the trail we had visited just a few weeks earlier. It was a hike of only 25 miles or so, requiring just two nights on the trail, and the elevation was between 4,000 and 5,000 feet above sea level, an easy beginning.

In the ensuing 11 years, BJ and I hiked nearly the entire length of Washington State's share of the PCT, from the Columbia River north to the Canadian border, almost 500 miles. We did this in 30 to 40 mile segments and were never on the trail for more than five days, our "endurance" limited by the amount of food we could comfortably carry. On many of these hikes we walked through some of North America's most spectacular mountain scenery. It was a wonderful experience, my only complaint being that BJ often would insist that we hike "just another mile" near the end of an already-tiring day.

Part Eight – Ultimate Fly Fishing

Chapter 33

Kamchatka

The Kamchatka peninsula is a California-size landmass that reaches about 900 miles into the Pacific Ocean, between latitudes 50 and 60 degrees, about the same northerly location as Alaska's Aleutian Islands. On a map, it appears as a dagger, pointed at the islands of Japan, more than a thousand miles to the south. It is eight time zones east of Moscow and, in a sense, the end of the earth for many Russians.

The peninsula also happens to be home to *Oncorhynchus mykiss*, the scientific name for the steelhead trout. The "steelhead," as this magnificent game fish is known, has been an important part of my life for more than three decades. That is why the steelhead, steelhead fly fishing and the Kamchatka peninsula will occupy a good deal of space in this autobiography.

KAMCHATKA

© John Sager

The Kamchatka Peninsula

I learned at age five, maybe six, that my father loved to take me fishing. Sometimes he would even persuade my Iowa-born mother, who never learned to swim, to come with us. We would sit in a slightly-leaking rowboat, put a salmon egg on a small hook, toss it overboard and wait. My dad had learned that to catch fish that egg had to be just about twelve inches off the lake's bottom. Soon enough that kind of fishing began to bore me and I longed for a little more action, never complaining to Dad, however.

Later, during World War II, my dad was able to save up enough gas rationing coupons to drive all the way to British Columbia. We made several trips there, high up on the Okanogan plateau, where there were some really big fish. We stayed in a rustic lodge on Beaver Lake and the lodge owner-operator told us that the best method for catching the large rainbow trout in that lake was to troll flies. I had never used a fly rod but the lodge operator provided one for me and one for my dad and we fished with those flies for a whole week. Whether it was luck I'll never know, but one day, just at dusk, I caught my 16th fish, a daily limit. At the time it was the biggest achievement a 15-year-old kid could imagine.

Trolling those flies did not require me to learn to cast a fly, just toss it into the water, strip out 50 feet of line, row the boat very slowly and wait. When a fish hit that fly there was no doubt about what was happening: "Fish on!" was a happy cry.

Those Beaver Lake Kamloops trout averaged about 16 inches in length, not huge but bigger than anything I had ever seen. We learned that there were even bigger fish in another lake but it required a five-mile hike to get there. The lodge operator provided a horse to carry our overnight gear to a waiting cabin and off we went, my dad and I alone, big adventure ahead.

The fishing method was the same, trolling flies, but when one of those fish took that fly it was another story. Four, five, six pounds of flashing rainbow color, lots of jumps, slashing runs and if we were lucky we could get the fish to a landing net. We kept only a couple for the table. Fortunately, my dad knew how to cook fish and we both enjoyed eating them.

I made a few other fishing trips when I was in high school but those Canadian rainbow trout were the best, pretty hard to duplicate.

One of my earliest recollections of fishing for big fish in rivers goes back to high school. Fishing for those large rainbow trout in British Columbia's lakes was one thing. But to go after big fish in a river would be something new.

Joe Stone and I had become good friends and he knew of my interest in fishing. Joe already had passed his driver license test and was driving a beat-up pickup truck that belonged to his father. One Saturday morning we piled into the truck and drove to Voights Creek, a small tributary of the Carbon River, just downstream from the town of Orting, Washington, about a 20-minute drive from Sumner.

Orting, by the way, provides the best view of Mount Rainier in the entire state. But we weren't interested in looking at Mount Rainier. Joe knew that the "Humpies" were running up the creek toward the fish hatchery where they had been spawned several years earlier.

The "Humpy" is one of the six species of Pacific salmon, otherwise known as the Pink Salmon. It is an unusual species because it returns to its natal rivers only in odd-numbered years, and it has a distinctive and unusual "hump" in its back, especially in the male. The hump, in a large Humpy, can extend nearly two inches above the rest of its back and when the fish are moving upstream in the shallow waters below a fish hatchery, such as at Voights Creek, that hump actually creates a wake in the water, making the fish easy to spot.

In those days, neither Joe nor I had learned the fine art of fly fishing. But we did know how to use a spinning rod. Joe knew how to get to the creek below the hatchery, located about a half-mile upstream of the creek's mouth. We beat our way through some brush to the creek's edge and, sure enough, there were Humpies all over the creek. With the brush extending right down to the creek, we had to step into the water to have enough room to cast. It was late summer and the water was neither too cold nor too deep.

I don't remember if we were fishing out of season, or if the creek was closed to fishing. I do remember that our fishing "technique" no doubt was illegal because instead of expecting the fish to go after the treble-hooked spinners we were using, we deliberately tried to cast over the backs of individual fish and *snag* them, That so-visible hump provided a cant-miss target. Further, when a fish is hooked anywhere other than its mouth it can provide some unbelievably exciting "sport," dashing every which way through the shallow water.

I seem to remember that Joe and I did a lot of whooping and hollering that morning on Voights Creek, before we decided to call it a day, before a game warden came along to see what the excitement was all about.

Years later, when I was working at the American embassy in Tehran, my friend John Aalto and I would go fishing in the Karaj River, a mountain stream less than 50 miles west of Tehran that flowed out of the Elburz Mountains. For me, this was a different kind of fishing. The river ran cold, clear and swift. Years earlier, a German construction crew had built a railroad for the Iranians, a project that lasted many years. To help make themselves feel at home, the Germans imported some German Brown Trout, put them into the Karaj River and within a few years these "Brownies" had established themselves and provided a fine sport fishery.

It appeared to John and me that very few Iranians knew about this place. The few times we fished there, we were all by ourselves. That changed dramatically when an Iranian "enforcer" showed up and demanded that we stop fishing. He was shouting at us in Farsi but we understood: We were fishing illegally, he claimed, and had to surrender our fishing gear. John and I both had expensive spinning rods, fitted with the latest Italian Alcedo spinning reels, and no way were we going to "surrender" to this Persian vigilante. The young Iranian had grabbed John's spinning rod and was threatening to break it in half when along the riverside road appeared a Mercedes sedan driven by a well-dressed Iranian who spoke English. He stopped and asked what was going on. We explained the situation to him and he delivered a rapid-fire lecture to the young vigilante. This was clearly a face-saving issue for our antagonist and he began to direct his invective at the driver of the Mercedes. After a few more tense moments the young man gave up and went stomping off into the woods. We thanked our benefactor and he explained that, as far as he knew, the river was indeed closed to fishing and that we had better go home before a real law enforcer appeared. We thanked him, put our rods away and drove back to Tehran.

But it had been a worthwhile fishing adventure. Before we were obliged to stop fishing, we had caught several beautiful Brownies and probably could have caught a few more. The experience left me with fond memories of fishing in a remote, wooded mountain stream—and catching beautiful fish—something I had not done before. Years later those memories would stick with me as I began to learn about steelhead.

After I moved myself and my family to Seattle, it wasn't long before the fishing itch began to appear. I decided to concentrate on big trout, the bigger the better, and I soon learned that the rivers flowing through Washington state were populated by steelhead trout, a sea-going rainbow trout that spends most of its life in the ocean but returns to spawn in the stream in which it was born. The steelhead has an uncanny, natural way of finding its way back to its natal stream, much like the Pacific Salmon does, except that the steelhead, instead of dying after spawning, will return to the ocean for a second or even third time, repeating the process, so long as it is healthy enough to do so.

The spawning process is something to behold. The "hen," or

female, turns on her side and with her thrashing tail digs a shallow depression in the river's bottom. She then deposits some of her eggs in the nest, then moves upstream, digs another nest and drops more eggs. She may repeat this process as many as six times, and the series of nests is known as a "redd." There is a reason for these several nests because if one or more are wiped out by the vagaries of the river, chances are that some of the female's progeny eventually will survive.

However, the female does not exert all this effort until she has mated with a male steelhead, a "buck." This underwater romance can last for several hours and often the female will find more than one male fighting for her attention. After that struggle has been decided, the winning male fertilizes the eggs by covering them with his "milt," the female covers the eggs in each nest with river-bottom sand or gravel and then Mother Nature takes over. Depending somewhat on water temperature, the eggs hatch within two months and the "fry" then find themselves in a very precarious position. They are small, less than an inch long, and very vulnerable to predators: larger fish, birds, river otters, and, sometimes, to drastic changes in water temperature should they become stranded away from the river's main channel.

Assuming the fry survives these dangers, usually after two years, it will attain a length of seven or eight inches—feeding mostly on aquatic insect life—and then it answers Nature's call to head for salt water. This trip also is full of danger, especially if the young steelhead must negotiate the many dams that have appeared on Northwest rivers. Today most of these large hydroelectric dams have built-in devices that guide the fish to collection points from which they are then trucked below the dam(s), returned to the river and then they head out to sea.

Once in the ocean, the steelhead still is far from "home free." Larger fish and seals are his worst enemies but if he can evade these predators, he will grow rapidly on the abundant food he finds there. Most steelhead return to their natal rivers after one year in the ocean and they are called "one-salt" fish. Some stay at sea for two years and some even three. A typical three-salt steelhead may weigh 20 pounds, some even as much as 30. But even the one-salt, at four to eight pounds, is a very strong game fish and a match for most anglers.

The steelhead's return to his birth place has its own set of problems. In some rivers, commercial netters are waiting for him. If his river has dams across it, and many do, he must ascend a series of fish ladders; in some river systems he repeats this process as many as seven times over hundreds of miles. Many rivers have very fast-flowing rapids and chutes that only the toughest fish can ascend. Over the centuries, the steelhead's gene pool has made him one of the most enduring of the animal species.

Knowing what the steelhead has endured, before he grabs the fisherman's fly, guarantees the steelhead fly fisher an almost mystic, religious, experience. I know, I've had it happen many times.

My first real exposure to steelhead fly fishing came by an unusual route. I had been writing letters to the editors of Seattle's newspapers, about the Soviet Union and its recalcitrant and propagandistic relationship with the United States, something I thought I knew more about than the average newspaper reader. In those days, Seattle had two daily newspapers, the *Seattle Post-Intelligencer* and *The Seattle Times*. My letters usually had an apparent "conservative" slant and the *Times* had a conservative letters editor, something of an anomaly for a usually-liberal newspaper. The *Times* published a few of my letters but I found a more receptive attitude at the *Post-Intelligencer,* or the P-I, as we knew it.

One of my letters reached the desk of Jack deYonge, the P-I's editorial page editor. He liked my letter and wanted to talk to me about it so we arranged to have lunch near his downtown office. I had to tell him that I had been working for the CIA, thus explaining my above-average understanding of things Soviet. His only concern was that I was not working for the CIA *now*. As I had retired, I could say no, not any more. With that concern out of the way we somehow got to the subject of fly fishing.

To my surprise and delight, Jack turned out to be an avid steelhead fly fisherman and he knew a lot about fly fishing and fly fishing clubs. He told me that if I were serious about learning about local fly fishing, I should join one of two clubs, The Washington Fly Fishing Club or the Washington Steelhead Fly Fishers. Each of these clubs met once a month and would welcome a new member. So I decided to join both of them.

The Washington Steelhead Fly Fishers was largely social in its outlook, choosing not to work on conservation or legislative issues, whereas the WFFC was quite active. I enjoyed both clubs and soon after joining the WFFC found myself on one of its conservation committees.

But it was the Washington Steelhead Fly Fishers that gave me an unexpected opportunity, one I had been waiting for without even realizing it. At one of their meetings their members talked about steelhead fly fishing in Kamchatka, a place I vaguely remembered to be in the farthest eastern reaches of Russia. They were aware of a 1970s scientific study, recently translated from Russian into English by the University of Washington's School of Fisheries, authored by two of Russia's foremost fish biologists, Ksenya A. Savvaitova and Valery A. Maksimov. Their study, titled *The Noble Trouts of Kamchatka*, was the first-ever scientific exposition of steelhead, based on their in-field studies on the Kamchatka peninsula. The data already were 20 years old but the study was something never before seen in the United States. As the Soviet Union had collapsed a few years earlier, it seemed quite possible that American and Russian steelhead "advocates" might be able to join together. They had the fish but no money, the Americans had plenty of money and very few fish!

I found the club's one translated copy of *Noble Trouts*, read most of it and decided that this was something we should look into.

By that time "we" meant The Steelhead Committee of the Federation of Fly Fishers. The FFF was a national organization, then interested mostly in conserving trout and those warm-water species that appealed to fly anglers, but it had yet to expand its reach into the Pacific Northwest. When the FFF leaders learned that a few dedicated fly fishermen in the Seattle area wanted to "do something" to help steelhead and salmon, it was an easy call to welcome the freshly-minted Steelhead Committee.

Bob Arnold was the new committee's first chairman and we held monthly meetings in his Seattle home, talked about current problems, our fishing experiences and, most importantly, what kinds of articles should appear in the committee's brand-new "voice," a typewritten newsletter which we called *The Osprey*.

The osprey is a "fish hawk," slightly smaller than a bald eagle, and it forages for food along those rivers that hold trout and steelhead. The name was an apt one for a newsletter dedicated to the protection and preservation of wild steelhead. After attending a few of the committee's meetings, I volunteered to publish the newsletter on a computer. The newsletter's mailing list was growing and it was obvious that the committee needed to modernize its publishing methods.

Nearly more than I had bargained for, I found that publishing a newsletter is not so easy. I had never owned a computer, much less a printer, but I was determined to improve on *The Osprey's* heretofore typewritten format. The newsletter was published three times a year and in Issue Five, January 1989, it said goodbye to the typewriter.

The committee's leadership rotated between Bob Arnold and my new friend Stan Young. It was Stan who introduced me to the committee after I first met him through the Washington Fly Fishing Club. We had driven to Olympia, Washington's state capital, to jawbone a legislative committee about conservation issues and during the hour-long journey to and from we discovered in each other a passion for steelhead and a mutual willingness to devote serious time and energy to "the cause." (Stan and I still are good friends and fish together whenever our tired bodies permit.)

The committee gradually earned a reputation, among steelhead fly fishermen, as a small group of guys who were serious about helping to save steelhead. It was obvious to anyone who fished for steelhead that each year there were fewer and fewer of them in our rivers. And we knew the causes: too many hatcheries, dams, nets, overfishing, habitat degradation, imprudent regulations from the state's controlling agencies and, worst of all, a state-sponsored management philosophy that supported the "meat eaters" among those who fished: A fish that is caught belongs on the dinner table. We conservationists, on the other hand, believed that nearly all wild steelhead should be returned to the river, unharmed and allowed to live another day. "Catch and release" was the byword, a contentious concept that persists today, more than 20 years later.

Within a few years of its inception the committee attracted the attention of a man who would become its chairman for many years. Recently-retired U.S. Navy Captain Peter Soverel had been the officer-in-charge of the University of Washington's naval ROTC program. His history included a decorated stint in Vietnam and duty with President Reagan's White House. He also happened to be one of the most dedicated and skillful steelhead flyfishers on the planet, recognized by the "fraternity" as such, and he had an encyclopedic memory that captured anything and everything having to do with steelhead.

It was Pete's leadership and the ever-increasing influence of *The Osprey* that began to make the difference we all wanted.

In *The Osprey*'s January 1991 issue I published an article (reprinted in the Appendix of this book), strongly influenced by the *Noble Trouts* research, in which I dreamed of fly fishing for steelhead in Kamchatka. The article was an appeal to readers for awareness of the presence of steelhead in that far-off place, which many readers—as I earlier—had never heard of or knew little about. The article concluded: "So, do we dream in vain? Maybe there are readers out there who might want to share ideas about putting something together beyond dreaming. If so, *The Osprey* could serve as an information central and catalyst. We'd be happy to try."

Enter now Serge Karpovich, like myself a retired CIA officer and a long-time colleague and friend. I had introduced Serge to steelhead fly fishing on the Wenatchee River in central Washington state and it was there that he caught his first-ever steelhead and, as it is said, "he was hooked."

Serge was one of *The Osprey*'s many readers and when he saw my article about fly fishing in Kamchatka, he phoned me and asked if we (our committee) were really serious about Kamchatka steelhead. I said that indeed we were, why was he asking?

Serge's parents had escaped from Russia just before the 1917 revolution and his father became a professor of Russian studies at Harvard University. Serge spoke beautiful Russian, learned at his mother's knee, and through adulthood he was able to maintain his contacts in Russia. In his retirement, Serge had developed a small business in Moscow, with the help of a family member, and he was about to go there again. After hearing my reassurance that our committee was serious about Kamchatka steelhead, he told me that while in Moscow he would see what he could do.

I may have forgotten to tell Serge about the *Noble Trouts* research but he knew that the answer to his query lay somewhere in Moscow's "academic world." One day while taking the obligatory tour of Red Square, he found a small museum which displayed, among other things, information about steelhead. He asked the curator where he could get more information and was told how to reach the Ichthyology Department at Moscow State University.

Once in the hallways of "MGU," (the Russian acronym for the university) Serge quickly found Dr. Savvaitova's office. He knocked on her door, entered her office and began to tell his story. Needless to say, she was more than surprised and, probably, a little suspicious. Serge's story sounded too good to be true: an offer of a serious and formalized partnership backed by American dollars, probably involving American fisheries scientists, and certainly backed by a well-established group of American anglers who were passionate about saving steelhead, just as the Russians were.

When Serge returned from Moscow he called me and reported what he and Dr. Savvaitova had discussed, making it clear that the Steelhead Committee now was committed to follow through. Serge said he was willing to fund the travel—Moscow to Seattle and back—of Dr. Savvaitova and her colleague Valery Maksimov, but it would be up to the Committee to do the rest.

In Spring 1994, and with Serge's so-optimistic report in hand, the Committee arranged to hold conferences, Savvaitova and Maksimov included, at the University of Washington's School of Fisheries, with the head of that department presiding at the first meeting. Other—technical—discussions would follow. We also knew that the visiting Russians would appreciate talking with our state Wildlife Department and its supervising Wildlife Commission, to get a better understanding of the state's management strategies and practices. It would be a whirlwind experience for the Russians, barely a week to shuttle back and forth between Seattle and Olympia.

And we needed an interpreter, my Russian was not good enough for the rapid-fire discussions we knew would take place. John Aalto was just the man for the job.

In fact, it had been John, Serge and I, while fishing together a few months earlier, who speculated how great it would be to fish for steelhead in Russia, now that the Soviet Union had collapsed and we could cast our flies without the KGB's watching us!

I mentioned earlier that Pete Soverel had assumed the chairmanship of the Steelhead Committee. Pete also began putting together an organization which he named the Wild Salmon Center. Pete's vision for salmon and steelhead conservation extended beyond the capabilities of the Steelhead Committee. He obtained a 501.c.3 designation from the Internal Revenue Service, thereby establishing the WSC as a legitimate charitable organization. With that "official" endorsement, the WSC was the natural choice for partnering with the Russians.

The meetings in Seattle and Olympia were even more successful than we had hoped. This was, after all, the first time that Russian and American scientists were able to cooperate with each other outside the confines of Soviet watchfulness. Several formal agreements were signed, one of them stipulating a 20-year program of joint cooperation between Moscow State University and the Wild Salmon Center. (As

I write this that agreement is still in effect and already has achieved most of its objectives.)

Before Savvaitova and Maksimov returned to Moscow, we planned our first expedition to Kamchatka. They had done their research there in the 1970s, as young biologists, and were as anxious to return as we were to join them.

This was now the Wild Salmon Center's operation and Pete Soverel decided to keep things as simple as possible, knowing that in post-Soviet Russia there would be plenty of glitches to get in the way of whatever plans might be in his notebook.

While worrying about the early logistics support, he also was signing up paying customers, fly fishers from around the country who were eager to spend the $6,000 required for a week's fishing in Kamchatka. These paying customers were informed, before they put down their money, that Kamchatka would not be their usual comfy tourist/fishing experience. It was wild country and few, if any, foreigners had yet visited the place, certainly no fishermen.

Pete's "clients" also understood that whatever fish they managed to catch would be released, unharmed, into the river. This would be catch-and-release at its finest.

Pete's informational brochure reminded his potential clients of an important piece of Kamchatka's history. During the period following World War II and up to the Soviet Union's collapse in 1989, the entire Kamchatka peninsula had been off-limits to foreign travel. For the past 30 years, the northern part of the peninsula had been used as a guided missile test range and impact center. Avachina Bay at Petropavlovsk was home to the Soviets' Pacific Ocean ballistic missile submarine base. The only people allowed to live in Kamchatka were those already-established populations in the region's capital, Petropavlovsk, and a few smaller towns, and those indigenous peoples scattered in small villages. This virtually-uninhabited region, the size of California, was thus free from the ravages of human development, one of the few places on Earth where Nature had been undisturbed for generations. It was little wonder that its native steelhead populations had thrived like nowhere else.

To make sure the expedition got off to a good start, it was essential that a skillful "advance man" go there ahead of everyone else, to handle the complex arrangements needed for such an expedition. Of course, this man had to know the Russian language and, one would hope, something about the Russian people.

Pete knew, from his recent experience with the Russian visitors to Seattle, that John Aalto was the perfect fit for this critical assignment.

Meanwhile, in Moscow, Dr. Savvaitova's colleague Valery Maksimov was making the necessary arrangements within his department at MGU: record books, partially-completed studies to be amplified in the field, measuring tools, arrangements with his staff for staying in touch—all the things that a responsible scientist would want to have ready and on hand in the wilderness. We later speculated that Valery may have been under more emotional stress than he could handle because shortly after he arrived in Petropavlovsk, he suffered a major heart attack.

When news reached us of Maksimov's incapacitation, John was at his home in Texas. Pete and I contacted him and asked him if he could come to Seattle immediately, go to Kamchatka (this was several weeks before his planned departure) and try to hold things together until the situation became clearer. He said he was on his way.

After a hurried consultation with Pete and me, John boarded an Alaska Airlines flight bound for Petropavlovsk. Pete gave him $11,000 in cash, most of which eventually would be paid to the Russian outfitters who would support the expedition.

John's reception at the Petropavlovsk airport was anything but cordial. A Russian *Pogranichnik*—a Border Guard official—singled him out of the group of arriving passengers and escorted him to what appeared to be a small jail cell. The official wanted to know if John had "friends in Moscow." Was this a probe into his former CIA connections or an honest question? And if the latter, why? John thought quickly about the Serge Karpovich business activity in Moscow, told the official that, yes, he did have friends in Moscow but they were business people whom he had not seen for some time.

The official seemed satisfied with John's reply but it reminded him that he probably was known to these Russian officials, 3,000 miles from Moscow!

John knew that Valery Maksimov was in a local hospital and that Valery's son Sergei would be meeting him. Before doing anything else, John wanted to visit Sergei's father. He had come to know Valery well, during their meetings in Seattle, and the two men liked each other. John found that his visit to Valery's hospital "room" was one of the most depressing events of his life. The "room" was nothing more than a concrete cell, cold and damp, a dim light bulb hanging above. Apparently the hospital staff already had decided that Valery was beyond help. And they were right because Valery died a short time later, after being flown to a hospital in Moscow.

So the expedition got off to a gloomy start. Sergey's concern for his father would certainly dampen his enthusiasm for the mission. Nonetheless, John and Sergei boarded an MI-8 Russian helicopter and flew north to the town of Tigil, which would become the logistics center for the first Kamchatka expedition.

Any fishing camp, when built from scratch, needs all kinds of materials: lumber, tents, cots, stoves, a field kitchen, rudimentary plumbing, some kind of clean water supply. These items had been assembled in Tigil by the contracted Russian outfitter. Now the task was to move them to the camp site. The Russians already had designated the Kvachina River as the first such camp to be used by the Kamchatka expedition. Savvaitova and Maksimov had done some of their 1970s research on this river and believed it would be a good place to start in 1994.

Some of the camp materials would be moved by helicopter over the 60 miles between Tigil and the Kvachina camp site. Other pieces would go by the ubiquitous Russian *vezdekhod*, a tracked vehicle left over from World War II that is a combination unarmed tank and a cargo/personnel carrier. *Vezdekhod* means "go anywhere" and indeed it can so long as the water courses it must cross are not too deep. Every fisherman who participated in the Kamchatka expedition had to ride in one of these beasts, probably the most uncomfortable vehicle ever devised by man.

Go Anywhere

After the camp was set up, John was joined by Pete Soverel and Dr. Savvaitova, henceforth to be addressed as "Oksana," the diminutive version of her given name, Ksenya. Oksana proved to be a charming lady and she fit in very well with the five American paying customer/fly fishermen who accompanied Pete to the Kvachina camp. She certainly was anything but a "stuffy scientist" and she enjoyed her new American friends from the get-go.

The week passed all too quickly and the American fly fishers did their job as they were taught to do: Every steelhead brought to hand (and there were many beautiful specimens, some up to 20 pounds) was measured for length and girth (from which to accurately estimate its weight), several of its scales removed (to determine the fish's age), a ventral fin was clipped for later DNA analysis, and—most annoying to the fish—a uniquely coded tag was placed just behind its dorsal fin. The tag was "inserted" by a powerful spring-loaded "gun," about the only painful part of the procedure. The fish had to be handled deftly and quickly to avoid keeping it out of water for more than a few seconds and whenever possible another fisherman would help.

After the five paying customers departed for the United States, John, Pete and Oksana helicoptered to Polyana, the regional capital of northern Kamchatka. By prior arrangement they met with several officials who identified themselves as local fishery experts. After listening to Oksana's description of the Kamchatka Steelhead Project, just completed on the Kvachina River, one of the officials launched a loud and verbal tirade at Oksana, telling her she was out of line to be encroaching on what should be the responsibilities of the local experts. The diminutive Oksana was in no mood to accept this barrage lying down. She stood up, pointed at her accuser and told him he was the one "out of line." She had come all the way from Moscow, was one of the most knowledgeable authorities on steelhead, she had worked years at MGU's laboratories, had spent months on Kamchatka's rivers doing her pioneering research. To top it off she had the official blessing of Doctor Dimitry Pavlov, an academician of the Russian Academy of Sciences.

Oksana's accuser was so baffled by this outburst, which he knew to be fully justified, that he huddled with his companions and then offered a "compromise." Would Oksana and her two American friends consent to appearing on the local "nightly news" television show? Of course they would and that evening the three of them found themselves under the lights with the TV camera whirring in the background. The experience no doubt was the only time in John Aalto's life that he appeared on Russian television, interpreting an interesting and informative discussion.

Back in Petropavlovsk, on his way to the United States, John was awakened about two o-clock in the morning by a loud pounding on his hotel room door. He opened the door and found a uniformed army colonel standing there, scowling at him. He had a message to deliver: Would John please join his commanding officer for dinner the next evening. Despite his fogged response to the two a.m. awakening, John had the good sense to reply that he would be happy to have dinner but only if it were understood that John would pay. The colonel nodded his head and left. Both surprised and perplexed John went back to sleep, wondering if this is just the way Russians "do things."

As requested he appeared in the hotel dining room, with Pete for company. Within moments a two-star general officer walked into the room, the grumpy colonel's boss. The general was accompanied by his wife and two teen-age daughters. He identified himself as the commandant for all airport and transportation security activity in the eastern half of the Russian Federation, from the Ural Mountains to the Pacific Ocean. The general's wife sat next to Pete and she soon demonstrated an adequate proficiency in English. The six of them enjoyed a pleasant meal and a very comfortable atmosphere, owing entirely to the general's pleasant demeanor. Unspoken was the reality that the general's often-missed pay check would never have allowed him to buy dinner for himself and his family in Petropavlovsk's finest restaurant. But just before the group got up to leave the general spoke to John, quietly, directly and with a smile, "We know from Moscow who you are: You are a "*bol'shoi spetsialist*," a "big specialist," meaning to John, clearly enough, " a CIA guy."

As I think back on this event, it seems obvious enough that the KGB and its successor Russian intelligence service had correctly identified John Aalto, Serge Karpovich and myself as "big specialists." But how were they to understand our obvious "connection" to the Kamchatka Steelhead Project? As some kind of cover for more nefarious CIA snooping, this time in Kamchatka? Hardly. But it certainly gave them something to think about. One would hope, as I do, that this eternal suspicion by the Russian authorities of most things American can someday be laid to rest. I believe that the

Kamchatka Steelhead Project has made at least a small contribution toward that end.

By the time Autumn of 1997 rolled around it was my turn to go to Kamchatka. The years 1995 and 1996 had seen two successful seasons pass, with many fly fishers participating and catching lots of fish. And another camp had been added to the expedition's list, this one on the Utkholok River, about 30 miles south of the Kvachina River camp that John Aalto had set up in 1994.

As the *Noble Trouts* 1970's research had shown, only those Kamchatka rivers that flow west to the Sea of Okhotsk hold steelhead. The peninsula's volcanic "spine," which runs north and south nearly the entire length of Kamchatka, neatly divides the peninsula. Its eastward-flowing rivers run to the Pacific Ocean and are home to very large rainbow trout and all six species of salmon, Chinook, Coho, Pink, Chum, Sockeye and Cherry.

The flight from Seattle to Petropavlovsk, with a stopover in Anchorage, was uneventful but for a 55 miles per hour headwind that slowed our flight by at least 30 minutes and the landing that followed. The airport was a leftover from the bad old days of Soviet management and its runway was a series of frost heaves which made its surface all but unsafe. As I would soon see first-hand, Petropavlovsk was nearly a forgotten city, eight years after the collapse of Soviet communism. Many of its buildings were gloomily empty, most of their windows broken or missing. It was obvious that the city had little or no money for routine maintenance and the airport's runway was just one item on a long list of waiting repairs.

I was traveling with six other fly fishers, all of us part of the Kamchatka Steelhead Project, and as we approached the airport's customs and immigration officials, it was clear to them that ours was an unusual group. Each of us was carrying at least one fly rod case, many of us had duffel bags instead of suitcases. It was natural enough for the customs and immigration officials to ask "Who are you guys?" And as the group's only Russian speaker, it was up to me to explain. At first, the *pogranichnik* (border guard) officer seemed incredulous that a bunch of Americans would come to "his" Kamchatka to catch fish. I explained that we were part of a scientific expedition, sponsored in part by Moscow State University, and that we were visiting Kamchatka with the knowledge and approval of the Russian government. I added that this was the third year of our project and that many others had come to Kamchatka before us.

The officer apparently was unaware of all this but he accepted my explanation and stamped each of our passports. As we moved away to our waiting bus, I heard him say to one of his colleagues, "Now I've seen everything."

When we left the airport's control room, we found Sergei Maksimov waiting for us. By now Sergei was an old hand at meeting and greeting American fly fishers and his English had improved enough that my services as an interpreter were rarely needed.

Sergei explained that we were on a fast-track schedule, that we would have dinner at the airport's restaurant and then board our bus for the drive to the village of Mil'kovo, probably not arriving there until nearly midnight. Dinner at the airport's restaurant was my first authentic Russian meal since I left Moscow 31 years earlier. And it was typically Russian: baked coho salmon, mashed potatoes, black bread and boiled cabbage.

The 130 mile bus ride to Mil'kovo proved to be a depressing experience for our first night in Kamchatka. It began to rain just before nightfall, the road was unpaved, muddy and full of potholes, and we were dead tired after the long flight from Seattle. Just before midnight, we stumbled into the town's only hotel, a lodging that would have been illegal by any Western standard, and collapsed onto lumpy mattresses.

Mornings have a way of making things look a little better, even though on this morning it was still raining. But we were hungry and found that the next-door "bistro" turned out a pretty good breakfast of *pel'meni* soup—a kind of Russian ravioli in beef broth—a chewy but tasty Russian bread and, of course, *instant* coffee. Even in

Mil'kovo the bistro's operators had learned that Americans usually prefer coffee to Russian tea. We spoke to a few of the locals who were having breakfast and they told us that Mil'kovo, a typical agricultural town in central Kamchatka, had at one time been much larger, with a population of 5,000 people. Now, everyone was trying to figure out a way to move far to the west because there were few jobs and even fewer markets for their products. The town was down to about 2,000 people, with little hope that things would get better. This gloomy assessment seemed to match the weather and we were glad to get back to our bus for the 100 mile drive to our next stop, Esso.

The rain persisted and the road became even worse but the scenery was beautiful. The Fall colors already were upon us at this far-north latitude and the hillsides and valleys, even in the rain, reminded me of the beautiful birch forests of western Russia that I had seen, many years earlier, while riding the train from Moscow to Helsinki. But here there were also many evergreen trees which our Russian bus driver identified as the Siberian Pine, a species I had not remembered.

We arrived in Esso in time for lunch. Esso was a small town, somewhat larger than Mil'kovo, and the temporary Headquarters of the Kamchatka Steelhead Project. Pete Soverel had arranged for year-round storage of all of the project's equipment—boats, motors, field-tent furnishings and much more—in a rented warehouse. The family who owned this facility would be our luncheon hosts. There were about a dozen of us, mostly fly fishers but a few Russian helpers, seated around a large oblong table. And what a groaning board it was: large bowls of steaming-hot borsch, sour cream, fresh cucumbers, tomatoes and cabbage from the hosts' garden, bread, spicy sausages, mashed potatoes, cookies, soda and, of course, tea.

And there were the usual Russian toasts: a toast to our hostess family, a toast to the success of the project, a toast to the successful piloting of our waiting helicopter. I wondered at the time why all this toasting was happening with nothing stronger to drink than tea; where was the vodka? It dawned on me, soon enough, that even the Russians knew better than to send these American fly fishers off into the afternoon skies with several shots of vodka under their belts. The heavy drinking could come later in the day.

Russians, especially since the collapse of the Soviet Union, are a "hurry-up-and-wait" people. Our group had come to Esso to board an MI-8 helicopter that would take us, finally, to the rivers that we had traveled so far to fish. When we finished our long lunch it was still only two in the afternoon, plenty of time for our helicopter to cover the 140 miles to our Utkholok River camp. Then we were informed that the helo would be ready at four o'clock. More waiting. Finally, at six in the late afternoon, our Russian group leader arrived and said, "Let's go." We piled into our waiting bus, waited another half-hour, drove to the airfield and the waiting MI-8 and finally took off about seven.

Fortunately, enough daylight remained that we could enjoy the hour and a half trip. Below us was the *real* Kamchatkan wilderness: We flew over several rivers that probably had never been fished by anyone, there were no roads, no signs of human habitation or activity. The hillsides and valleys were in full and breathtaking fall color: alders, birches, the Siberian pine, larch trees and a very large bush that had turned a golden-red.

But evening was advancing and the helo had to deliver part of our group to the Utkholok River camp and then fly again to drop off the rest at the Kvachina River camp, then return to Esso. We later learned that these MI-8 helicopter pilots could fly just about anywhere at any time and they knew the Kamchatkan landscape better than anyone. Considering that Kamchatka has more mountains per square mile than just about any place on the planet—more than 100 volcanoes that have erupted in the last 200 years—one had to admire these pilots and their crews.

Pete Soverel was waiting for us at the Utkholok camp and it was good to see his broad grin as the helo door opened. We had all waited a long time for this moment and, finally, we were about to begin our Kamchatka fly-fishing adventure.

I had been traveling all the way from Seattle with my fly-fishing friend Howard Johnson, long a fixture in our FFF Steelhead

Committee. Several years earlier Howard and I had fished the remote Dean River in British Columbia, a helo and float adventure enjoyed by relatively few anglers. The helo dropped Howard and me about 30 miles upstream from where our float would end. We assembled camp, inflated our 14-foot Achilles raft and fished for seven days, making a new camp every two days as we moved downstream. I still have on my office wall a photograph Howard took of me, briefly holding a steelhead buck that weighed about 20 pounds. Howard and I had talked about those Dean River steelhead, wondering if "our" Utkholok River could hold fish that big and feisty.

Dean River Steelhead

After the helo had taken off for the Kvachina camp, Howard and I learned that we would be sharing Pete's tent, so we stashed our gear and got ready for our first meal on the banks of the Utkholok River. In the dining tent we met the Russians who would be working with us. The camp cook was Boris, the Russian camp director a man named Vasiliy, and a person we had not expected to be part of our group, Vladimir Plotnikov who worked for the regional wildlife conservation office in Tigil. His job was to make sure we obeyed all the "rules" about collecting the research data that we had come to gather. He turned out to be very friendly and already he had learned how to use a fly rod, having done this job in previous years with the project.

Dinner began about 9:15 and included much vodka-inspired toasting. After we finished eating, Howard, the other fly fishers and I, were introduced to a Russian fishing camp tradition we had not known about. It was called "The Talking Feather." We gathered in a circle, sitting on the floor of the dining room tent. One of the Russians produced a giant primary wing feather from a Steller's Sea Eagle, one of the largest birds anywhere, native to Kamchatka. The feather was passed from one fly fisher to another and while he held that feather he was expected to describe his day, just completed. Pete told me that he and the Russians, who had been in camp for just three days before our arrival, were unable to perform this little ceremony, until now, because there was no one among them who could interpret from Russian to English and back. He said to me, "You're it!" Fortunately for me, everyone had had enough vodka by this time not to notice, or care about, my less-than-sterling performance.

It had been a long day. Two hours later, a little before midnight, we returned to Pete's tent, crawled into our sleeping bags, thoroughly exhausted but high with anticipation of the day ahead.

My notebook tells me the "day ahead" was September 14, 1997. It also says that I got my first decent night's sleep since leaving Seattle, six and one-half hours. The camp staff had installed steel bed frames—with real springs—in the camp tents, so I didn't bother to inflate my air mattress. It rained off and on during the night but was not cold. The outhouse for our camp was some distance from our tents and in the dark and rain not a very comfortable trip, so I used my trusty pee bottle, a plastic quart container with a fool-proof screw top. By 7:30, It was light enough to move around without a flashlight.

We all were anxious to see how the river looked after the night's rain. At full light it appeared to be too high for ideal fishing and had picked up some color but certainly was far from being "out," as steelheaders refer to a river that is running too high to fish. Boris, the camp cook, wanted to make a good impression with our first Utkholok breakfast and he succeeded: fried eggs with chopped wieners, lots of fresh Russian bread and real American black coffee.

Most of our fishing would be on parts of the river some distance from camp and we would get to those places by jet boat, a large, sturdy and fast river craft that could handle up to five fishermen. The expedition also had two banana boats, inflatables that could carry two anglers but only downstream as these pontoon-supported craft did not have motors. At the downstream end of the float, the anglers would wait to be picked up by one of the two jet boats and ferried back to camp. In this way it was possible for all nine fishers to be on the river at one time.

When the steelhead returns from the ocean to its natal stream, its natural instinct is to conserve energy as it awaits its time to spawn. Spawning sometimes can be months away and so the energy-saving strategy is critical. Thus the steelhead always seeks some kind of obstruction on the river bottom behind which to rest, when it is not moving upstream. Most river bottoms in the Pacific Northwest are heavily strewn with rocks of all sizes and shapes. Not so in Kamchatka where most of the river bottoms are composed of silt, clay, sand or a mixture of all three. But these rivers flow through vast areas of sub-arctic tundra and the rivers' currents are constantly eroding the tundra so that large chunks of it fall into the water, thus providing the cover which the steelhead need.

For the steelhead fly fisher, this means that he can expect the steelhead to be lying close to the river's bottom, always facing upstream and in a position to see the fisher's fly swimming by. If the river's water is crystal clear, the steelhead can see the fly for some distance, perhaps 20 feet or more. If the river is cloudy or murky from rain, visibility can be reduced to a few feet, sometimes less. In those conditions the fishing is more difficult because, even though there may be steelhead present near the river's bottom they can't see the fly and, for the fisherman, hookups are hard to come by.

Knowing all this, when fly fishing for steelhead, the fisher always is wading in the river; he never fishes out of a boat. The "protocol" requires the fisher to make a few casts, allowing his fly to swing downstream in the river's current, then take five or six steps downstream, repeating the casting, and so on until he/she believes that the water—often referred to as a "drift"—has been covered. This allows another fisher, usually 50 to 70 yards upstream, to move downstream at about the same pace while allowing the water to "rest" that has just been covered by the downstream fisher. Being the first fisher to move down through an untouched stretch of river usually gives that fisher the advantage over his upstream partner but occasionally the upstream fisher will hook a steelhead that, presumably, his downstream partner has missed.

It took Pete most of the morning to get everything ready so we fished the camp water, without much enthusiasm and no success.

We ate lunch in the dining tent, Russian noodles in chicken broth, bread and cheese, with tea or coffee. I had become accustomed to this kind of Russian food many years earlier in Moscow, but it was apparent that some of Pete's "clients" would need some time to adjust.

After lunch the whole group set out on the river, one jet boat going upstream, the other down. With nine rods on the river, we expected to get a few fish each day. Mark Chilcote, a fish biologist from Oregon State University, and Pete demonstrated to each fisher how to do the scientific collection work that was the *sine quo non* of the expedition.

There were two "musts": *Do not* harm the fish but *do* collect the required data. That required that each of us fish with barbless hooks. It also meant that, at least for the first few days, the fisher landing the steelhead would need help from a nearby partner, which is why we always fished in pairs, never alone. Once in hand, the steelhead would be measured with a soft cloth tape measure, both length and girth (to estimate its weight), a few scales would be scraped from just behind one of the pectoral fins (to determine the age of the fish), one of the ventral fins would be clipped and saved for later DNA analysis, and a tag would be inserted by a spring-loaded "gun," just behind the steelhead's dorsal fin. The tag was a green piece of "spaghetti," about an inch long and stamped with a unique coding. No tagged fish, anywhere in the world, would have that same coded number and if that fish were captured again, the tag would be obvious and, usually, reported to a recording authority.

Mark Chilcote, the OSU biologist, brought with him another "tagging" system, one new to biologists' studies even in the Pacific Northwest. These were radio tags, a battery-powered miniature radio transmitter that would emit a unique frequency, a different one for each fish. Mark's radio receiver was tuned to track these radio emissions, thus enabling him to record the movements of each fish as it moved up and down the river. But the radio tags were relatively expensive and only ten fish received them. By the time our party left the Utkholok River, Mark had been able to locate eight of the ten radio-tagged fish, a significant achievement for this brand-new technology.

To make the radio-tagging system work, Mark had one more hi-tech trick up his sleeve. He had with him a GPS (Geodetic Positioning System) transmitter-receiver with which he located each of fourteen "holes" along the river, marking their precise locations on his map of the Utkholok River. That word "hole" (sometimes called a "drift") is something unique to anglers, a specific location along a river's bank that usually holds fish. Almost always these "holes" are christened with a name, sometimes the name of the fisher who first fished it, others for other reasons. On the Utkholok we named a bunch of them: the North Wind hole, the Last hole, the Confluence hole, etc.

One of the more interesting and important findings, over several years of Kamchatka Steelhead Project experience, was the discovery that Kamchatka steelhead often returned to their natal rivers as many as three, four, five, even six times between trips "home," after spending a year or two in salt water. The green tag made this discovery possible and it proved beyond doubt that the steelhead, if spared the onslaughts of humankind—as was the case in Kamchatka—could reproduce itself at nearly astronomical numbers, something that had not happened in the United States for two centuries.

That first day on the Utkholok River gave me an unwarranted sense of optimism: I caught, tagged—with Pete's help—and released one steelhead, an eight-pound male. Only one other of our group had been able to do the same, catching and tagging a nine-pound female. All the other fish taken by our group were the lowly "Kunzha," the East Siberian char that is easy to catch and of no interest to the Kamchatka Steelhead Project. Along the river banks we saw many dead or dying Pink ("Humpy") salmon, those salmon familiar to Pacific Northwest rivers that migrate into their spawning rivers every odd year.

As if to make up for the slow fishing, the jet boat I was riding in provided us with an impressive introduction to bear country. For years Kamchatka has been known to be home to more Kodiak bears, per square mile, than anywhere else. Our flight to Kamchatka from Seattle, just a few days earlier, had stopped in Anchorage. During that layover, some of us visited the wildlife museum on the airport's below-ground level. The museum displayed most of Alaska's wildlife, each animal a life-size replica of the real thing, done by expert taxidermists. Included in the display were two Kodiak bears, one standing on all four feet, the other fully upright, on its hind legs. That upright bear's front feet extended ten feet off the floor and the animal weighed about 1,500 pounds. In Kamchatka, we were to learn later, this same bear—a slightly different sub-species—is even larger.

As our jet boat rounded a bend in the river we could see, no more than 50 yards ahead of us, the head of an animal that was swimming at full speed to get away from us. For an instant my eyes told me it must be a hippopotamus, nothing else in a river could be that big. But not in Kamchatka. It was a Kodiak bear and, in mid-stream, his feet could not quite reach the river's bottom. Within a few seconds he was able to run rather than swim and within a few more seconds he reached the river's bank, crashed into the tall grass and disappeared.

A few minutes later Pete beached our jet boat and revealed to his now-nervous clients some essential facts about Kodiak bears. The bear's eyesight is his weakest sense, his hearing is about average and his sense of smell may be the keenest in the animal kingdom. Pete told us a parable, probably Native American: "A pine needle fell to the forest floor. The eagle saw it, the deer heard it, the bear *smelled* it."

The bear we had just spooked had heard us coming up the river and before we saw him he was already trying to get away. Bears, unless threatened, will do whatever they can to avoid humans. But for the fly fisher in Kamchatka, it was important to pay attention to wind direction. Along the Utkholok River, where we would be fishing, there were vast stretches of dense, tall grass, reaching right to the water's edge. The grass was too dense, in fact, for a fisherman to walk through it but, fortunately, there were many bear "runs" in that tall grass and that was about the only way a fisherman could move up or down stream. Pete warned us that if we wanted to walk through one of these bear runs we had best be sure that the wind was at our backs so that any nearby bears would catch our scent and move out of the way.

Throughout the rest of the expedition we never saw another bear. But we did see, often enough, their tracks in the soft sand along the river's edge. Some of those footprints measured as much as fourteen inches across, a reminder that we were indeed fishing in bear country.

Bear Tracks

My Best Utkholok Steelhead

We came back to our river camp about 5:30 that afternoon, and Pete radioed the group on the Kvachina to learn that they had tagged five steelhead. As we had managed only two, that news put us in a kind of sour mood. Besides, we were cold and damp from the occasional showers that had persisted all day—tired and ready for a hot shower and dinner.

So how does one take a shower in the midst of the Kamchatka wilderness? In a *banya*, that's how. "Banya" is the Russian word for "bath" or, more likely in Americanese, a shower. While we were out on the river, the Russian camp staff had erected one of the most clever, yet simple, instruments of human hygiene I had ever seen. In one of the camp's large orange-colored tents, staked downhill from the tents in which we slept and out of sight behind some large bushes, they installed a wood-burning pot-bellied stove, with a long metal stove pipe up through the tent's roof. Inside the stove were coiled copper pipes, fed with cold water from the river below, pumped up to the stove by the gasoline-powered electricity generator that supplied 220-volt power to the camp's kitchen and dining tent.

The bushes provided a modicum of privacy and each fisher walked into the tent, one at a time, disrobed, and enjoyed a hot shower that, in those circumstances, equaled any hot shower he/she had ever experienced in the comfort of home. And the bonus feature was the "sauna" effect: The moisture and the hot stove provided a virtual steam bath to go along with the hot running water from the shower head above.

A perfect way to get ready for dinner, anywhere.

And dinner was special: fresh Kamchatkan crab and huge bowls of steaming borsch, Russian bread, tea, coffee and, of course, several vodka toasts during the meal. The Talking Feather routine went much better than it had the night before, mostly because each of us had some kind of fishing story to share. Exaggerations received a few chuckles and cat-calls but we agreed that our expedition was on the right track. Pete confirmed this belief by giving a brief "thank you" speech—which I interpreted—to the Russian staff and his paying clients. By midnight, everyone was in his/her tent and our propane lanterns gave way to a clearing night sky, its swiftly-moving clouds revealing a nearly-full moon. Maybe better weather tomorrow.

Just before dinner that evening I had wandered into the camp kitchen to chat with Boris, our cook. I wanted to get to know the staff a little bit before trying to talk to them about their faith, or lack thereof. Because I would have to do this evangelizing in Russian, I needed to have some idea about where they were in their faith journey: Did they know Jesus, or was He just part of a long fairy tale?

When I found Boris in the kitchen, hidden from the dining room by a heavy piece of canvas, he was hovering over a huge pot of borsch. I was surprised to see an attractive young blonde woman standing beside him, rubbing the back of his neck. Maybe I was interrupting a tryst?

At least not yet. The young *blondinka* introduced herself as Yulia. She had arrived in camp a few days earlier, coming directly from Moscow State University's ichthyology department where she was working under the direction of Ksenya Saavaitova, our own Oksana who at that moment was with our group on the Kvachina River. Yulia said she was doing the necessary field work which, when completed, would be the last requirement for her PhD in fisheries science. She had never held a fly rod but was anxious to learn.

Over the next few days at our Utkholok River camp, I learned that Boris had brought with him his ten-year-old son Kolya, even though his school in Tigil already had begun its Fall session. Kolya was a cute kid, with a big smile, typical Russian blond hair and wide blue eyes. His teeth were a mess, owing to the backwoods dentistry as practiced in Tigil. But Kolya was fascinated when he watched these American strangers casting their flies into the river. He had seen a few of the fish that we were allowed to bring back to camp for table fare and so he had learned that there was something to this fly fishing, after all!

It seemed to me, as a would-be ambassador for Jesus, that I had just identified three people with whom I could talk about my own Christian experience; three people, each much different from the other. Boris seemed to be typical of the kind of Russian one might meet in a place like Kamchatka: pleasant enough but with rough edges, big and strong physically and, likely, not very well-educated. Kolya was the epitome of youthful innocence, he probably had never set foot in a Russian Sunday school. Yulia was a highly-educated female Muscovite, probably more cosmopolitan than she realized and, with her passion for science, she might have a healthy suspicion of anything "religious."

Now my challenge was to find times and places where I could chat with these three, one-on-one, without drawing attention to myself or to them. It seemed to me that my "missionary work" should be of no concern to anyone else in our camp. If the three Russians wanted to talk about our conversations, that was okay with me.

A few days later there was a lull in the fishing schedule so I walked into the dining room tent, hoping to find a cup of hot coffee in Boris's adjoining kitchen. I found Yulia sitting at one of the tables, sipping a cup of tea. She was reading a book and there was no one else in either the dining room or kitchen tent. I found my coffee and asked if I could join her. She smiled and said, "Sure."

I told her that Oksana was very pleased with her advanced-degree work at MGU and that the ichthyology department was expecting big things from her. What was she planning to do after her PhD was in hand? She said she hadn't decided, that she had some "family concerns" to deal with in Moscow and that she was trying to decide whether to marry her boyfriend or pursue her career as a single woman. That seemed like a good opening so I asked her if she were to marry, would it be in a church or one of Moscow's traditional civil ceremonies. For seven decades the Soviet system had tried to erase Christianity from all aspects of Russian life but now, eight years after Communism's collapse, how were young Russian couples thinking about weddings and other "religious" questions?

Yulia smiled at this question and told me that even though her parents had been persuaded to atheism by the constant barrage of Soviet propaganda, she considered herself to be a believer, but one with many questions. She had grown up without any church life but as a scientist she had concluded that there had to be "something" more out there to explain all that she could see and experience.

I then told her about my own path to Christian faith, how I had been a serious skeptic until I was in my early forties but once I had figured it out my life had made a huge change for the better.

We chatted some more, Yulia seemed pleased to know that I was interested in her future. I told her that I had brought with me to Kamchatka several books about Christianity, written in Russian. Would she like to have them? "Of course," her smile said it all.

The two books I had in mind were Josh McDowell's *More Than a Carpenter* and a testimonial written by Billy Graham. Both had been translated into many languages, including Russian. McDowell's book was a simply-written but powerful apologetic about the Christian faith, Graham's a review of his many years as the world's most far-reaching Christian evangelist.

I gave these two books to Yulia a few days before I left the Utkholok River camp. She was very happy to have them and I've often wondered, over the years, how Jesus might have impacted her life.

The fishing had been only so-so on the Utkholok River and the paying guests were beginning to grumble about the weather, the high water and, surprisingly to me, Boris's food. Within a day or two of the group's arrival several of them came down with mild diarrhea and within ten days only Pete, Howard Johnson and I had escaped Montezuma's Revenge.

One afternoon, on a cloudy, showery day, Howard and I decided to take the blue banana boat downstream from camp, arranging with Pete to come get us in his jet boat in time to get back to camp for dinner. We had fished this part of the river before but without much success and we thought we knew where the fish ought to be holding. About half way to the point where we expected to stop fishing, we rounded a slight bend in the river, to the left, and it looked to me as though the water under that left bank should hold a fish or two.

I said to Howard, "Let's stop here and give it a try." He answered, "Nah, why bother?" I persisted. We stopped the banana boat, got out on the opposite bank and I insisted that he go through the drift first. Howard had as good an eye as anyone for finding fish and he dropped his first cast just at the edge of that far bank. Nothing. On the second cast, after his fly had moved no more than 20 feet, his rod suddenly bent nearly double and about 30 yards downstream a huge steelhead exploded out of the river. Howard's reel already was screaming as the fish took off for the ocean. Howard had had this happen many times before, in other parts of the world. He calmly braked the reel, turned the fish around and worked him for the next 15 minutes. The fish came to hand, I photographed it, we did the required data collection, and Howard released his beautiful steelhead; he would live to fight another day.

As I have said, on a river rarely fished before, a fisherman who catches a fish is expected to put a name to that specific part of the river. On the Utkholok River, in far-off Kamchatka, is a spot forever to be known as the "Why Bother?" drift.

Howard in the Why Bother Drift

Howard's Fish

One morning, about two weeks into our Utkholok River fishing, Pete asked me to pair up with Vladimir Plotnikov, the regional wildlife conservation official from Tigil. Vladimir had visited the earlier expeditions in 1995 and 1996, he knew the Utkholok River pretty well and he had become a very good fly fisher. So, for me, it would be a good learning experience, not to mention a great opportunity to practice my Russian. And, if I could create an opportunity, perhaps I could talk to him about Jesus.

It was a windy morning, and wind never helps the fly casting, but about noon Vladimir found a spot along the river that was shielded from the wind and, as was apparent, it would be a good place to have lunch. Vladimir was a real outdoorsman—a man in his line of work had to be—and he soon had a small fire going, over which he roasted a kind of pheasant that one of the camp staff had brought down with a shotgun the previous day. Out of his small rucksack came some Kamchatkan caviar, slices of black rye bread and two bottles of Russian beer. We were set for lunch.

I didn't think I knew Vladimir well enough to jump right into my Christian testimony; he could easily be offended by what I said, especially if he had accepted the long-running Soviet line about atheism, to which he had been exposed since he was a child. The beauty of our lunch setting, right along the river, with the wind pushing puffy white cumulus clouds overhead, was not lost on either of us. I said something like, "God could hardly improve on the beauty of this place, don't you think?" He chuckled softly: "So, you know about God?" I said, "I try to learn more about Him all the time." Vladimir, warming to the subject, replied that for that one needed a Bible.

This conversation lasted for at least 30 minutes, as it became clear that here were two believers, from opposite ends of the earth, suddenly talking about the same thing: their belief in God and in Jesus.

Vladimir explained that he had been an Orthodox Christian since he was a teenager but before the collapse of Soviet Communism, eight years earlier, he had to be careful about how and where he worshipped. Now, he and his family openly attended a small Orthodox Christian church in Tigil. He said that he knew some Seventh Day Adventists who had an even smaller congregation in his home town.

I told him that I belonged to a Lutheran church in the Seattle area and, after I heard him talk about his congregation's financial struggles, I told him I would find out if my church could "pass the hat" and send his group some financial help. Vladimir was visibly surprised, but pleased, to hear that Lutherans would be willing to help Orthodox Christians, especially such a small group, so far away. I reminded him, with a smile, that Christians have been helping other Christians since St. Paul's days in the first century.

We chatted about our families and Vladimir told me that he has a nine-year-old daughter who is just learning about Christianity at his church. I thought about that for a moment, thinking of my ten-year-old granddaughter, Nicole. Nicole was growing up in a Catholic family and she certainly knew about Jesus. Why not put these two kids in touch with each other, a kind of "hands across the seas" Christian fellowship? Vladimir loved the idea and we talked about how to make it work: Nicole would write to Vladimir's daughter, in English of course. I would translate her letter into Russian and send Nicole's letter, along with the translation to Vladimir. Vladimir's daughter would respond in Russian, mail the letter to Nicole and I would translate it back into English. Vladimir already knew the value of his daughter's efforts to learn English, a very tough thing to do in far-off Tigil, but our just-contrived pen-pal arrangement should help.

Before we put away our lunch scraps and headed back into the river, I told Vladimir about the books I had brought with me: the Josh McDowell *More Than a Carpenter* and Billy Graham's testimony. Vladimir had not heard of McDowell but, as he said, "Everybody knows Billy Graham." These two books would be among the gifts that Vladimir carried back to Tigil.

As I had planned my witnessing for Christ with Yulia, I wanted to talk to our camp cook, Boris, in a private setting. But he usually was busy in his kitchen, with his occasional helper Igor scurrying in and out. Finally, one mid-morning, I found him alone in the empty dining tent, having a smoke and drinking some American instant coffee. I asked him, did he mind if I had some coffee with him. He motioned for me to sit, with a big, rough smile and *Pozhaluista,* "please do."

I knew that his young son, Kolya, was not in school in Tigil and I asked Boris if this concerned him: Would Kolya miss enough class work to set him behind the others? Boris said that might be so but that the experience Kolya was enjoying in our camp more than made up for it, part of his growing-up. I told Boris that I had learned from Vladimir that there is an Orthodox Church in Tigil; did Boris ever take Kolya to that church, as part of his growing up? At this, Boris's eyes narrowed a bit and I wondered if I had offended him. Turned out he was deciding how to answer my question. He said he did go to church "now and then," but he wasn't sure about the Christian faith—too many years of hearing his radio tell him that there is no God and that those who think otherwise are fools. I told him about the two books I had brought with me, books that could explain Christianity, in Russian, much better than I ever could. Would he like to have them? Of course, he smiled. Then I asked him if he would mind my talking to Kolya about "these things." Boris seemed pleased that I would bother to do such a thing and he said, "By all means."

After we finished our coffee and chat, I asked Boris where I could find Kolya. He thought Kolya would be down by the river, waiting for some of the fly fishers to come back for lunch or, as likely, looking over the fly rods and reels stacked in the fly rod rack near the boat launch. Kolya was fascinated by this Western fishing gear, something he had never imagined as a youngster growing up in Tigil.

Sure enough, that's where I found him. He was looking intently at one of the fly rods on the rack and—I could imagine his young mind asking himself—"how do these things work?" He had watched a few of the adult fly fishers practicing their casting—some of them were new to fly fishing and needed help—but Kolya had not yet handled a fly rod himself. I walked up to him and asked him if he'd like to practice. One of my rods was in the rack, ready to go, and when Kolya's eyes lit up at my suggestion, it was easy enough to grab the rod, take him down to the river's edge and give him his first-ever lesson.

I may have been the first adult in camp to take this kind of interest in the youngster but whatever it was, I sensed that a real bonding was taking place. It was easy from there to ask him about his school, his friends and, did he go to Sunday School in Tigil? He said he had been a few times with his dad. Did he know about God? "I think so," he said. What about Jesus? That question puzzled Kolya and it seemed he wasn't sure about what I was asking him. I told him that I would be giving his father a couple of books that explained all about Jesus and that if Kolya couldn't read them himself, his dad would be happy to help him.

The next day I pulled out of my fly rod case a third, spare, seven-foot graphite Loomis fly rod. I had brought along an extra reel, loaded with line and leader and ready to go. Then I made up a small box of the many extra flies I had brought to Kamchatka. All of this was to be my remembrance for Kolya. I still remember the broad grin on his young Russian face as he thanked me for the gift.

The tents that we all slept and ate in, in our Utkholok River camp were, if not uniquely Russian, different from any tent I had ever seen—and I had seen many of them over the years. For one thing they were a gaudy orange color; on a clear day you could see one for miles. To cope with the below-freezing nights, even in September in Kamchatka, each tent was fitted with a wood-burning stove, planted exactly in the center of the tent. From the stove, a long-enough metal stovepipe exited through the peak of the tent. The stove and its pipe radiated the heat and, depending on how much wood was fed into the stove, the inside of the tent could become very warm. In fact, Pete Soverel later described Oksana's need for early-morning warmth—before she would get out of her sleeping bag—as a temperature that would melt nylon, maybe an exaggeration but not far off.

Most of us newcomers to Kamchatka, as we snuggled into our sleeping bags and stared upward at the tent's ceiling, had to wonder how that hot stovepipe might avoid igniting the tent fabric through which it passed. The Russian tent-makers had anticipated this problem and each tent ceiling was fitted with a flame-proof collar around the pipe that connected to the tent's orange fabric. So far, so good, but what if - - -?

Well, "what if?" happened to the tent I was sharing with Howard Johnson. One morning while we were eating breakfast in the dining tent, we all heard the loud clanging of the camp's fire alarm. We rushed outside to see our tent burning furiously. The Russian staff already was throwing buckets of water, inside and out, and they quickly subdued the flames. But as in any fire-extinguishing exercise, the water damage is often worse than what the flames have done.

None of my stuff had been singed but it was all soaked and stunk of smoke. Drying out wet clothes, a sleeping bag and heavy wool socks, in 40-degree weather, is not something the average fly fisher enjoys doing. No one dared say to Howard and me, "Have a nice day."

As it happened, one of our Utkholok River gang was a recently-married young couple who had been assigned one of the largest tents in the camp, of course instantly dubbed The Bridal Suite. They were leaving on today's helicopter, heading back to Esso and, eventually, the USA. And so Howard and I moved into the Bridal Suite, real class in the wilderness and not a bad way to spend the final few days of our Utkholok River adventure.

Speaking of class in the wilderness reminds me of some of the nitty-gritty things our Russian camp staff contrived to make our visit a little more comfortable than it might otherwise have been.

For one, there was the "outhouse." This was not a building, not even a very small one. It was a trench, dug in the ground and, of course, downhill from the rest of the camp. Above the edge of the trench was a heavy tree branch, supported by three upright, knee-high limbs, its bark carefully peeled away to offer a smooth surface on which the user could sit. The staff dealt with the privacy requirement by draping a large piece of canvas from a tree limb on the uphill side of the trench, large enough to shield the trench and its user from view. So far so good, but there was only one trench and our camp's population included several women. Alas, there was no outhouse door on which to post an "occupied" sign.

I learned later that when John Aalto first came to the Kvachina camp, in 1994, the Russian camp crew had not done anything about providing an outhouse: "Just walk about 50 meters or so, down hill and away from camp, and do your thing." That's what they had been doing for generations. That wasn't good enough for John and he designed his own "occupied" sign.

The "sign" was a long tree branch—only local materials were used—which was bolted to a sawed-off sapling, about waist high. The bolt was drilled through the long tree branch just at its pivot point. At one end of the branch was a round yellow disk, easily visible from anywhere in the camp. The other end was counter-weighted so that the user had only to lower the branch from its usually-upright position to signal that he or she occupied the facility.

I have used many "outdoor facilities" in my lifetime but never one quite like our Utkholok outhouse.

Another "facility" was of interest only to the men in the camp. Even on the Utkholok River, miles from civilization, the guys needed to shave now and then and this was not easy. One of the staff nailed a slightly cracked mirror to a small tree, not far from the kitchen tent. Boris's kitchen had the camp's only hot water and he guarded it. He would let us have a coffee mug full of his precious hot water for shaving, only. Hand washing was to be done at the river's edge or in the *banya*.

I still remember my last shave in our Utkholok camp. It was mid-day and chilly, and I was standing shirtless in front of the cracked mirror, enduring an over-used disposable razor, with a mug-full of Boris's hot water resting on a small stand beside me. Suddenly, in the mirror, I saw something that made me pivot for a better look. About two hundred yards behind me were two men on horseback, indigenous Koryaki tribesmen leading a large herd of reindeer, heading for better grazing land. The camp staff walked out to meet the two men. I could barely hear their excited chatter, a mix of

Russian and Koryaki, but it soon became apparent that our Russians had invited the herders to have dinner with us. When they had staked their horses, they left two well-trained dogs to keep the reindeer herd in check and walked into the kitchen tent carrying several large pieces of recently-butchered reindeer meat. Later, at dinner, we feasted on Boris's roasted reindeer, and the table talk extended far into the evening. The vodka-inspired stories grew louder and funnier, as the herders and our staff caught up on events in their separate lives. Our Russians knew these men from previous visits, which were only occasional and determined by the grazing needs of the herd. Boris and Igor invited the two herdsmen to share their tent and the rest of us went back to our own tents, to spend our last night in the Utkholok River camp.

Koryak Reindeer Herder

Although we were leaving the Utkholok River we were not through with our adventuring. The Kamchatka Steelhead Project was expanding. By now there were established camps on the Kvachina and Utkholok rivers, in operation for three years, and the Moscow State University directors wanted to study other rivers.

The Saichek River was one of these because it was different and never before had been studied. It was smaller and shorter, tree-lined and in heavy tundra country. And it was a short helicopter flight to the south of our Utkholok camp.

We had a brief but poignant going-away "ceremony" before we boarded the MI-8 helicopter that would take us to the Saichek camp. It was good-bye to the Russian staff with whom we had become good friends. In the traditional Russian way it was a time for gift giving. I gave Vasiliy, our Russian camp director, a Swiss Army pocket knife and a liquid butane-powered hand warmer, two items beyond his reach in Kamchatka. Boris, our indispensable camp cook, had always grumbled about the poor lighting in his work area. I gave him a pocket flashlight and a large package of batteries, enough to last through the rest of his stay. Boris's helper, Igor, a heavy smoker, was happy to receive three cigarette lighters.

When the MI-8 arrived, we learned that the "brass" from Moscow were aboard: Dmitry Pavlov, the renowned academician and head of MGU's ichthyology department, his "right arm" Oksana, and another top-level Russian biologist whom we had not yet met but certainly had heard about. Kirill Kuzishchin was an up-and-coming part of Oksana's team, working for his PhD. He would become the most effective working field biologist in all of Kamchatka.

When our MI-8 helicopter approached the Saichek River camp, its pilot saw below him something much different: A dense green forest and not much room to drop his bird within a reasonable walking distance of the orange tents already in place along the river. And our pilot knew that at least two of his passengers were big wigs from Moscow, not to be inconvenienced by having to walk hundreds of meters from his chopper to their new accommodations.

But Dimitry Pavlov and "our" Oksana were far from the stuffy bureaucrats that our pilot had every right to expect. Dimitry was the first off the helicopter and he nearly sprinted into the arms of the waiting camp director. Oksana was next, her sprinting days were over, but she greeted the waiting camp staff with a big smile and hugs. The rest of us, including Oksana's talented assistant, Kirill Kuzishchin, followed, already assured that this camp and the fishing would be something new.

The Saichek River surely was different from the much-larger Utkholok. Trees crowded its shorelines and in some places it was so narrow that a flyfisher could nearly reach the far bank with one cast. We fly fishers could hardly wait to get out and go fishing.

The project's Russian workmen already had set up the requisite tents: sleeping, dining, a kitchen and this time, a real outhouse. They also had constructed a log-built stairway that led down the steep bank to a somewhat precarious boat launch. No long, flat convenient sand bars here.

The camp had been located, purposely, a relatively short distance from the river's mouth at the Sea of Okhotsk. This would allow one of our jet boats to go downstream to the mouth and have enough time to return to camp in daylight. The Russians knew that some industrial-grade poaching was going on in salt water, just off the river's mouth, illegal netting of salmon and steelhead heading into the river to spawn. They wanted to document the poaching and, if possible, learn the names of the guilty so that legal action could be taken against them. Poaching was the one thing over which Mother Nature had no control. She had gifted the Kamchatka Peninsula with free-flowing rivers, no dams, and essentially no people to despoil the hundreds of miles of natural habitat. The poachers had to be stopped.

Some years before the first KSP expedition, and because of the poaching, Kamchatka's steelhead populations had been listed in Russia's "Red Book," the equivalent of the United States' Endangered

Species Act, and steelhead fishing in Kamchatka had been given special permission by the Russian government with the understanding that the fishing would advance the survival of the fish.

We flyfishers soon were reminded of the special needs for fly casting in close quarters. In many parts of the river that looked to hold fish there was little or no room for a typical back cast. Vladimir Plotnikov knew how to deal with this inconvenience and he caught the first fish ever recorded on the Saichek River. He named the drift where he caught it after his wife, *Nadezhda* ("Hope"). When the rest of us learned about this, at the end of our first day on the river, it seemed like a good omen with which to begin our Saichek River adventure.

However, it would take more than "hope" to control Kamchatka's fickle weather. The Russian helicopter pilots had learned that a storm was brewing to the west, over the Sea of Okhotsk, and moving our way. Before we had finished our first dinner in our new dining tent, it had begun to rain. The news about the storm, the steady tattoo of the rain on our tents, and an increasing wind put everyone into a sour mood as we headed for bed that Sunday evening.

Sea of Okhotsk Shoreline

Kirill Kuzishchin's reputation as a brilliant young scientist had preceded him and I managed to have both of us assigned to the same two-man tent. I wanted to try to talk to him about faith and his younger years in the atheistic Soviet Union, and being his tent mate should provide plenty of opportunities. Neither of us was very tired that first evening and with the rain pounding on our tent, it was a good time to talk. I asked him what it was like, growing up in Communist Russia. As a Christian myself I had wondered how much influence the atheism drumbeat would have on a young Muscovite.

Kirill made the rest of our conversation easy by telling me that he had grown up in Moscow with his grandparents, both of whom were believers. He went through the obligatory atheism school-room classes but quietly rejected most of what he heard. Now, he was disappointed in the newly-free Orthodox Church's treatment of its parishioners. The priests he had listened to seemed to be trying to tell everyone how to live without leaving much room for personal differences. And for Kirill, personally, there was the inevitable tug-of-war between his understanding of Christianity and his years of training as a biologist: how to square the "real world" with what the Bible teaches?

As I had spoken to Yulia that day in our Utkholok River camp, I described for Kirill the Josh Mc Dowel *More Than a Carpenter* Christian apologetic. He had not heard of it but if it dealt with the conflicts between science and faith he would certainly want to read it. I reached inside my sleeping bag, found my last copy of the book and told him it was his to keep. I drifted off to sleep thinking, "Not a bad Sunday!"

Kirill with Nets

The next morning it was still raining and the river already had risen nearly eight inches. Water clarity was down to about two feet and likely to get worse, and the wind had picked up considerably—far from ideal fishing conditions. It was a large storm—later described in world weather reports as a near-hurricane—covering most of the Kamchatka Peninsula and Pete was concerned about the expedition's two camps farther north, on the Utkholok and Kvachina rivers. Owing to the flat terrain in that region, it was possible that the two rivers could come up enough to cause serious flooding. Pete wanted to know if the staffs and clients were prepared to move to higher ground, should that become necessary. Pete was able to get through to both camps, by radio, and he was assured that they were ready for whatever came their way.

To add to the excitement, an MI-8 helicopter arrived, coming north from a river camp on the Sopochnaya River, 50 or so miles south of the Saichek. (The descending helicopter blew over the camp's outhouse, adding disgust to the excitement.) This camp was not part of the Kamchatka Steelhead Project but rather a competitor of sorts, operated by an aggressive American entrepreneur, Tony Sarp. Sarp's operation charged its clients nearly twice what we fly fishers had paid to fish with the KSP, the extra money going to pay professional fishing guides brought in from the United States and to provide somewhat more comfortable camp facilities than were available to our groups.

Pete Soverel was well aware of Sarp's operation and he rightly worried that if the fly fishers on the Sopochnaya were not abiding by "rules"—collecting and recording the required data on each caught steelhead—there could be serious trouble with the Kamchatka authorities.

To make certain that Sarp's group was indeed obeying the rules, Pete had asked my old friend from the Seattle *Post-Intelligencer*, Jack deYonge, to go to the Sopochnaya and assume the role of "camp cop." Jack was ideally suited for this job, himself an excellent steelhead fly fisher with years of experience on Pacific Northwest steelhead rivers. He was also a pleasant but no-nonsense guy who could be counted on to be an effective enforcer.

At dinner that evening, with the rain and wind howling outside our dining tent, Jack reviewed his Sopochnaya experience. When he arrived two weeks earlier he quickly learned that Sarp's "guests" were paying no attention to the rules. They were catching lots of fish—one fly fisher claimed to have caught and released 17 in one morning—but not bothering to collect the required data. They even said they were unaware of the requirement, and if true that claim would have shown the entire operation to be illegal and a direct threat to the legitimacy of Pete's three-year-old project.

Jack lamented the situation there: The guides and the American clients had nothing to do with the Russian camp staff, their meals were taken in private, no Russians allowed. Three of the guests were wealthy young men from Manhattan with a know-it-all attitude. When he left, he said, there was an obvious animosity growing between the Russian staff and the American clients. Not good.

As the next day wore on and the rain intensified we gave up any hope of going out on the river to fish. It had turned a muddy brown and had already inundated the boat launch. Pete again radioed the camps on the Utkholok and Kvachina and to his horror learned that the Utkholok camp had been flooded out and its guests forced to leave their tents about two o'clock in the morning. They had to boat across the river to get to higher ground and the whole camp was a shambles. Fortunately, no one was injured in the emergency evacuation but the flooding had ended the fishing for that group.

The storm by now had finished my group's fishing. We were scheduled to helicopter back to Petropavlovsk in two more days so we spent the rest of the time drying out clothes, packing our duffle bags and tidying the camp for the next group of fly fishers. The storm would pass, the river would drop—although ever so slowly in the vast and spongy tundra—and life would go on.

The rain did let up the next day, the sky cleared a bit and, to kill time, we decided to look for mushrooms, which always pop up after a good rain in this part of Kamchatka. Serge Karpovich had joined our group and he knew mushrooms like no one else. We walked across the small meadow that the helicopters used as their landing site and into a small wooded area. Sure enough, there were new mushrooms all over the forest floor. Serge pointed out which ones were safe to eat and which ones to avoid. We gathered a small gunny sack full and brought them back to our kitchen tent. That evening we enjoyed fresh sautéed mushrooms, which made even the canned corned beef hash enjoyable.

The next day, our helicopter arrived about mid-morning. The weather was still squirrelly and it would be a rough ride back to Petropavlovsk, but it had been one month since I arrived in Kamchatka, I had seen my 68th birthday pass and it was time to go home.

When the calendar turned to the new millennium, in year 2000, BJ and I had been married for 28 years. Like most married couples, we had had our share of ups and downs. She had brought to our marriage four children from a previous union, Randy, Janice, Jeff and Shirley. Randy and Janice were already of an age to be out on their own, Jeff and Shirley five years younger. These four had become my "step children," of course, and by and large we got along pretty well. And so did their step-brothers, my two sons, Scott and Mike.

Eventually, as must happen, all six of our children moved on to marriage and families of their own, leaving BJ and me as "empty nesters." I've never known exactly why, but we seemed to drift apart in those later years, finding fewer and fewer things to do together and to talk about. In 1993 BJ had decided that we should leave our home in Normandy Park and move to our old home town of Sumner where she had several friends who were now widowed and living there alone. The move to Sumner meant that our Lutheran Church near Seattle was too far to drive to each Sunday, so we began attending services at Sumner's Presbyterian Church. As I had been doing at Prince of Peace Lutheran, I quickly moved into a Bible-teaching role at Sumner Pres. BJ was now much closer to her long-time friends and I was happy enough to be back in Sumner, after an absence of nearly 50 years.

Still, things weren't quite right and they got progressively worse. I knew that God expects the *man* in the family to make things right but I felt that my marriage was slipping away, not His fault, nor BJ's, but mine. I tried to talk it out with Betty Jean but that didn't work either and so, reluctantly, I filed for divorce, making me a "two-time loser." At one of my Bible studies, a visiting pastor learned of my decision and told me, "For you, divorce is not an option!" Of course he was wrong, but his admonition surely didn't make me feel any better.

Part Nine – Two Brothers in Christ

Chapter 34

Coach

It's not uncommon, when a couple of guys get together, and each knows the other is a Christian, to say something like, "Hi, Brother," or "Good to see you, Brother."

With that in mind, I can write about two men, two "Brothers in Christ," who are not, biologically, "brothers" at all. One is my son, John Michael, the other my old pal Duane "Coach" Magee. Each of these "Christian brothers" has played an important part in my life.

My first recollection of Duane Magee probably goes back to Fall 1945, just a few months after World War II had ended with the surrender of Japan. Duane was living near Orting, Washington at the time, a town even smaller than Sumner, about ten miles south on one of the roads leading to Mount Rainier. A year earlier, he had transferred from the Orting school system to Sumner's, to begin his high school years there. Duane already was a good basketball player and made the Sumner Spartan team as a sophomore.

As juniors, we both turned out for football, neither of us making the first team. It was a rough season, with the Spartans losing seven of their nine games. As I have written earlier, our senior year was much better. We went 7 and 2, but one of those losses was to Puyallup. Not a good thing.

Duane's basketball team didn't do much better, losing nine of 13, including a one-point nail-biter to arch rival and undefeated Puyallup.

That same year, Duane and I decided to try out for the annual school play, *Ladies of the Jury*, and in that environment—after-school rehearsals several times each week—we got to know each other and became good friends. There was something about him that I noticed to be different from the other guys I knew: He never cussed. I didn't know it, and Duane didn't talk about it, but he was a Christian. He went to church every Sunday and already had learned about Jesus.

As seniors we both had achieved something of that "BMOC" (Big Man on Campus) reputation. I had been elected student body president and Duane was making a name for himself as one of the Puget Sound League's best basketball players. And we both found ourselves on the school's debate team, with June Schlauch as our coach. Our team traveled all over the state—in "Miss June's" car—winning many more than we lost.

Duane still kids me about our experiences on the gridiron. As seniors we were on the first team, I played center and Duane played quarterback. In those days most high schools used an offensive formation known as the Notre Dame Box, in which the center passes the ball to one of the running backs, but occasionally we would try to fool our opponents by shifting, without warning, to a T-Formation alignment. In the "T," the center snaps the ball to the quarterback who has his hands right under the center's butt. At first, this required more than the usual practice time and during one set of drills, I snapped the ball to Duane and in my rush to get into a blocking stance I hit him in the nose with my left elbow. I don't remember this, of course, but Duane does. He said I just about broke his nose and he was sore for weeks.

That winter saw Duane's basketball team have one of its best seasons in years, even though it lost one more regular-season game than it won. Three of its losses were by one point but, most important, the team beat Puyallup twice.

Duane was elected to the Puget Sound League's All-Conference first team, the league's finest point guard. Later he would wise-crack to anyone who would listen: "There are three things in life you can count on: death, taxes, and Magee from 16 feet." It's a line I still enjoy hearing.

After graduating from Sumner High School in the spring of 1947, Duane and I lost track of each other for quite a few years. He went on to Seattle Pacific University and I to the University of Washington. Duane quickly established himself on SPU's basketball team, played four years and was good enough to catch on with a semi-pro team soon after he graduated. He went on to become a teacher-counselor and basketball coach in several of Washington's high schools. His former players now number in the hundreds and he meets with many of them at least once a year. They still refer to him as "Coach Magee." Even his cell phone answering service uses that moniker.

After being out of touch for years, it's not surprising that it was our love of Jesus that brought Duane and me back together.

Not long after I committed myself to Christ in 1972, I began looking for groups of Christians beyond my own church. Promise Keepers was one of those and the organization held one of its huge gatherings in Seattle's Kingdome, home to its professional football and baseball teams. I had already been to Billy Graham's Seattle crusade, the second-ever event to be held in the new domed stadium. That Crusade packed in more than 80,000 people. The Promise Keepers event wasn't quite that well attended but during the registration process I noticed Duane's name on one of the lists. After I found him, we sat together during each of the PK sessions and then agreed to get together regularly.

That Promise Keepers experience led to a renewed and long-running friendship. Duane and I met at a local restaurant once a week for breakfast. We brought our Bibles, prayed together and examined scripture passages that we had agreed to study. It was a bonding experience like none I've had with any other man. And the "glue" is just as well set today as it was more than 30 years ago.

When my wife Joan died, Duane was one of the first people I turned to for the kind of support a guy needs at a time like that. A week later, he attended her memorial service and, along with our mutual friend Frank Sato, delivered a beautiful eulogy.

I'm convinced that that's the kind of friendship only a common Christian faith can support and I thank God for it, for Duane, "Coach" Magee.

Chapter 35

Mike

I've written about "Son No. One," Scott. Now it's "Son No. Two's" turn.

Mike was born at the American military hospital in Tehran on October 11, 1957, just seven days after Sputnik blasted off from a far-away missile launch pad in Soviet Russia, an event about which I have written earlier in these pages.

Colleen and I named him John Michael and within a few hours of his birth, I told my friend Serge Karpovich—a colleague at our CIA station in Tehran—about my son's name. Serge said it was a good choice, because his own name was Serge Mikhailovich ("Mike"), the Russian patronymic that identifies, in this case, the name of Serge's father. Not so, here, because my name is John and to have been consistent, Mike's middle name should have been "John," but John-John didn't work, so we settled on John Michael. It didn't matter, because almost immediately everyone called him "Mike," including his two proud parents.

For the first two years of Mike's young life, he and his two-years-older brother Scott got along famously. Scott couldn't do enough for his little brother. But as they grew older—and as an only child I never understood this—they became very competitive and eventually rather combative. It was a situation that eventually led to some serious friction between Colleen and me. Her attitude was, "Boys will be boys" so let them duke it out if they must. I took the "Tough Dad" approach and insisted that they not be allowed to pummel each other. Scott and Mike soon learned that when they were alone with their father the "rules" were much different than when Mom was around.

But, thankfully, over the next few years the two boys developed a kind of 'truce" between themselves. They still fought with each other more than their parents would have liked but our family life settled into a pleasant rhythm, thanks to the oh-so-slow maturation of our two sons.

Years later, when Mike was in his senior year at the University of Washington, he telephoned me to say that he had just met a former high school friend who told him he was part of an on-campus group that called themselves "The Way," the same name that Jesus' followers had used to identify themselves 2,000 years ago. It was apparent from Mike's enthusiasm that he believed he had found a path to Christianity, through this new group. I encouraged him to talk to its members and, if he felt comfortable with them, to join their organization.

But something about this bothered me, because Mike told me that he needed some money to join the group. How much? One hundred dollars to join and then another fifty each time he reached a new "plateau" through his studies which, he was assured, would be a regular part of his new association. Each new plateau would bring him closer to Jesus.

That sounded fishy, to say the least, and I began asking questions about "The Way." I learned that it was a legally-registered group of young men and women on the University of Washington campus. It had met all the requirements for an on-campus presence. It was an okay group. Anyone could join, so far as the university was concerned. But why would young men and women have to *pay money* in order to come closer to Jesus?

A few months earlier I had been contacted by a young man who identified himself as a member of Campus Crusade for Christ, an organization I had never heard of. He told me about the organization's history, about its president Bill Bright, in 1951 a student at the University of Southern California at Los Angeles. Bill had decided that the only way to help America become a truly Christian nation, on the heels of World War II, was to reach out to college students, those young people who eventually would become America's leaders. If they could be led to Christ, the nation's future would be in much better hands. I told my new friend that I would like to learn more about CCC (as it was called) but what about my son, Mike, and his infatuation with "The Way?" I didn't like that.

He told me that Mike had been beguiled into joining a group that intended to make a handsome profit, that its organizers knew exactly what they were doing, a kind of alliance with the Devil.

After hearing this, I asked Mike to join me for coffee and after our hour-long meeting he agreed to meet my new Campus Crusade friend. Neither I nor Mike knew it at the time but the young man was the head of the university's CCC chapter. He liked Mike and decided—he later told me—to try to bring Mike to Christ. CCC was, after all, an organization devoted primarily to evangelism and Mike was but one of many undergraduate students on the campus who were seeking something new in their lives.

Mike graduated from the university in June 1979, with a degree in economics. He went to work for Seattle's office of Merrill Lynch, as an apprentice stock broker. He had been meeting regularly with other Campus Crusade enthusiasts and, with their help, he decided he wanted to commit his life to Jesus Christ. As he grew in his new-found faith, he could see himself better investing his life in eternal things rather than temporal. Merrill Lynch was not the place to do this.

A year later, Mike enrolled at Talbot Seminary, at La Mirada,

California. During his seminary years, he attended the Fullerton Evangelical Free Church, home of Dr. Chuck Swindoll and his *Insight for Living* ministry. This is where Mike began to discover and greatly appreciate The Evangelical Free Church of America. Many of Talbot's graduates have gone on to become pastors in that denomination.

Mike was one of these and after graduating in 1985 he accepted a pastoral internship in central California. But first he married his sweetheart, Holly Freed, a Wyoming girl he had met at the Fullerton Free Church. Holly would become the mother of three of my six grandchildren, Steven, Kristi and Luke. Mike and Holly moved to their new home in Walnut Creek, and after serving there for 13 months, Mike was called to his first church, as the pastor of the Evangelical Free Church in Morris, Minnesota.

He served in Morris, a town in western Minnesota of about 5,000 people, and he and his church fit well together for ministry. Morris is home to a branch campus of the University of Minnesota and there were many college-age students to whom Mike was able to minister. It was good experience for him, including his early challenges as a marriage counselor.

After 19 years in Morris, Mike and Holly sensed it was time for a change. Mike's district superintendent asked him to consider a church in Austin, Minnesota. Following the normal candidating process, he was called to assume the lead pastor role in that church. He is still there as I write this and doing well. After years of putting it off, he earned his Doctor of Ministry degree from Trinity International University, donning his cap and gown in May 2012. I had never considered addressing my own child as "Doctor," and Mike tells me, with a chuckle, that it's not needed.

I think it is normal for any Christian to ask him or herself, "What have I done to further God's kingdom here on earth?" In my case, aside from my own meager contributions to God's kingdom, I can always point to "Son Number Two," my "Brother in Christ," who has been so influential in the lives of so very many.

Part Ten – Joan

Chapter 36

The Girl of My Dreams

Isuppose a first-time autobiographer might approach his story by asking himself, "What's the most important thing that has ever happened to you?" Your readers—you'll be thankful if there are more than a few hundred—want to know about *you.*

In my case, that's an easy question to answer. Next to Jesus, "Jo-ANN" is the most important thing that ever happened to me. I have written about my efforts to share my faith with others, especially when I was in Kamchatka, and Jesus was front-and-center in those moments. But I have to admit that a "love affair" with Jesus is not the same as a love affair with the woman you've longed for for 70 years.

As I will explain, Joan and I first "connected" on the playground of Sumner, Washington's grade school in September, 1935. She would much later remember, and tell me, that she was a "naughty little girl," chasing around that playground during the recess hours, trying to kiss whatever boy she could stop long enough to receive her child-like affection. As I learned as her husband, many years later, she was then, and forever, a "people person." Joan loved people, some kind of God-given gift that told her that, in Jesus' image, everyone was to be loved. How she sensed this at age six, I'll never know, but as I look back on her beautiful childhood, I know for sure that God had chosen this precocious six-year-old as an instrument of His love. That she lavished that love on me, some 70 years later, is another story which I can tell with joy.

First off, we need to get the pronunciation right. Her name is pronounced Jo-ANN, not Joan (rhyming with "loan.")

Joan Elizabeth Kohl was born February 1, 1930, at the Tacoma General Hospital in Tacoma, Washington. Although her father, Gerald Kohl, was a surgeon, he did not become an OB/GYN until after his return from Europe and World War II. Thus, it is unlikely that he delivered his first child. He did say later that Joan was the most beautiful baby he had ever seen, and by that time he had seen many of them.

The Kohl family lived, as did my family, in the small town of Sumner, Washington, at that time population probably no more than 1,600. Joan was the first of four children, two sisters, who followed about two years apart, and a "little brother" who followed eight years after Joan's birth. Their names are Barbara, Patricia ("Trish") and Alexander ("Alex").

Joan was a precocious child. Her mother arranged for her to sing a song on the radio, at age five, on Tacoma's only radio station in those days, KVI. That song, "The Isle of Capri," had been written just a few years earlier, was popular at the time, and five-year-old Joan performed it beautifully.

Seventy years later, after Joan and I were married, she explained to me how she happened to sing that song on the radio; some of her story is speculation, because her parents never told her about it, but the puzzle's pieces fit. It is a story I have shared with many friends, since Joan's death in 2011, and it is worth repeating here.

Joan and I lived, as I've said, in this small town of Sumner. We were both five years old and had not yet "met" each other; that would come about a year later when we entered first grade. Joan's father was the town doctor and my dad happened to be the town lawyer. The two of them worked in the same building and their second-floor offices were no more than a few hundred feet apart.

They surely drank coffee together at the drug store coffee bar on the street level below.

At that time, 1934, my grandmother was living with my parents and me. In those days that's how "grandma" was cared for, each of her children taking turns caring for her; as she had had five children, of whom my mom was one, it was my mother's turn to have her live with us.

For reasons I've never understood, my mother arranged for me, age five, to recite a poem at the Christmas gathering of Sumner's Methodist Church. I guess I was, as was Joan, a "precocious" kid, or at least my mother thought so. Anyway, I had to learn to recite, by heart, *The Night Before Christmas*. This required some rehearsal time at home. I vaguely remember reading the poem, aloud, getting ready for the "big show." My grandmother was usually within hearing and I later understood that she, a staunch Iowa Methodist (she was born in 1865, the year President Lincoln was shot) was offended when I spoke the words of the poem, "His little round belly shook when he laughed, like a bowlful of jelly." Apparently Grandma thought those words, especially "belly," were not dignified.

So, fast-forward a week or so, I'm up in front of this Christmas gathering of Methodists (probably no more than a hundred or so, but it seemed to me to be at least a thousand) and I began reciting "my" poem. When I reached the line about Santa's belly, offensive to Grandma, I stopped in mid-sentence and said, "Grandma doesn't like this part."

To my very young amazement, this brought the house down, the audience laughed long and loudly, and I wondered "why?" I must have finished the poem and then forgot the whole thing.

Well, as Joan and I reconstructed this event 70 years later, it seemed certain that my dad and mom had been in that Methodist audience to watch their wonderful child recite his poem, which would have gone unremarked had it not been for the "Grandma doesn't like this part" ad lib. Then, probably the next day, my dad and Joan's dad have coffee together and what do they talk about? Their kids, of course. My dad tells Joan's dad what happened at the Methodist Church. Joan's dad tells Joan's mom, after getting home from work, and Joan's mom, not to be outdone, arranges for Joan to sing on the radio.

I should add that at that time, in little Sumner, everyone knew the politics of everyone else. My parents were hard-core Democrats, Joan's were staunch Republicans. After hearing Joan's recounting of this story, I've wondered if that might have had something to do with it.

In any event, after hearing Joan's account of this so-personal story, I went online and downloaded a sheet-music copy of "The Isle of Capri." It was simple enough for me to bang out on Joan's piano and we often sang it together. It became "our" song.

And speaking of Joan's piano, that's another story.

As I said, Joan was a precocious child and her parents managed to have her enroll in Sumner's grade school at age five, five months shy of her sixth birthday. (She had to take some kind of special "exam," which she no doubt aced.) I was within a month of being six, so Joan and I wound up enrolling in the first grade at the same time, September 1935. We were not, however, in the same classroom. There were two first grade classes, across the hall from each other.

Second Grade, 1937
Joan is first on left, front row; John, 2ⁿᵈ from left, 2ⁿᵈ row. Geneve is 3ʳᵈ from right, 2ⁿᵈ row. Frank Sato is first on left, 2ⁿᵈ row.

But it was on the playground of that school, during recess time, that Joan caught my attention, big time. I developed a huge crush on this little brown-eyed beauty, with her deep-brown hair in pig-tails. I never got over this feeling about Joan and somewhere along the way the crush became a real love, a love that has lasted, now, for 78 years.

Joan's artistic interests and talent showed up very early. In the first grade—she was across the hall in a different classroom—she was cutting out paper dolls, coloring the various "outfits" she put on them, trying out different color combinations and "fashions." In the second grade we were now in the same classroom and she was always better than any of the other kids when it came time to get out the Crayolas and draw and cut.

When she was in the third grade she did a painting and framed it. Her teacher was so impressed that she told the school principal about it. He, without saying anything to Joan, decided to hang it on his office wall, as an example of how well some of his students were doing. Joan soon found out about this and although she was irked at the principal's appropriation of her painting, she was too shy to complain about it. But before she left the Sumner school system, eight years later, she went back to that same principal and asked him for her painting. It was still hanging on his office wall and he had no choice but to return it to her. Needless to say, he was embarrassed, but by that time Joan was grown-up enough that her former principal's discomfort bothered her not at all.

Back to that piano. I still remember being invited to a fifth-grade kids' party at Joan's home, in her downstairs recreation room. There were about a dozen of us and one of the games Joan's mom had helped organize was "spin the bottle." The reward for having the bottle stop and point: The kid pointed to could kiss any one in the room and you can imagine my anxiety level as that bottle spun and stopped. But not at me, and the "rules" were that the bottle would be spun only three times. So I was denied something I had longed for, probably more than anything else, for quite some time.

I don't recall why I was called upon to do this but during the party's festivities I was asked to play something on the piano, sitting there in the recreation room. I had been taking lessons for about a year and the only thing I could play from memory, without music, was a piece called "Cow-Cow-Boogie." Apparently this performance made an impression, at least on one of the kids at that party.

That "kid" was a neighbor of Joan's, Geneve Purvis. They were already best friends and remained so, right up to Joan's death in 2011.

Sometime, probably in 2007, Joan received a note from Geneve, who then was living near Lake Tahoe, in Nevada. In the note, Geneve included a copied item from the diary she was already keeping at the time of that fifth-grade party. She had made some notes about the party, one of which said "John played the piano."

The piano Geneve was referring to now rested on the floor in Joan's Mercer Island home. Being the gifted artist that she was, Joan had painted the piano a lovely Chinese Red.

Joan and I were married in Honolulu in November 2005 and within a few days of returning to her (now "our") lovely home, I began playing around on the Chinese Red upright piano, never imagining that it was the same piano on which I had played Cow-Cow Boogie some 64 years earlier. That was until Geneve's letter arrived a couple of years later and Joan and I (we both had long forgotten about this) learned what had happened. The piano was impossible to keep in tune, as old as it was, so for my 80th birthday Joan presented me with a brand-new Yamaha upright piano, a thing of beauty. I'm still practicing on it, nearly every day, and only wish I could do it justice, such a generous gift it was.

I have written a book about the love affair that developed between Joan and me. Its title is *A Tiffany Monday*, published in 2012 by WestBow Press and available on Amazon.com for about $14.00. Its sub-title is "An Unusual Love Story," and indeed it is "unusual" because the book is made up, almost entirely, of the more than 200 pages of email messages that Joan and I exchanged during the Spring, Summer and Fall of 2005. But that happy story is just about our courtship. It says nothing about the many sorrows that Joan endured, beginning when she was only 15 years old, a ninth grader in that Sumner, Washington school system.

As I've said, Joan's father was a surgeon. In early 1941 he believed that war was coming, with either Japan or Germany, or both, and he enlisted in the U.S. Army Medical Corps. Fort Lewis, Washington, was not far away and he reported there for duty soon after his enlistment. On the morning of December 7, 1941 Pearl Harbor was attacked by the Japanese. When the news reached Joan's home, her father was installing the first-ever electric/automatic dishwasher to be available in little Sumner. (Gerald Kohl, in addition to being a skilled surgeon, also had been a carpenter in his younger years in Iowa, and was very handy with tools, so the dishwasher installation was, for him, "a piece of cake.") He quickly finished his work, jumped into his car, and drove off to Fort Lewis.

As Joan recounted to me many years later, her father had a wife and four children at the time of the Pearl Harbor attack, so it was not necessary for him to enlist. Apparently his fierce patriotism (which Joan inherited) was his primary motivation.

Captain Gerald Kohl, after establishing himself in England as an Army field hospital surgeon, went ashore at Normandy, France on D-Day Plus One, June 7, 1944. He was already in command of a field hospital team which, eventually, saw duty at the Battle of the Bulge, in Bastogne, Belgium. Just before the war's end, in May 1945, he was assigned to duty in Norway. There, he worked with a Norwegian nurse with whom he fell in love.

When he returned to his family in the summer of 1945, Joan's father told her mother that he wanted to leave her, to return to Norway and marry the nurse. Joan's mother, quite naturally, was devastated. She confided the whole story to Joan, her eldest daughter, but insisted that Joan tell absolutely no one what had happened.

So Joan, at the tender age of 15, a sophomore in high school, had to try, somehow, to hold her family together, without telling anyone. It was only the first of many sorrows that would come her way.

During that high school sophomore year, which I continued to share with Joan because we often found ourselves in the same class room, I learned quickly that she was "going steady" with one of the high school seniors, a very nice young man. He had just returned from military service and was a few years older than the rest of us. He apparently fell in love with Joan (who would not have?) and talked to her about, someday, marriage. As Joan related this story to me many years later, she never understood what happened, but after the young man left high school he never came back to Joan. She thought of him as a very nice guy but far from someone to marry and besides, she knew she was much too young for such serious thinking.

Of course I had been in love with Joan, by that time, for about ten years but I never dared asked her for a date, and not just because she was going with someone else. In our junior year in high school, she was "free." But I was so enamored of her and so fearful that she would turn me down, that I never asked her for a date. I could never have lived with the humiliation.

Three years later, Joan was the innocent victim of another "family decision." Her father had seen so much death and destruction in Europe that he decided to become an OB/GYN, a surgeon who could promote life, rather than try to save it. He went to Harvard University for the necessary additional training and returned to Sumner. But Sumner was a small town, with relatively few women who would need his services. So he decided to move to Tacoma, Washington, the second-largest city in the state.

Joan, now an about-to-be high school senior, found herself to be a new student at one of Tacoma's largest high schools. She dreaded leaving the comfortable surroundings of Sumner but she had no choice. One of her mother's friends had belonged to a high school sorority at the same high school and insisted that Joan should join. So she did. What she learned almost immediately was heartbreaking: The girls at the new high school all were wearing the "new" style clothing, skirts down to the ankles, shoulder-length hair. Joan, coming from "provincial" Sumner, had short hair and shorter skirts. To make matters worse, her new sorority sisters had a (stupid) "rule" that forbade them to speak to the new pledges. This might have been acceptable to incoming tenth-grade girls, but Joan was already a twelfth-grader. So she was obliged to spend her first half-year at her new "swish" high school being ignored by those "sisters" who were her own age. It was a humiliating experience which she never forgot.

Joan's High School Portrait

Joan's experiences, four years later, were even more heart-breaking. She had pledged the Alpha Phi sorority at the University of Washington. While there she befriended another Alpha Phi sister, a year older, and because she was a year ahead of Joan, she would graduate a year earlier. The two of them became close friends and decided that, together, they would begin their adult careers as airline fight attendants (in those days known as "stewardesses"). Joan Taber graduated from the university and immediately got a job with United Airlines as a new stewardess. She kept in touch with Joan, writing about how much she enjoyed her work. Then one winter night, on a flight out of Spokane, Washington, her United DC-3 aircraft encountered severe icing conditions, crashed, and everyone aboard was killed.

As Joan related this terrible experience to me, many years later, I could not help but think that, had it not been for her deep immersion in her studies of art at the university, she might very well have quit school and never finished her studies. That would have been a tragedy as lamentable as that of Joan Taber's death, given the huge talent that lay within Joan's being, waiting only to be revealed through the genius of her paints and brushes.

Joan married Clifford O. Johnson on July 14, 1951, in her parents' home in Tacoma. She had hoped to be a stay-at-home mom, anticipating that four or five children would be "just about right." Another disappointment appeared within the next six years when the young couple learned that Cliff could not give Joan children. So they adopted a boy and a girl, two years apart. Joan's OB/GYN father, by then well-established at Tacoma's General Hospital, provided the links for the adoptions. Joan, true to her unselfish nature, let everyone assume the child-bearing problem was hers, not her husband's and, so far as I know, she never revealed the truth to anyone outside her immediate family.

Cliff Johnson, also an undergraduate student at the University of Washington, had enrolled in a U.S. Marine Corps reserve program, to help fund his education. The Korean "conflict" was brewing at the time but Cliff's Marine unit never was called up. Between his junior and senior years he decided he wanted to get into the fray and joined the Army; his previous Marine Corps experience earned him a second lieutenant commission. As a result, when he set out on his honeymoon with Joan, he knew he could be shipped out to Korea at any time. The newlyweds drove south from Tacoma but no sooner had they arrived at their destination in California than Cliff received his orders to report to San Francisco. So back they went.

It was on this drive that Joan experienced another setback to her young life. She was still learning to drive and was behind the wheel, Cliff sitting beside her, when she decided to pass a log truck, which was climbing slowly up a hilly piece of the highway. She sideswiped the truck, the driver lost his load trying to avoid Joan's car, the logs went tumbling over the highway and Joan's car slid off the highway and rolled onto the front lawn of a road-side home. This was before seat belts, of course, and miraculously neither Joan nor Cliff was hurt. They were obliged to spend the night in a nearby small town and to appear before a local judge the next morning. He fined Joan $50 and, as she told me later, she's quite certain he pocketed the money.

The experience was so unsettling for Joan that she didn't drive a car again until 16 years later. She took herself and, eventually, her small children, everywhere by bus. Anyone who knew Joan well saw her to be a gentle but determined woman, nowhere better demonstrated than here.

Cliff's responsibilities in Korea—he was there for just one year—mostly were to command a company of GIs who guarded a prisoner of war camp near Seoul. As Cliff wrote to Joan often, she soon learned that he spent a lot of his time pulling his soldiers out of Seoul's many whore houses, not very stimulating duty. On one occasion, however, the prisoners in his camp rioted and Cliff's nerve-wracking job was to prevent his men from opening fire. This incident made headlines in U.S. newspapers and Joan read of it before Cliff's letter reached her, telling her that he was all right. As Joan told me much later, that year was a very scary time for her and her daily prayers helped her through it.

After Cliff returned from Korea, Joan moved out of her parents' home in Tacoma and she and Cliff rented a first-floor apartment on Capital Hill in Seattle, close enough to the University of Washington that they had an easy commute to their classes. Then, as now, Capital Hill was a very quirky neighborhood and it wasn't long before Joan realized that some of the local boys were trying to peek through her apartment windows, especially if they suspected she might be in the bathroom, getting in and out of the shower. This happened often enough that Joan soon had had enough and she insisted to Cliff that they move, somewhere—anywhere.

As luck would have it, they found a log cabin on Mercer Island, recently vacated by its owners. The rent would be $10 a month less than the Capital Hill house of horrors. That move was the beginning of a love affair with Mercer Island that Joan enjoyed until the day she died. She and Cliff soon bought a small house on the Island's north end and began raising their family. But as the artist she was, Joan had her sights set much higher. In 1966 she designed a new home and soon found a piece of property at the Island's south end, just right for what she wanted. The home was built by the Buchan Brothers, two young contractors in their 20's who went on to become the Island's most successful builders. Joan's home was a bi-level rambler with its four bedrooms and two baths on the lower level and her living room, dining room, kitchen, guest bathroom and family room above. Joan loved the lake and her design provided a spectacular view of it from every room in the house.

It was while Joan and Cliff were living in the log cabin that Joan, new to Mercer Island, joined the Orthopedic Guild of Seattle's Children's Hospital. At age 23, she was about ten years younger than most of the women who volunteered to support the hospital but her artistic talent made up for whatever disadvantages her youth might have suggested. One of the group's major projects was the construction of mobiles that the ladies hung above the beds—many of them cribs—of the sick or injured children. The women came to her home once a week to paint, cut out and put together. The mobiles were made of heavy paper and were painted and strung so they turned properly. Each one had a theme and they were changed once a month. For12 years Joan designed every one of those mobiles. The experience was, for her, only the beginning of a life-time of giving to others, through her artistry and her love of people.

Joan's first sister, Barbara, had married Don Adams the same year that Joan and Cliff were married, in 1951. Barbara had three daughters, Catherine, Cynthia and Kerry. On the evening of Kerry's high-school graduation, while driving to one of its celebrations in her new Volkswagen Beetle, Kerry ran a stoplight, was struck by another vehicle and horribly injured. Her emergency room surgeons contacted Kerry's grandfather, Joan's dad, and explained Kerry's condition, telling him that even if they could save the girl's life she most likely would remain in a vegetative state. Gerald Kohl then made one of those wrenching decisions that many doctors have to make: "Let her go." Kerry was 17 years old. The Kohl family—Joan's parents, Joan and her three siblings—always had been very close and Kerry's so-untimely death was a shock that stayed with them all for many years.

About ten years later, in 1983, Joan's husband Cliff underwent open-heart surgery in Seattle's Swedish Hospital. Early-on, during his recovery, the routine hospital tests revealed that he had contracted Hepatitis C from one of several blood transfusions that had been needed during the surgery. His doctors told him, and Joan, that with a proper exercise regimen and a "heart-safe" diet, he could expect another 20 years of relatively good health. And, as it happened, Cliff died just 20 years later, in March 2003.

Cliff's illness put an enormous strain on Joan throughout those 20 years as he refused to tell anyone about his condition and insisted that Joan not reveal it . She quickly changed her family's eating habits, no fat, no salt, but keeping Cliff's "secret" was never easy, especially when they traveled. Some of his medications needed constant refrigeration and there were other regimens that Joan needed to follow, all the while trying to give the impression to others that everything was okay.

Joan told me several times during our married years together that, through all of those difficult times, several of them tragic, she had determined to be a happy person. Her faith in God and her knowing Jesus were a huge part of this "process," and I believe her devotion to her art work also helped a great deal. By the time she died, Joan had produced well over 100 paintings and sketches, nearly all of them cheerful and bright. I look at them every day, on the walls of my apartment.

Tap Dancing is Happiness

One of those paintings—there are 61 of them—is an oil of Albert Einstein. On the back of that painting is a very old price tag from the University of Washington's book store which suggests that Joan did that painting while she was still taking courses at the university's school of art. Some of the other pieces on my apartment walls are her early batiks, probably dating to the early 1970s when that complicated process was popular. The 61 paintings tell a story, a progression of her skill and growing imagination and diversity. Nearly everyone who sees Joan's work comments about that—her diversity. It would be difficult to assign a "style" to her work.

Not long after coming to Mercer Island from Seattle, Joan began to connect with other artists on the island. In 1961—she was just

31 years old at the time—Joan and her friends formed a group and called themselves the Mercer Island Visual Arts League, MIVAL. They wanted to meet regularly to discuss art, show and sell their artwork, and provide art demonstrations to their members. The group's biggest production was (still is) its summer arts festival, a three-day event in which all the Island's artists displayed their work, paintings, sculpture, glass, jewelry, ceramics and photography.

Joan had always wanted to be a stay-at-home mom and she kept herself busy raising her two children, painting in her home and helping with the many chores related to her MIVAL membership. Her leadership qualities were recognized by her artist-colleagues when they elected her MIVAL's president for the year 1986.

At the same time, Bellevue, Washington was still a bedroom community for Seattle but as it grew to become a major city in its own right, its community leaders decided they should have their own art museum. The city is just five minutes away from Mercer Island and most islanders go there for the shopping, restaurant and other amenities that Mercer Island doesn't provide. Joan was one of these and soon she was drawn to the beginnings of the city's art museum "movement," a group of mostly young women artists who wanted to help. They saw a cultural void in their growing city and wanted to fill it.

The fledgling museum's biggest challenge was to raise money, enough to pay for building space and a small paid staff to complement the work of its many volunteers. These volunteers organized themselves into three guilds, one of which, Joan's, was the Miller Freeman Guild, named for Bellevue's most influential citizen, Miller Freeman. Over the years Joan served as her guild's secretary and president.

Every summer, in July, the museum—BAM, the Bellevue Arts Museum—sponsored a weeklong outdoor arts fair, on one of Bellevue's streets, and invited artists from all over the state to come and display their work. Joan played a major role in the fair as she and a few friends were responsible for hanging the work of the displaying artists. It takes a keen eye to do this seemingly mundane task well and Joan was very good at it.

Joan also was a fund-raiser for the museum, often participating in its auctions by modeling clothing and hats. She loved this action, knowing that it gave her a chance to display her good looks while helping the museum's bottom line.

Sassy Show-off

Joan's guild made good use of her organizational skills in another important way. Each year the museum organized a "Patrons' Party," an event to which the museum's financial supporters were invited, to show them the museum's appreciation for their giving. Museums never make enough money on memberships and admission sales to cover their costs. Joan was well aware of that part of museum operation and was a key player in organizing these events.

One of the first things I learned about the depth of Joan's

commitment to her world of art, soon after we were married, was the size of her "budget" for giving to the museum. When membership renewal time came each year, she expected that both of us would open our wallets. I had never been a member of a museum of any kind, but in the case of Joan's "BAM," the Bellevue Arts Museum, I was more than happy to be counted, beside her, as a regular member.

When Joan died, the museum lost one of its longest-serving and most dedicated volunteers.

Chapter 37

Traveling With Royalty

B ack to my first book, *A Tiffany Monday*. Page 55 tells the reader
about the first time I ever heard Joan say to me, "I love you, too,
John." She said that—it was April 30, 2005, a place on the calendar
I'll never forget—at the end of one of our many phone calls. From
that moment on, as the story unfolds, our love for each other grew
deeper and deeper.

A Tiffany Monday is a collection of emails that Joan and I
exchanged during the six months that preceded our marrying, on
November 25, 2005. In several of those emails I referred to Joan as
"My Goddess." It was an appellation she loved to hear, believing, of
course, that I was jesting. Maybe I was but I really did, in my heart
of hearts, have her on a beautiful pedestal, just where "My Goddess"
belonged. So we toyed with the "royalty" idea during our lighter
moments together; she loved it.

The book's dedication reads: "To my beloved Joan, easily the
most beautiful person I have ever known." It would be difficult to
list all the things about Joan that made her the beautiful person she
was. She certainly was beautiful to look at, but it went much deeper

than that. We truly were soul-mates because we loved so many of the same things and had such fun together.

Part of Joan's personality that all but her closest friends would never have guessed was her penny-pinching view of money. She hated to spend it. In fact, I heard her brother call her a "tight-wad," right to her face and in front of other family members. She just smiled and said something like, "Of course, why not?"

After Joan and I decided to marry, and like most about-to-be newly-weds, we talked about "family finances," who would pay for what? Each of us was bringing our own assets to the marriage and it made sense to work out some ground rules. Many marriages have foundered on the shoals of family financing and we certainly didn't want that to happen to us. As the so-practical person she was, Joan's "solution" was simple and straightforward. She told me it wouldn't cost her much more to feed me than she was already paying for her own upkeep—insurance, house maintenance and the many other things any homeowner pays for, whether living alone or with a spouse. In exchange, I would pay for our travel expenses. Neither of us had done a lot of traveling, aside from mine on Uncle Sam's dime, and we wanted to use whatever time God gave us to see the many parts of the world not yet visited.

We made two other decisions before marrying, one of which brought to me a huge sigh of relief. I told Joan that forever more I wanted to be "uncovered." No longer would I continue to live my cover story, that of a retired "other-agency" official. I was 75 years old and, as I had to admit to myself, rather proud of my service for the CIA. I didn't want Joan to have to go around fibbing to her many friends, telling them I was something I was not. And, as we both agreed, nobody would notice or even care.

The other decision was Joan's alone. Her daughter, Libby, had insisted that her mom and I draw up a pre-nuptial agreement, a legal document that would specify how we would spend the money that each of us was bringing to the marriage. Joan telephoned the Seattle attorney who had taken care of first-husband Clifford's business needs and the two of us then visited him in his opulent skyscraper office. I've forgotten what the lawyer's fee was for this service, but it was huge. The irony of this whole affair was that Joan and I immediately ignored the pre-nup. She had done it just to placate her daughter: How we spent our money was no one's business but ours.

Back to our travel plans, we agreed that no matter what other kinds of travel we might do, going back to Honolulu every November to celebrate our wedding anniversary would always come first. While Joan was still married to Cliff they had established a "preferred customer" relationship with the Diamond Head Beach Hotel, as its name suggests, located just below Diamond Head. The hotel was just a few doors away from the Outrigger Canoe Club, the very place where Joan and I were married, under a palm tree. Joan and Cliff had been members of the Washington Athletic Club, which had a reciprocal arrangement with the OCC, so we could use their facilities for lunch, dinner, sun bathing and swimming. When we went back to Honolulu in 2006, just a year after our palm-tree wedding, we stopped by Honolulu's Christian book store and bought about a hundred Christmas cards to send to our friends, most of them Joan's, on the Mainland.

Honolulu Wedding at the Outrigger Canoe Club

We went to Honolulu in November 2010 and by that time Joan's dementia had advanced to the point that I could see she wasn't enjoying the experience nearly as much as she had just one year earlier. Because I had never learned to play bridge very well, we had used gin rummy as a substitute and played it often. Our win-loss record was about even over the first five years but this time in Honolulu, I was winning far too often, another depressing sign that Joan would never be the same again. So it was our last visit and I'll never go back.

I really believe that Joan and I were truly blessed by God during those first years of our lives together. It was as though He wanted us to make up for all the years we had missed, a sort of "cram session," two lovers with so much to do and see and so little time.

China was one part of the world that neither of us had ever been near. We had heard from a few members of our church about river boat cruises in China. This was something neither of us had considered but after we looked into the possibilities, we booked a cruise on a river boat that would take us from Shanghai, up the Yangtze River to Chunking, from there by plane to Xian, thence to Beijing and back to Seattle. In May, 2006, just six months after our Honolulu wedding, we flew out of SeaTac airport—no time to waste!

Shanghai is an amazing city. We spent two nights there in an opulent hotel, took scads of pictures of its super-modern and almost-impossible skyline, visited a school for young girls (of money-privileged parents), visited a beautiful pagoda, and ate *real* Won Ton soup. We visited a silk carpet workshop where I lost my head and paid too much for a beautiful two-by-three foot silk carpet—which now hangs on one of my apartment walls. When Joan learned how much I had paid for the carpet, she could hardly believe her cost-conscious ears. I reminded her that our pre-nuptial "deal" called for me to pay for the travel and for her the rest, so not to worry.

From Shanghai we took a short airline hop to get to the Yangtze River boat terminal, from there to Chungking. Along the way we passed through the five massive locks that are part of the Three Gorges dam project, all part of the Chinese monster-plan to dam the Yangtze, flooding out millions of peasants who have lived there for as long as history knows.

Another Chinese jet airliner took us to Xian, something Joan had been wanting to see for many years. This city—more than three thousand years old—now is home to one of the most remarkable archeological digs ever, the Terra Cotta Army discovery, going back only to the 1970s. The Chinese have excavated an area the size of more than two football fields and enclosed it with a massive roof and walls. On close inspection every one of these soldiers and archers has a face as individual as though the artisan, more than two thousand years ago, was working from a photograph. Many of them are mounted on horses, or chariots, every one is armed. Anyone interested in sculpture, as Joan surely was, had to marvel at the scene.

We learned that this enormous display of artistry had been accomplished by thousands of slave laborers, all for the sake of the greedy, inhumane emperor Qin Shi Huang who wanted to be buried with an army of protectors.

From Xian we flew on to Beijing. We walked on top of the Great Wall and took pictures to prove it to our friends back home. On Day Two in Beijing, the traveling tummy finally caught up with me and I let Joan do the picture taking while I stayed in our hotel room.

The flight back to Seattle seemed much longer than it had going to Shanghai; I suppose that's always the way it is. Fourteen hours is a long time. We arrived at our Mercer Island home tired but satisfied, and even more in love—if that were possible—than when we had left. This was the kind of togetherness each of us had been longing for, for much longer than we had realized.

Joan, Sister Barbara and John on The Great Wall

A few months after returning from China, Joan and I decided to try something a little less strenuous, an automobile trip to Yellowstone National Park, which she had not visited. But not in just *any* automobile. We would drive Joan's beautiful silver Mercedes convertible, a 1993 CLK model that had all of 20,000 miles on it, this in 2006, the quintessential little old lady's car. I called it her "Silver Bullet," and it matched her beautiful silver hair, which is why first-husband Clifford bought it for her.

Packing that convertible—we intended to drive it top-down as much as possible—was a challenge but we managed to get everything stowed away and headed east on Interstate 90, 70 miles an hour, top down. For a couple of senior citizens, pretty exciting!

Before leaving I had contacted my old friend John Aalto to learn that he would be having a group of fishing buddies at his home in Ennis, Montana. Could Joan and I stop by for a day or two, Ennis is right on the way to Yellowstone Park? We'd be happy to fix dinner for John and his buddies. That was an offer John couldn't refuse so we pulled into his driveway the next afternoon, having stopped at a local grocery store to stock up on the dinner fixings Joan needed.

Joan had always been a great cook and she moved into John's kitchen as though it were her own. I've forgotten what was on her menu but everyone loved it. We drank wine and chatted far into the evening. The guys warmed to Joan as all men did, something I had learned to expect within a few months of marrying her.

The next day, John took his fishing buddies out onto Ennis Lake, leaving Joan and me to get ready to move on to Yellowstone Park. But Joan was so enamored of the view from John's deck—the Madison River was a stone's throw away and the snow-capped Madison Range stretched for miles, just across the valley—that we decided to stay another day to give her time to paint that awesome scene. Joan sometimes painted from photographs but she preferred "the real thing" and this was an opportunity she couldn't expect to have again.

I took a picture of her, at work with her paints and brushes, which appears in *A Tiffany Monday*. It may be my all-time favorite picture of Joan, showing her doing what she loved most.

Painting the Gallatin Range

We spent several days in the Park; Joan loved all the scenery, the wildlife. We saw several swans on one of the rivers and Joan spotted a wolf, a real thrill for her because such sightings were quite rare.

We spent our first night in the park in a small cabin. We found that it was fitted with two single beds, with the cabin's front door between them. Joan and I were no longer "newly-weds" but we didn't much like the bed arrangement so we pushed them together, even though that blocked the front door. There was another door that led to the outside so we figured the local fire marshal wouldn't object. The two young women who cleaned the cabin saw our bed arrangement, looked at the two 70-something marrieds who were responsible for it and, together, we all had a good laugh.

After taking a zillion pictures of Yellowstone Falls, upper and lower, the geysers (especially Old Faithful), a number of bison, a few elk, we headed back toward Mercer Island, driving through Idaho to have a change of scenery on our way. The journey through Idaho was the only time we had to put the top up: The weather was so warm that we needed the Mercedes' air conditioner, full strength.

Joan had always joked with me, after she learned about all the out-of-doors experiences that had been part of my life, that "I don't camp." It was her gentle way of reminding me not to try to change her ways. And indeed she didn't "camp." Any kind of outdoor toilet would have been anathema. She much preferred hot and cold running water, indoors, to the alternatives. Fortunately, our "camping" in Yellowstone Park did not require her to change anything. We both enjoyed the experience tremendously, especially because we were able to do it *together*.

Joan and Her Silver Bullet

In August 2006, just nine months after Joan and I were married, we decided to visit Washington, DC. It had been at least ten years since Joan had visited our nation's capital and I thought it would be great if we could tour the city together. I would look up some old colleagues and she would be free to roam about and reacquaint herself with some of the beauties of Washington.

We visited the Lincoln Memorial and its adjacent Reflecting Pool—its surroundings now refurbished with lovely lawns and trees, a far cry from the days I had worked in those "temporary" buildings as a young CIA officer. Nearby was the FDR memorial, the Korean Veterans' memorial—of special interest to Joan because Cliff had served there—and the Vietnam Veteran's Memorial Wall. At the eastern end of the Reflecting Pool, we saw Washington's most recently-constructed monument, the World War II Memorial. It already had become an architectural controversy but Joan loved it and I took her picture as she was seated beside one of its many fountains.

The Washington, DC WWII Memorial

We had rented a car, and from Washington we drove north into New Jersey to visit my cousin, Kitty Katzell, one of the few remaining relatives on my mother's side of the family. Kitty is the daughter of one of my mom's brothers. A few years older than I, she has become a very dear friend, and as the "Acknowledgments" page of this book will remind readers, she has been oh-so-helpful as an editor of these pages. Kitty loved Joan, as I knew she would. We stayed overnight at her Medford Leas retirement community and then drove farther north to visit Joan's sister, "Trish," in Woodstock, Vermont. Trish and her husband, Sandy, were busy re-modeling the home they had recently purchased, a 19th century "fixer-upper." It was a labor of love and they were doing it very well. From Woodstock we drove to Boston's Logan airport for a non-stop flight back to Seattle. Our tickets had been mishandled and the airline put us in first class seats, up front, an experience that we would remember some years later as our travel schedule picked up.

For many years, beginning in the mid-1980s, I had been going to the Grand Ronde River every October. "The Ronde" guaranteed some of the most satisfying fly-fishing experiences a man could hope for, especially in October with eastern Washington's Fall colors in their full glory.

The Grand Ronde River headwaters in Oregon's Blue Mountains and flows generally north and east until it joins the mighty Snake River near the junction of the Washington, Oregon and Idaho borders. It is not a large river but one of the most beautiful I have ever fished, as it cuts its way through a 2,000-foot deep canyon below Washington's wheat-growing high plateau. The narrow, twisting two-lane highway that descends into the canyon is known, locally, as The Rattlesnake Grade, and although only 16 miles long, is one of the most spectacular automobile trips anywhere.

I wanted Joan to experience the grandeur of this place. She had never heard of it until I began talking about it, part of my fly-fishing life and lore.

So in October 2006, we packed up the Silver Bullet and drove to the bottom of the canyon, a seven-hour trip that was, in itself, a thing of beauty. I have always thought that, at least in Washington state, October is the finest month of the year. We were not disappointed.

We had reserved a modest cabin at Boggan's, a restaurant-gas station operation at the bottom of the canyon, situated just below the long, south-bound ascent up into Oregon's high plateau. Boggan had a package deal, breakfast and a box lunch included with the cabin rent. We chose to stay there two nights.

I had become very familiar with the Ronde's steelhead holding water, those places along the river that might hold a fish or two, but catching a steelhead was not what I had in mind this time. I wanted to find a place where Joan could go to work with her paints and brushes; that was the purpose of the trip.

After a restful-enough night in Boggan's cabin and a huge breakfast in his small restaurant, we drove a few miles up the river to a place I had fished many times before. For Joan, it was the perfect scene. The river danced through a long riffle, populated by the smooth boulders that steelhead need, and the far bank was a riot of fall colors. Joan positioned me about 50 feet out into the river, fly rod in hand, and went to work. I "posed" long enough for her to do a carefully-penciled sketch and to get the color mixes she wanted. Then I retrieved my digital camera from my fishing vest and took her picture from my spot in the river. Back at the cabin, she continued to rough out the painting and, after we returned home, she finished it, signed it, framed it and presented it to me as my "major" Christmas gift for 2006.

That painting still hangs on my office wall, a permanent reminder of the impossibly-beautiful experiences that Joan and I shared.

But our Grand Ronde adventure was not over. Before leaving Mercer Island, we decided to take in some of southeast Washington's wine country. The region already was carving out a niche of its own in the state's highly-competitive wine industry and we wanted to visit some of its wineries.

We had reserved a room in the Whitman Hotel, Walla Walla's best-known and most-comfortable. The drive to Walla Walla—site of the infamous Whitman Massacre in the then-Oregon Territory in November, 1847—from Boggan's, took most of the day and we arrived just before six that evening. The registration clerk informed us that the room we had reserved was not available, some kind of mix-up deep inside the hotel's computer. The only room left was something she described as "The Eisenhower Suite." Would that do? Joan and I looked at each other, her money-conscious mind whirring away. How much would it cost? The clerk explained that the hotel's policy required the suite to cost just what our reserved room would have cost; it was not our fault that we had to use a different room.

It took only a few moments for Joan and me to realize this was not a joke and we asked the clerk, just what *is* The Eisenhower Suite?

In the 1950s, during the Eisenhower administration, the federal government built a succession of dams on the Snake River, hydroelectric, flood-control and navigation-enhancement projects that remade the region's economy, making it possible for large river barges to carry products from the mouth of the Columbia River all the way to Lewiston, Idaho. At the completion of one of these dams, Eisenhower and his wife Mamie were to come to Walla Walla to dedicate the dam. But there was no accommodation in Walla Walla, or within several hundred miles, suitable for the First Family.

The Whitman Hotel, already the region's finest, quickly rebuilt its entire top floor. The president came and went and that suite, ever since, has carried his name. I have thought since then that it was right for Joan to have those two nights of unexpected luxury. She was, in my heart, a Goddess, and she deserved the best.

Paints on the Grand Ronde

A Typical Grand Ronde Steelhead

The following February, just nine months after returning from China, the overseas travel bug bit us again. Joan and I had never been to South America and we decided the best way to do that would be an ocean-going cruise. The Holland America Line operated one of these, from Chile to Brazil. Just getting started would require a very long flight, from Seattle to Santiago, Chile's mountainous capital.

Our bus tour of the city, the day after we arrived, took us past the burned-out presidential palace in Santiago's downtown center, deliberately left there as-is as a reminder to Chileans of the bloody coup d'état of 1973, led by Augusto Pinochet, which led to the indiscriminate torture and killing of thousands of their countrymen.

The same bus tour provided much happier scenes as it ascended the mountainsides that surround Santiago, beautiful vistas of a now-prosperous city.

Our cruise ship would leave from Chile's port city of Valparaiso, 70 miles to the west and downhill from Santiago. The drive to the ocean took us through some of Chile's finest vineyards, scenes not lost on Joan's keen artistic eye and her interest in wine. She had painted vineyards at home, several of which I have in my collection of her works on the walls of "Jo-an's Gallery."

From Valparaiso our ship headed south, stopping along the way at two interesting and different small towns. When we finally reached the sometimes-feared Cape Horn, we were somewhat disappointed. Instead of our ship's plowing into roiling seas and 12-foot waves, the surface was nearly mill-pond still.

Coming up the east side of the South American coast we visited Buenos Aires, Argentina's bustling capital with its 24-lane-wide central boulevard and intriguing wine cellars. At one of these we tasted several Argentine wines. The wine guide explained to us that the reason Argentine wines are so much more expensive in the United States—than are Chilean wines—is that the Argentines *drink* most of their wines, while the Chileans have the good sense to export much of theirs. Probably just a local joke, but an interesting one.

By the time we reached Rio de Janeiro, Joan and I had recovered from a nagging cough that we each inherited during the long American Airlines flight from Seattle to Santiago. The coughing and hacking had been so bad during the first week of the cruise that we avoided meals in the luxurious Holland America dining room, not wanting to be a distraction to our table partners. As soon as we recovered enough to join our friends at dinner, I asked one of them to take our picture, the only one I have showing Joan and me together in festive formal wear. Today, that photograph reminds me that even at age 76 she was a beautiful woman.

We spent two days in Rio, in a hotel right on the beach. Joan always had been a sun worshipper, and Rio's December summer skies were bright and clear. She felt at home almost immediately, the scene reminded her of her beloved Honolulu beaches. With our too-long coughing spell behind us we savored every moment.

One of the shore excursions out of Rio was the tram trip up the jungle mountainside that leads to the city's world-renowned landmark, the huge, glistening-white statue of Jesus with His outstretched arms—"Come to Me, all of you who are weary and burdened and I will give you rest."

Standing there, at the base of that enormous monument, holding hands and gazing through misty eyes at His outstretched arms, surely was the spiritual highlight of our South American cruise.

Formal Night, South American Cruise

Even before we were married, Joan had told me about her fondness for California's wine-rich Sonoma Valley. She and Cliff had gone there many times, he always searching for "cheap-but-tastes-good" wine. I learned that there was (still is) an event in the nearby Dry Creek area, called "The Passport Weekend." It always happens over the last weekend in April, and people from all over the country want to join in the festivities. To be issued a "passport" you must apply for it well in advance. The organizers then hold a drawing and the lucky winners receive their passports in the mail.

Joan and I had applied in 2006 but our names weren't drawn. In

2007 we were luckier. So we flew to Oakland, rented a car and drove to Geyersville, the hub of the festivities.

Saturday morning we drove to the first of the six vineyards we would sample that day, six more on Sunday. Each of these places had musicians at work, lots of interesting food, at least six wines to sample and, of course, order sheets for purchasing wine. We decided we preferred the local Zinfandel to the other offerings and ordered two cases, but only after Joan had determined that the price was right.

On Monday, on our way back to Oakland, we detoured over the mountains from the Sonoma to the Napa Valley. One of Joan's long-time friends lived there, with her family. She, her husband and son had built a lovely home, grown and gathered their first year's grape harvest and were in the process of marketing. Joan's friend gave us a private tour of the winery and then offered us a bottle of their first year's crop. At $100 a bottle—which Joan reluctantly agreed to let me pay—we assumed the wine had better be good. When we got home and tried it, we agreed that it was.

The family-owners of this winery, not so incidentally, are an unusual story in themselves and meeting them reminded me of Joan's uncanny knack for attracting interesting friends. Louis Kapscandi, a Hungarian by birth, escaped the uprising in that country in 1957 and came to the United States. In his native Hungary, he had been an outstanding soccer player and it wasn't long after his arrival in America that he caught on with the Los Angeles Rams' professional football team, as its place kicker. After his career with the Rams, he moved to Seattle and developed a successful heavy-equipment company. He and his wife always had wanted to "dabble" with grapes and after his retirement he moved his family to the Napa Valley.

During the longer fall and winter evenings, and before dinner, Joan and I would sit in front of a crackling fire in our family room fireplace and talk about all the places we had yet to see. We loved to day-dream, aloud, about far away places, and my experiences in Kamchatka only added to her enthusiasm that we should go someplace "different." One evening, over our usual straight-up martinis, we agreed that there was a lot of the United States that neither of us had seen. So Joan—who easily admitted to being "not very swift" with her computer—suggested that I get out my trusty desk-top computer's Microsoft *Streets and Trips* program and work out an automobile tour of the Southeastern United States, a good place to begin.

During my Washington, DC tours with the CIA, I had visited near-by Monticello, President Thomas Jefferson's home, but never farther south. For years my interest in flying had reminded me that the Wright Brothers' Kitty Hawk, North Carolina was not so far away and Joan's love of history and the gentle culture of the Old South brought Charleston, South Carolina to mind. These places were enough to form the outlines of another travel adventure.

I should mention that just as we were planning this trip, I bought my first-ever portable GPS, a 4 x 6 inch electronic marvel. Before we left Mercer Island, I programmed into the GPS the names and addresses of every motel we were likely to use, even the few airports we would be flying into or out of. That miracle in a box saved Joan and me a ton of frustration—probably even a few sharp words while trying to find *the* motel in the dark. As the old ad used to say, "Don't leave home without it."

We ruled out the idea of driving all the way to the East Coast and decided, instead, to fly to Charlottesville, rent a car, and drive from there. We would go as far south as Charleston, then double back through Asheville, Tennessee, visit the Biltmore Estate, go through Great Smoky Mountains National Park, do the Skyline Drive to Front Royal, Virginia and from there to the Gettysburg National Military Park which commemorates the turning point of America's Civil War and President Lincoln's immortal Gettysburg Address. It should be a fun and inspiring trip, and indeed it was.

As millions of Americans have discovered, Jefferson's home at Monticello is a national treasure. The man was a genius and his well-preserved mansion displays most of the reasons for that assessment.

The only part of the experience that troubled Joan and me were the slave quarters, very much the same as they had been in the early 1800s, a reminder that as brilliant as he was, Jefferson was far from perfect.

Kitty Hawk's Kill Devil Hill, even in the foggy weather that greeted us, was more than we had expected. The original takeoff "grid," which the Wright Brothers used to get their craft airborne, was marked off on the ground, a distance about the same as the wingspan of today's largest commercial jet aircraft. The original Wright flyer is in the Smithsonian Institute's aviation section in Washington, DC but there is a perfect duplicate on display at Kitty Hawk. Seeing all this caused me to think my "prowess" as a sailplane pilot was pretty puny stuff.

Charleston proved to be more than we could have expected. We saw a real plantation, just as it had been when Cotton was King and, as at Jefferson's home, there were rows of slave quarters. We could look inside several of these 10 x 10 foot cubicles and see what these mistreated Americans had to live with, not much, and we wondered how the Republic survived its Civil War.

As if all this never happened, Charleston's splendid mansions were even more opulent than we had anticipated. Every one of these ornate homes had employed at least a few of the slaves whose quarters we had just seen. Were we looking at the South's best finery or at something less? For two Pacific North Westerners, Joan and I were left to ponder the truth about a part of America's history of which we knew so little.

From Charleston we motored northwest to Asheville, North Carolina and the one-of-a-kind Biltmore Estate, built by one of the Vanderbilt billionaires in the 19th century. Joan and I knew little about this exhibition of early-American opulence. The home is America's largest, more than four *acres* of floor space, 250 rooms. The grounds surrounding the estate were probably the most beautiful and expansive that Joan and I had ever seen, on a par with the Buchart Gardens near Victoria, British Columbia. Joan, the gardener that she was, could not have been more thrilled.

From Asheville we drove northeast to intersect the Skyline Drive, a scenic highway that I had traversed several times, not far from my home in Northern Virginia. This route eventually led us to the Gettysburg National Military Park. The Park operates a self-guided tour that stops at the many battle scenes, where the Civil War's outcome turned to the North. We were reminded of the horrific losses in the conflict where every casualty was an American. Joan posed for a picture alongside one of the then-modern field artillery pieces, another snapshot of her that has a special place in my heart.

From Gettysburg, we returned to Charlottesville, returned our rental car and flew back to Seattle. It had been a wonderful trip, a time to reflect on the storied history of our beloved America.

Joan at Gettysburg

That summer, 2008, Joan and I worked hard in her shade garden, a quiet, cool and lovely spot behind the large wooden deck that surrounded two sides of our Mercer Island home. The garden was about as natural as Nature could provide, lots of ivy, a heavy stand of evergreen and deciduous trees—home to several families of grey squirrels, chickadees, Steller jays, finches, an occasional humming bird, bush tits, spotted towhees and too many crows. One of my assigned tasks was to control the slugs, so prevalent in the Pacific Northwest's cool, moist environment. Another was to ensure that the garden received enough water during the dry months.

For years Joan had been hand-watering about 80 boxes and clay pots, in which she grew arugula, basil, two kinds of mint, garlic, parsley, a few other herbs and at least three varieties of tomatoes. As I've mentioned more than once, Joan was an excellent cook and she preferred her own fresh garden produce to anything available in the local grocery stores. But these indispensable pots and boxes needed watering every day so, to reduce her workload, I installed an automated drip irrigation system.

It became a Mother's Day tradition for me to purchase for Joan some kind of hanging flower basket. The nearby nurseries came up with beautiful combinations of mosses and flowers and choosing just the right colors was always a challenge; Joan's keen artist's eyes were quite demanding. She was equally particular about the colors of the many geraniums and the shade-loving impatiens that I planted for her. The end result was always a summer-long display of Nature's beauty.

During those long summer afternoons and evenings, after we decided we'd done enough gardening, it was time for our before-dinner martinis. Joan and I made it a habit—a tradition, eventually—to have a straight-up martini, each with two olives, and to talk about the day's accomplishments and the next day's opportunities. Joan had purchased a set of sturdy teak outdoor furniture and we sat in two of its chairs, her peaceful shade garden behind us and all of that color before us. It was in that setting that the two of us enjoyed our most intimate and meaningful conversations.

During one of these we began thinking out loud about "where do we go next?" Although I don't think we ever spoke about it to each other, I'm pretty sure each of us had a quiet feeling that there was a lot more of our world to see and probably not enough time.

Joan had heard me speak about several of my visits to Arizona and the Grand Canyon and I had made another trip to Utah, some years earlier. She had never been to either of these places so it was easy enough for us to decide that this would be our next "togetherness adventure."

We would do it in The Silver Bullet. This would be even more a challenge than had been our trip to Yellowstone National Park: Our plan called for a 21-day trip and there would be much more "stuff" to take along, including Joan's paints and brushes. On a beautiful late-summer September morning, we left Mercer Island and headed south.

This trip would have double meaning for Joan. Her best friend from childhood, Geneve Purvis Geer, was living near Lake Tahoe, a place that Joan had visited many times with first-husband Cliff, and we could drive there on our way to the Grand Canyon. She loved the lake and its mountain-forest surroundings, and she already had in mind a scene she would paint, something that had eluded her before.

Our top-down drive to Lake Tahoe took us through eastern Oregon's high plateau pine-studded forests, south to Reno and over a high mountain pass that, once crossed, gave us our first glimpse of the lake, far below, appearing as an emerald jewel. It was my first experience driving down the eastern side of the Cascade-Sierra Range, and Joan had to nudge me now and then to keep my eyes on the highway.

We spent four nights right alongside the lake, in a motel that Joan had used many times. One day, when the breezes had subsided a bit, Joan took her paints and brushes right to the edge of the lake, to paint the scene she had expected to see. It was a group of small pleasure boats, anchored about 100 yards distant. They were bobbing up and down in the choppy water and I wondered how Joan would be able to capture this constantly-moving scene. She sat quite close to the shore, her brushes constantly moving, a dab here, a dab there. The painting materialized before my eyes and it was, to me, a perfect rendition of what I had been looking at over Joan's shoulder. But

Joan didn't think it was up to her standards, so she never finished it. I decided then that Joan probably had painted hundreds of scenes that I, and most others, would have thought beautiful works of art; but for her, "perfection" was the standard.

The next morning Joan and I hopped into the Silver Bullet to begin a drive that would take us all the way around Lake Tahoe. It would be nearly a day-long trip, as we had arranged to have lunch with Geneve and her husband at the half-way point. It was a long lunch as the two best-friends needed a lot of time to catch up on the goings-on in their lives. We said our good-byes and continued our circumnavigation of Lake Tahoe. We could not know that it would be the last time, after being best friends for 73 years, that Joan and Geneve would be together.

With Best-Buddy Geneve, High School Reunion

Joan had driven around the lake many times during her previous visits and she had favorite places along the road to pull over and savor the scenery. This was all new to me, of course, and at every stop I took a picture with my digital camera. At one of these, which I now realize was one of her favorites, she asked me to stop the car. I did and we spent some time there looking out over the lake. I took another picture, we finished our drive and the next morning we left Lake Tahoe and continued our journey southward.

Four years later, a few months after Joan died, I discovered in a lower level storage area of our home more than 100 of her paintings, one of which, an acrylic, she had painted on one of her earlier visits to Lake Tahoe. It matched perfectly that one digital camera picture I had taken of the lake. Joan had never given the painting a name. It now hangs on the bedroom wall of my bachelor-pad apartment, right above my head. I named it for her: *Tahoe Splendor.*

We left Lake Tahoe and set out for Arizona. But first we had to navigate the gaudiness of Las Vegas. Our overnight motel was on the north side of the city, and the next morning we left early enough to see that its patrons were not yet out and about. Even at ten in the morning, the Las Vegas' strip was alive with its neon lights and come-on-in-get-rich-quick appeals. Joan and I were glad to be able to keep the Silver Bullet headed due south, without stopping. With the warm Nevada morning, and our top down, we soon found ourselves back on the highway that would take us to Boulder Dam.

At that time, another miracle of American engineering was taking place for all to see. As we crossed over the top of the dam, we could see, downstream and to our right, the beginnings of a monster bridge that would span the broad and deep canyon below the dam. When completed, the bridge would re-route the traffic that for years had been required to crawl across the top of the dam. (As I write this, the bridge is complete and has been in use for several months; it's worth an Internet look-see.)

From Boulder Dam we drove directly to Sedona, Arizona. This is Red-Rock country, complete with rattlesnakes, scorpions and the oh-so-shy Roadrunner. It was Joan's first opportunity, since we left Lake Tahoe, to get out her paints and go to work. The red rock formations, she knew, would be a challenge: get the colors and shadows just right. She worked on that painting for an hour but, like so many others, she didn't think the results were good enough and so she never finished it.

Sedona was not far from the Grand Canyon's south rim and, even though I'd seen it before, the views are so spectacular that it's impossible to be bored. Joan could hardly believe her eyes and, unfortunately, the crowds of tourists were such that she decided not to try to set up her easel and paints. We came back the next day for a second look and then headed for Lake Powell and Utah's fabulous canyon country.

The drive north through Utah took four days and we wished we had more time. There are four national parks and one national monument in this part of Utah—Natural Bridges National Monument and Zion, Canyonlands, Capitol Reef and Arches National Parks. We decided to skip Zion but spent all the available time in the other four places. With the Silver Bullet's top down, we nearly developed stiff necks from all the gawking. It was beautiful and we hated to leave.

On our way home we skirted the northern edge of Salt Lake City, then, from the freeway, we could see the lake itself, a vista that one has to see to believe. Another day took us through Idaho and back into the more-familiar Washington. Three weeks after leaving, we drove into our driveway on Mercer Island, tired for sure but grateful that we could enjoy, together, another part of our beautiful country.

For many years, Joan had been leading an exercise class that met three times a week at her Mercer Island Presbyterian Church. As soon as we returned from our honeymoon in Honolulu, I joined this group and every Monday, Wednesday and Friday, promptly at nine in the morning, we left our home, drove to the church, and she would lead the class, nearly all women and most of them in their seventies. The routine lasted about 45 minutes, mostly stretching and bending but with enough exertion to produce some aerobic benefit.

At the end of each session, during the cool-down time, Joan read a few passages of Scripture.

In March of 2009, Joan began to experience pain in her left shoulder which, over the next few weeks, became so severe that she could no longer lead the class. A visit to a local orthopedic surgeon revealed a torn rotator cuff, a condition all too common among our age group. Surgery followed on April 30 and then began the long and painful rehab. The healing came slowly but Joan was never able to resume her leadership of the exercise class. It was depressing; the class had been an important part of her life.

At that time of year, the evenings weren't warm enough for us to sit outside on the deck. Instead we enjoyed our pre-dinner martini in the family room, sometimes in front of a quiet fire in our fireplace. But the atmosphere was the same as outside on the deck: We talked about today's accomplishments and tomorrow's opportunities.

Our river-boat cruise in China, even three years later, still ranked as Joan's all-time favorite travel experience. We wondered if there might be river cruises elsewhere and a little bit of research, with the aid of our travel agent, turned up several, most of them in Europe. Joan had traveled to France and Portugal and I had visited Germany and the Scandinavian countries. Neither of us had been to southeastern Europe. After having been under the thumb of Soviet Communism for so many years, those countries by now had emerged as free peoples, most of them still struggling to catch up with their neighbors to the west. And tourism was one of their major exports.

Our travel agent told us about river cruises on the Danube River, beginning near the Black Sea and extending north into Germany. It sounded exciting and fun and we booked a cruise with the same company, Viking, that had taken such good care of us in China.

Joan's sore shoulder was still a problem for her and she had learned that she couldn't walk as well as she had just a few years earlier. I thought about this and decided that my travel budget would support first-class accommodations. I also decided that I would request wheel-chair assistance for Joan at each of the airports we would have to negotiate.

We were to fly out of Seattle-Tacoma airport on July 10, on a Lufthansa Airbus A-330. The wheel chair request provided a benefit neither of us expected: priority "processing" through the airport security system. I thought then, and still do, that security screening at airports has reached absurd heights: Joan, all 5'-4" of her, silver hair, sitting in a wheel chair, looked about as threatening as a pet poodle. Still, she was asked to remove her shoes and when she walked through the metal detector the clips in her hair set off an alarm. She was required to remove the clips, her hair fell to her shoulders and she then had to put it up again after she had been "cleared" by a uniformed TSA woman. I growled at the lady for the way she had treated Joan and she snarled back, "I'm just following orders." But even after putting up with these indignities, Joan and I had a good laugh and agreed that the wheel-chair routine would become a permanent part of our traveling *modus operandi.*

That M.O. proved to be a godsend when we arrived in Frankfurt some nine hours later. The Frankfurt airport, which I had not seen in more than 30 years, had grown to an enormous complex and we learned that our connecting flight to Bucharest, Romania was leaving from a gate located about as far away as possible. But the wheel chair attendant who met us at the top of the jetway told us not to worry, he knew all the shortcuts and would get us to our next flight in plenty of time. And indeed he did, but it was a trip that neither of us could have managed without his help.

The flight to Bucharest, on an airplane much smaller than the A-330, was mercifully brief. We were dog tired, having had little sleep on the flight across the Atlantic. We really appreciated the first class seats; lots of leg room and wide, comfy seats, perfect for napping.

A Viking Cruise representative met us as soon as we cleared customs at the Bucharest airport and our Danube River adventure was about to begin.

The next morning our guide led us on a walking tour through one of Bucharest's oldest sectors, over uneven but smooth cobblestones dampened by a light drizzle. We saw one of the Eastern Orthodox churches that had survived the Communists' attempts to erase religion from the lives of the people. The square that fronted the church was rimmed with lovely flower displays, mostly red and white. As it happened, Joan was carrying a red umbrella and wearing a red tee shirt under her black jacket. It took her artist's eye no time at all to realize that, against that floral backdrop, I would have a beautiful picture-memento of our Bucharest visit.

Joan in Bucharest

We soon learned that paprika is the region's most abundant cash crop, exported throughout Europe. The next day, as we were traveling on our bus to reach the Danube River boat pier at Oltenita, we passed though acres and acres of blooming paprika. It resembled, I thought, our vast fields of mustard in Washington state.

The boat pier was a busy place and we knew that the *Viking Neptune* would be our home for the next two weeks. We were reminded that the Danube is a major commercial artery for all of eastern Europe, and beyond. It traverses ten countries, beginning its modest flows in Germany's Black Forest and then flowing for nearly 1,800 miles before reaching the Black Sea, second only to the Volga as Europe's longest river.

Our cabin was not large, at 170 square feet, but very comfortable, with a perfect window view of the river. We unpacked our suitcases and moved on to the dining room for lunch. Even though this was Romania, we were served Hungarian goulash, covered with paprika.

After lunch we transferred to a smaller boat for an afternoon trip downstream and into the Black Sea. The cruise company advertised this trip as going from the Black Sea upriver to Nuremburg, Germany but the company calculated that the *Viking Neptune* was too expensive to operate down and back through the Danube-Black Sea canal. This was the less-expensive short-cut to salt water at the city of Constanta which avoided the 200-mile longer trip north to the Danube's mouth. Our boat cruised the Black Sea for about an hour, and all of us took pictures to prove to our friends back home that we had really "sailed" the Black Sea.

We returned to the *Viking Neptune* in time for dinner and went to bed to the steady but quiet throbbing of the boat's diesel engines, pushing us upstream.

The next morning, after breakfast, it was time to get acquainted with our fellow cruisers, just 150 of us. Joan and I were hoping to find Christian passengers and, if possible, conservative ones. That would allow our dinner conversations to be more congenial and we could talk about faith and politics, the two usual no-nos, without upsetting anyone. By our third evening we discovered a dining room table populated by just the kind of people we had hoped to meet.

Two of these were Norm and Rosalie Newton, from Louisville,

Colorado. We soon learned that Norm was recovering from brain cancer, and that at most of the boat's stops along the river, he and Rosalie would head for the nearest hospital to check on Norm's progress. This made the trip much more difficult than they would have liked but Norm was a tough trooper. He talked about his illness, saying he doubted he had many years left. We soon discovered that each of us was passionate about fly fishing and when I told Norm about my experiences in Kamchatka, he said he'd like to add Kamchatka to his "bucket list." There weren't many items left on that list but Norm thought Kamchatka should be near the top.

After we returned to the States I wondered if it might be possible, somehow, to arrange for Norm and me to go to Kamchatka together, a great way to cross that one item off his bucket list. Sadly, within a year or so, the cancer won. Rosalie wrote to Joan and me that his memorial service played to a packed church. Knowing Norm, not surprising.

Joan and Rosalie hit if off immediately and shared many happy hours throughout the cruise. It was a good example of how Christians, from anywhere, have a head start when it comes to making new friends.

Our first stop after leaving Olenita was the Bulgarian port city of Ruse, on the river's true right bank, with Romania still across the river to the north. As with each of these "border stops," the Neptune's crew was required to show our passports to the Bulgarian immigration authorities, even though none of the passengers planned to stay in Bulgaria. That procedure seemed to me to be a sorry hangover from the bad old days of Communist rule.

At Ruse, our *Viking Neptune* entered the first of many locks that we would ascend as we moved upstream. The locks at Ruse were part of the "Friendship Bridge," built in the 1950s to connect Bulgaria and Romania, the only highway bridge joining the two countries over their 290-mile-long Danube border.

We encountered our second set of locks at the so-called Iron Gate, a place where the river makes a ninety-degree bend to the left and narrows considerably. Before a huge dam was constructed there in the 1970s, to control the river's flow, the Iron Gate was a dangerous threat to some river traffic, swift and boiling. The dam's construction included the installation of two locks and it took us about 90 minutes to pass through them.

During my CIA days I had known several officers who worked in Belgrade, in those days the capital of Yugoslavia. Now this storied city, only since 1992, is the capital of Serbia, a result of the violent breakup of Yugoslavia following the collapse of Eastern Europe's communist masters in the late 1980s. I had never been to Belgrade but had heard many favorable comments from men I knew who had served there. Joan and I were anxious to visit the city and the cruise plan gave us a few hours' free time while the *Neptune*'s crew resupplied its kitchen and fuel tanks.

We found the Square of the Republic and its adjacent pedestrian shopping center, bought a few trinket-souvenirs, found a convenient bench and watched the Serbian world go by.

Our next stop, Budapest, was probably the most spectacular "viewing" of the entire cruise. There really are two cities, historically, Buda and Pesht, divided by the river. The *Neptune* stopped there for several hours and timed its departure just as dusk was falling and both cities' lights were coming on, illuminating the huge parliament building on one side of the river and the post World War II office buildings on the other. All the passengers came to the top deck to view and photograph the scene. It somehow had a magnificent old-Europe feel to it and we were thrilled to be part of it.

We passed by newly-minted Croatia and eventually docked at Vienna, one of the busiest river ports in Europe. For me this would be the high point of the cruise, because I would be able to show Joan the precise location where she had appeared to me, years before, in a vision.

I was living in Sumner at the time, in my early 70s, and while sound asleep one night, I saw Joan, in a stunning yellow knee-length dress, walking down Vienna's Opernstrasse Ring Road. Her gait was visibly "regal," as I later described the vision to her. She had always had excellent posture and I recognized her immediately. In the vision, I was riding in a streetcar on that Ring Road and off to the left, on the broad boulevard sidewalk, was Joan, striding purposefully ahead, regally. The streetcar stopped at an intersection, I could see that Joan was crossing in front of the stopped car so I jumped off and followed her as best I could, into a women's boutique that she had just entered. I followed her in, looked around, walked upstairs to a small balcony, no Joan. At that moment I woke up, almost overwhelmed by a huge sense of loss and disappointment.

During our married years together, I shared this story with Joan several times, always coming to the same conclusion: From age six forward, this beautiful person was never very far from my consciousness.

Now we could visit that scene, the two of us together. And indeed we did, in a taxi that followed the same route. Joan and I were both surprised at how real the vision scene had been. After we returned to our *Neptune* stateroom, we gave each other an especially long hug, as if to seal the promise of that vision.

From Vienna upstream, the *Viking Neptune* passed through at least 11 more locks before reaching Passau, one of Austria's largest cities. From there the river becomes smaller, eventually giving way to another set of locks that lift the boat one last time before it crosses over Europe's spine and begins its descent through a long canal and more locks. Now we were in Germany, Regensburg first and then Nuremburg, site of the famous war-criminal trials that followed the end of World War II.

Nuremburg was our destination. At its airport, one of Lufthansa's airplanes was waiting to take us home. At our stopover in Frankfurt we did the reverse wheel-chair "voyage" through its cavernous airport and ten hours later we were back on Mercer Island, physically drained but so satisfied about what we had just done and, we agreed, even more in love than before we left.

One of the first things I learned about Joan, after we came home from our wedding in Honolulu, was that she loved to dance. This didn't surprise me. She was so talented about so many things, and even in Honolulu I had noticed that whenever a small group of Hawaiian musicians would begin playing in the Outrigger Canoe Club's dining room, Joan would begin moving to the music, even though she was seated at a table. As soon as I had figured this out I said to myself, "John, you have a long way to go."

Joan quickly, and forgivingly, realized that I was not a very good dancer. Sometimes we had some dance music playing on the television or radio and I would ask her to "give it a try," either on her smallish kitchen floor or out in the hallway. The practical but determined woman she was, she made a few phone calls and learned that there was a dance club right here on Mercer Island. It was called "Let's Dance," and they came together five times a year, on Friday nights, at the local Veterans of Foreign Wars hall. But before we joined the club, Joan thought it best that I take a few dance lessons.

For many years, Joan had been a member of Seattle's Women's University Club, probably the oldest of its kind in the Pacific Northwest. The WUC owned its own building at the corner of Sixth Avenue and Spring Streets, had its own parking garage and, as I soon learned, was a delightful place to visit. It was a "coat and tie" venue for the husbands of its members and Joan and I enjoyed many pleasant evenings in its chandeliered drawing room. I had noticed a grand piano, sort of hidden off in a corner of that drawing room, and one evening I summoned enough courage to play it—after most of the guests had gone home—so that no one would hear my halting performance of Beethoven's *Sonata Pathetique*.

The WUC offered all kinds of educational programs to its members, and one of these was a learn-to-get-better dance class, to be held once a week on its large, lower-level dance floor. I think Joan may have been hesitant to ask me if I'd like to enroll, but she was determined enough that she would pay for the lessons. I really did want to get better so I agreed to do it.

Every week Joan and I went to those lessons and every week I found myself dancing with a woman other than Joan. That part of it, I would tell her while driving home, was not fun. She would smile that patient, awesome smile of hers and remind me that I shouldn't expect to dance with no one but her. So we stuck it out, six or seven lessons as I recall, and by the time we finished the lessons I had managed the Fox Trot, Waltz and, sort of, The Swing.

All of this had happened in Spring 2009, before we did our Danube River cruise. The *Viking Neptune* had been too small to sport a dance floor, even a small one, so Joan and I weren't able to practice my new-found skills. But we did get to a few of the Let's Dance events at the VFW hall.

A few weeks before we left for Bucharest, we had received in the mail, as we always did, our copy of *The Weekly Standard*, Bill Kristol's weekly political opinion magazine, published in Washington, DC. This particular issue ran a large advertisement plugging the magazine's next ocean-going cruise, something it had been doing every year for some time. Up to that time, Joan and I hadn't paid much attention to those ads but something told us we should look into it, another one of those subliminal you're-running-out-of-time feelings.

I called the toll-free number of the travel agency that was handling the cruise, the Florida-based *Cruise Authority*, and learned that there were still a few staterooms available. After getting the details I asked the reservationist to give me a day or two to talk it over with my wife; I'd get back to her asap.

It didn't take Joan and me very long to decide this would be a real opportunity. On our cruise around South America we had spent most of the time in our stateroom, recovering from nagging coughs. Joan's previous cruise had been some time earlier, on the *Crystal Harmony* in 1990—the ship caught fire on its maiden voyage and drifted for three days through the tropical Caribbean. The entire vessel was without electricity: no lights, air conditioning or running water. That had been a rough experience for Joan and now she saw an opportunity for something much more pleasant.

The next morning I phoned the reservationist and booked

stateroom 6038 on Holland America Line's MS Noordam. On Deck Six, this would be the most comfortable accommodation either of us had ever experienced: HAL's web page described it as a "Deluxe Verandah Ocean View," and we had to wait two more weeks to see it.

We flew out of SeaTac, non-stop to Paris, on an Air France Air Bus A330, transferred through Paris' huge airport—using our now-familiar wheel-chair routine for Joan—for a flight to Rome. At Rome, there was a mix-up with our luggage so that when we finally got to the ship at Rome's sea port, Civitavecchia, we were so late that the passengers already on board were going through their mandatory life-boat drill. But that little miscue gave us an extra 30 minutes to explore our new "home."

The suite was nearly as large as an on-shore deluxe hotel room. It had a separate powder room for Joan, a huge bathroom, a lounge area, king-size bed and, yes, a verandah—large enough for four lounge chairs and a table. Just right for our before-dinner martinis. From the verandah we could look across Civitavecchia's harbor and watch several other cruise ships, one of them even larger than our *Noordam,* heading for open water. This would be the cruise of a life-time. Joan and I collapsed onto the king-size bed for a short nap, before going to dinner.

The next morning we met our *Weekly Standard* hosts. This was another "first" for Joan and me, to be in the company of nationally-known political pundits of the first order. Bill Kristol, the magazine's editor, was at the head of the reception line, with Fred Barnes, his executive editor, right beside him. The magazine's publisher, Terry Eastland, was there along with Mary Katherine Ham, all favorite television personalities. Another of Kristol's staff, Elliott Abrams, had served in President G. W. Bush's State Department and was the foreign policy expert among the magazine's team.

During the ten-day cruise, this team held four half-day seminars in the ship's theater, discussing all manner of interesting issues: domestic politics, the U.S. economy, America's position in the world, the operation of the magazine and some others. There were about

150 of us who had paid the extra fare to participate in the seminars and each of us wore a large name tag, identifying us as WS guests. At dinner, each of us was seated with one of the WS team so that we could chat with them one-on-one about whatever came to mind. My best opportunity came on the next-to-last night of the cruise when I sat next to Fred Barnes. We talked politics and my CIA career for more than an hour, each of us finding the other equally interesting.

That same evening was one of three "formal attire" events that the ship always organizes, a chance for everyone who wants to to come to dinner all gussied up, as my mother used to describe it. I wore the standard tuxedo, with a white dinner jacket. Joan wore an ankle-length black skirt and a sequined black and white jacket, with silver jewelry. She always dressed to compliment her gorgeous silver hair and in that outfit, even at age 79, I thought she was the most beautiful woman among the nearly 1,000 passengers.

Most, if not all, of Holland America's cruise ships have a lounge area, known as The Crow's Nest, on the top deck, at the ship's bow, surrounded by large windows. There is a bar, plenty of comfortable chairs and couches from which to enjoy the views and a place for a small orchestra. In the center of this space is a small dance floor. The live music begins a few minutes after dinner and plays on until the guests have gone to bed.

Joan and I had visited The Crow's Nest several times, but always during daylight hours. On this night, after dinner, we decided to join the fun. We both knew this would be my "big chance." Would I embarrass both of us, or would anyone notice? It didn't take long to answer that question.

We watched while the orchestra went through a few pieces too fast or complicated for me to deal with, but eventually it began a piece of music each of us recognized as a Swing rhythm. Almost immediately the postage-stamp dance floor filled with couples, Joan and I among them. Then, an amazing (to me) thing happened: As the other dancers began to focus on Joan's movements, one-by-one they stepped off the dance floor, giving the two of us the whole space. They just wanted to watch this beautiful 79-year-old woman doing her thing. I had the good sense to do my best to move with the music, realizing that nobody was watching me. When the orchestra finished the number Joan received an impromptu round of applause. She clearly stole the show that evening and, not surprisingly, it was a moment I'll never forget.

When I look back on that special formal-wear evening, I find it even more remarkable than I did at the time. Joan was still recovering from her rotator cuff surgery and dealing with the associated pain. And, unknown to either of us, her breast cancer had begun its slow re-appearance. So if she was hurting—and she surely must have been—she didn't show it, even to me.

The *Noordam* stopped at Barcelona, Spain and Joan and I did one of the shore excursions, a bus tour through that lovely city. The Moorish architecture in some of its older buildings was of great interest to Joan: She had studied the subject years earlier in one of her Art School classes at the U-Dub.

From Barcelona the *Noordam* crossed the Mediterranean to the southeast and stopped at Tunis, Tunisia's capital city. The interest in Tunis is nearby Carthage, a city at least 3,000 years old, with a history far ante-dating Christianity. It would be our only stop in Africa but the outdoor temperature had reached nearly 100 degrees and Joan was not feeling well. So we decided to stay aboard the ship and enjoy our comfy stateroom. From our verandah I was able to photograph an Arab hawker. He was standing at the bottom of the ship's gangway, with his camel, offering to photograph any of the Noordam's departing passengers who might want to climb aboard the ugly beast for an unusual photo op. I had done that years earlier, on a camel in front of the Sphinx, just outside Cairo, and decided I didn't need to do it again.

Salerno, Sicily, was our next stop. Joan and I had been high school classmates of a man of Sicilian extraction, several generations removed, and we knew he had visited Sicily within the past few years. I had asked him before we began the cruise if Salerno would be worth a look. He said it might be, depending on the weather and if the tour bus took us to the higher reaches of that mountainous island.

He was right about the weather. It was hot, very hot, but the bus was air conditioned and we enjoyed the ride, high up the mountain side above the city.

Naples was our last stop before returning to Rome. This was a special occasion for Joan because we would be doing a shore excursion into the Tuscany region, a part of Italy that Joan had visited with first-husband Cliff several times, the first in 1989. On that occasion she had done a painting—which hangs in my apartment—of a building in Borgo A Mozzano, a charming village with an even more-charming hotel, the *Milano*, in which she and Cliff stayed. Their second visit was in 1992 and now, 17 years later, we would be visiting the region together.

Our first stop was in Florence, whose museum housed the most-famous of all of Michelangelo's sculptures, *David*. Although Joan had seen the masterpiece years earlier, seeing it again may have been, for her, the highlight of the trip. We did a lengthy walking tour of Florence, then drove to Pisa, home of the world-famous Leaning Tower. Neither of us had seen it before and even though the bright afternoon sun illuminated the tower perfectly we both felt a little let down: It looked exactly like the many pictures we had seen of it, beginning with our junior high school geography text books!

The bus ride back to Naples was uneventful but there was still enough daylight that as we approached the city's sea port we could see, across the water and off in the haze, the Island of Capri, the subject of that song that Joan, as a five-year-old, had sung on the Tacoma radio station. That sighting brought back fond memories and a few chuckles as we relived the story.

Our departure from the ship in Rome was an emotional experience as we said our good-byes to our new friends on the *Weekly Standard* staff. They reminded us that they do a cruise each year, each time to a different part of the world, and that Joan and I would be on their mailing list.

At our request our travel agent had booked an after-cruise extension, giving us three days to explore the center of ancient Christianity. We soon discovered that our hotel was miles from the city's center. To make matters worse, it was the middle of August, stifling hot, and it seemed that the city had shut down for a couple of weeks. All the restaurants within walking distance of the hotel were closed, even the hotel's bar and restaurant had closed for the week and there was no room service and no ice available for our pre-dinner martinis. I walked several long blocks before I found a dingy Chinese carry-out hole in the wall, and we ate "Chinese," in our hotel room, for three nights. Not a very good way to top off a first-class tour of the Mediterranean. No matter, Joan maintained her usual cheerful disposition and I felt obliged to try to match it.

Despite the unpleasant circumstances, we did manage to see something of the city. We hired a young Italian driver to cover the long distance from our hotel into the city and we found his English to be just passable, enough words to describe most of the things we wanted to see. When we reminded him that it was time for lunch, he found a sidewalk cafe, on the shady side of the street and with a clear view of the Coliseum. He thought it was "cool"—as he said—that I would buy his lunch. It was a relaxing hour, probably the most comfortable of all our time in Rome.

The next day we used the same driver to deliver us to a pre-paid tour of the Sistine Chapel. We told the driver we wouldn't be needing him any more, thanked him for his services and sent him on his way.

Neither I nor Joan had ever seen Michelangelo's ceiling, something she had studied years before in her U-Dub art classes. What we found was that, despite the heat, there were probably 100,000 tourists milling about St. Peter's Square, and the lines into the chapel were blocks long. Our pre-paid tour was supposed to allow us to go to the head of the line but there were hundreds of other tourists who had paid for the same privilege. We waited and waited and out of the crowd surged an impatient and very large Italian man who, in his hurry to crash the line, slammed into Joan's still-tender left shoulder. She nearly fell to the floor in pain, tears began to flow. One of the uniformed security men saw her plight and helped her out of the building. After ten minutes or so her pain had subsided enough for her to enjoy an ice cream cone from a sidewalk vendor. We huddled in a shady spot, enjoyed the ice cream and then hailed a taxi for the long and expensive drive back to our hotel. We had seen enough of Rome and were happy to be leaving the next morning.

Rome had been a disappointing experience for both of us. But after we were airborne and nestled into our Air France seats for the long flight back to Seattle, we decided that our Mediterranean cruise might have been our best togetherness experience yet, especially as we recalled those magical moments on the Crow's Nest dance floor.

Joan had heard me talk, many times, about my experiences in the Soviet Union. I didn't say very much about the work I did at the embassy but I did like to describe the traveling I was able to do, away from Moscow. Among other things, I told her about my occasional trips to Helsinki. Each one of them took me through Leningrad (now St. Petersburg) and on two of these stopovers, I was able to visit the Hermitage Museum, next to the Louvre in Paris probably the world's most famous art museum. When Joan heard me talk about the Hermitage, she wondered out loud, "Why couldn't *we* do that, together?"

"Why not? Yes, why not do it?" I felt kind of stupid for not having thought of it myself several years earlier. It was late May, 2009, and we were already booked to go on our Danube River cruise in July, with the Mediterranean cruise to follow in August. We decided that to try to crowd in a visit to the Hermitage in what would remain of 2009 would be too much and so I asked our travel agent to look at the schedules available for 2010.

We had something a little different in mind for our trip to Russia, now 20 years free from the bad old days of Soviet Communism. And we well remembered our Viking river boat cruise in China and were looking forward to another one on the Danube River, just two months away. Our travel agent told us that Viking had a river boat cruise that would be just right: It would begin in St Petersburg, giving us three days there—enough time to see at least some of the cavernous Hermitage—then three days on Russia's Volga-Baltic waterway, including Yaroslavl and its beautiful pre-revolutionary onion-domed churches. From there, more river cruising to the Moscow canal, then three days and nights in Moscow with time to visit its most famous art museum, the Tretyakov Gallery. If we could make this happen, Joan would finally have an opportunity to see a good deal of the world's finest art.

It was a beautiful plan, but as it turned out, too good to be true. We probably over-did our touring in July and August, both the Danube River and the Mediterranean and by the Fall of 2009 it had become apparent that Joan could never handle all the walking that would be required to do justice to the museums, even though that trip was still a year out. So in November, I wrote a note to our family physician and asked him to notify our travel insurance company that we would be unable to make the trip.

We both knew that this was a terrible disappointment to Joan, and to me, too, because I would have been able to be her interpreter, Russian-to-English, and to show her some of the things that had been an important part of my life some 45 years earlier. But Joan was a tough trooper. I don't recall that she ever complained. Rather, we decided to do another cruise in 2010 that would require no walking at all, if we chose not to: the Panama Canal.

Joan and I often had lunch with a group of people who called themselves "The Presbyterian Dissidents." There were 15 or so of us who had left the Mercer Island Presbyterian Church when its leadership decided it would be "cool" to promote gay marriage and, eventually, to have a gay pastor in the pulpit. We could find no scriptural basis for such a position and had many "discussions" with our leaders about this; but they eventually prevailed and so we left the church.

At one of these luncheons, we learned that another couple recently had transited the Panama Canal. They did this on a Holland America Lines cruiser, much like the ships that Joan and I had come to love. We asked a few questions about their experience and decided to look into it.

Anyone who wants to know all there is to know about the Panama Canal must read *The Path Between the Seas,* by David McCullough. It is the most thorough and thought-provoking history that Joan and I had ever read and we devoured every word.

Our ship, the *MS Maasdam,* would sail in early February, 2010, from Ft. Lauderdale, Florida. By the time we were on board we were satisfied that we had learned as much as we could about our upcoming adventure.

The canal, for its day, was the engineering marvel of the world. The French had begun digging the canal in 1881 and by 1903 had excavated a "mere" 78 million cubic yards. But their efforts were thwarted by a monumentally-naive belief that the canal could be dug as a sea-level "ditch," between the Atlantic and Pacific oceans, much as had been the digging of the Suez Canal in the1870s. Ferdinand de Lesseps, the "Patron of Suez," and the bankroller of the French effort at Suez and now in Panama, insisted that what had worked in the North African desert should work in Panama. Not only did de Lesseps know—or care—little about engineering, but Mother Nature stood in his way as well. The Americans were still years away from learning how to control Yellow Fever; the mosquito controlled Panama.

The Americans took over the project in 1904, soon after President Theodore Roosevelt's election to his first term of office. By the time the canal opened in 1914, the excavation had moved more than 300 million cubic yards of dirt and rock.

To my way of thinking, the genius of the canal—which somehow had escaped the French—lay in the simplicity of its "mechanics." All of the power needed to operate its huge locks and its many auxiliary parts is "free." It rains in Panama as much as anywhere in the world and its lakes are always full. Water from one of these flows into the canal, assuring it plenty of water to float the huge ships that traverse its length every day. The water flowing through powerful generators provides more than enough electricity to operate all of the canal's moving parts, and electric power for the several communities in the Canal Zone.

"Our" MS Maasdam entered the canal at Colon, on the Caribbean side, just as dawn was coming on. The ship's open forward deck soon was jammed with passengers, most of them with cameras or binoculars or both. Joan, never "a morning person," remained in our cabin, offering me a sleepy "Have fun," as I scooted out the door to join the mob. For the next six hours I moved about the ship, taking pictures of all the things I had read about in McCullough's book. Those six hours were the most adventuresome of all my time on cruise ships.

Our voyage from the canal north to San Diego was a bit anti-climactic after the excitement of the canal crossing. Our ship stopped at San Isidro in Costa Rica, and our shore excursion took us by bus high up into the mountains to a farmers' market. From there we could see the spine of the continental divide, a view much different than what we were accustomed to seeing in our own Rocky Mountains back home.

Our next stop was Acapulco, at the foot of the Sierra Madre Mountains. We didn't get off the ship because we wouldn't be there long and, owing to the shallow water, the ship's lighters were used to take passengers ashore. But we could see, from our verandah, the glistening white beaches for which this part of Mexico is so attractive to tourists.

Our last stop before reaching San Diego was San Lucas, just north of the famous cape named after one of our biblical heroes, St. Luke. Here we did get off the ship and wandered along its planked wharf, admiring the many pelicans that were mooching free fish from the many fishing boats coming and going from the piers. I told Joan that I wanted to have a real Mexican beer in real Mexico so we dropped into a pier-side tavern. Joan was never much of a beer drinker, but in these circumstances she joined in and enjoyed the experience just as much as I did. It was another one of those "togetherness moments" that I will always remember.

MS Maasdam finally pulled into its assigned quay at San Diego's harbor. From our verandah, before we disembarked, we could see the U.S.S. Midway, tied to a nearby pier, one of America's aircraft carriers of World War II fame and now a museum. That sighting was a reminder to both of us of how precious our freedom is, ensured by the men and women who served on that warship and so many others.

In September 2010, Joan and I decided to try a trip much closer to home than had been our previous adventure. Just a month earlier, we had gone to Alaska on a Holland America cruise ship but Joan wasn't feeling well and we got off the ship only once, in Skagway. There had been a lot of fog along the way and after we returned to Mercer Island, we had to agree that the Alaska cruise was pretty much a bust.

Each of us, in years past, had visited Victoria, British Columbia, and for the same reasons. Joan's love of flowers—she always had fresh flowers in our home, usually from her own garden—drew her to the world-famous Butchart Gardens, just a few miles from Victoria. We both wanted to re-visit Victoria's equally well-known natural history museum. So we decided to go to Victoria the following month, October, a month that, in the Pacific Northwest, usually offers the finest weather of the year.

Just getting to Victoria would be something of an adventure. Even though Washington state has the largest ferry boat system in the United States, there were no ferries going from Seattle to Victoria. We would have to drive to Port Angeles, on the other side of Puget Sound, and from there board a ferry that would take us directly to Victoria.

Before leaving Mercer Island, I booked a room for three nights in the Union Club of British Columbia. The Union Club is not Victoria's largest or most expensive hotel but it does have a reciprocal arrangement with Seattle's Washington Athletic Club, of which Joan had been a member for many years. The room rate was reasonable, and Joan was happy about that.

We arrived at the hotel late enough in the day to find the hotel dining room closed. The hotel clerk told us there was a restaurant just a block away that would be open and after we got our luggage squared away in our room, we walked to the restaurant. It had a long bar and many booths but, because of the late hour, there were only a few patrons. We had the place pretty much to ourselves. The waiter came to take our orders and, of course, we both asked for a straight-up martini; the entree would follow.

What happened next still sticks in my memory as one of those unpleasant scenes one would rather forget. Joan took one sip of her martini and said to me, "This is awful, let's get out of here!" By now I had come to realize that Joan's dementia was never far beneath the surface of her now-troubled personality. I suggested we trade martinis, maybe mine would be different. We switched, she took a sip, and, Bingo, she smiled, resumed the conversation we had been having before the flare-up. It was as though it had never happened.

The rest of that evening passed by peacefully, we both had a good night's sleep, and the next morning we were ready to "do" Victoria. Fortunately, Joan's dementia remained in its "closet" for the rest of our visit.

The Butchart Gardens, for those who have never seen it, is a treasure begging to be discovered. It is a huge park, on two levels, with virtually every species of plant life to be found in North America. As this was October, the Fall flowers were at their best: yellow daisies, pansies, asters, chrysanthemums, even some late-season geraniums and many others we had never seen, a few never heard of. The deciduous trees were aflame and were especially beautiful because there had been little or no rain for the past month. But the flowers were the main attraction.

The artist she was, Joan had a wonderful sense for arranging flowers. She had done so many times for The Women's University Club in Seattle and for her Mercer Island church. She loved to arrange flowers at home for her bridge-playing guests. On one occasion she used some yellow (her favorite color) tulips which I had given her, telling me later that her "stunning arrangement" of the flowers had made a big hit with her guests. On hearing this, I told her that I thought those words, "stunning arrangement," applied to her as well as anything she did with flowers. She had posed a photograph of herself, taken when she was 60 years old, with a beautiful floral arrangement she had just completed. It is one of my favorite pictures of her and I look at it every day.

A Stunning Arrangement

For many years now, the Gardens have been "wheel-chair friendly." The long pathways have been paved with smooth asphalt and the grades re-built to accommodate visitors who must get around in wheel chairs. Recalling our airport experiences with wheel chairs, I rented one the moment we arrived at the Gardens' entrance. We took our time touring the Gardens, most people need a whole day to see everything. A break for lunch in one of the Gardens' restaurants gave us time to recharge our batteries but by 4 o'clock in the afternoon we were pretty well wiped out, I especially after pushing Joan's wheelchair for most of the day. On the way back to our hotel, she told me how grateful she was to be married to "such a nice man." It was another one of those "togetherness" experiences I'll never forget.

The next day it was time to visit the Royal British Columbia Museum, known to most of us as Victoria's natural history museum. It is located only a long block from the Union Club so we walked, but when we were inside the entrance hall, I found a wheel chair for Joan, this time a freebee, included in the price of admission.

The museum displays every species of animal life to be found in the Pacific Northwest, including a magnificent mount of a polar bear, nearly as large as the Kodiak bears I had seen in Kamchatka and northern British Columbia. The moose and elk in the north country are some of the largest to be found anywhere and the museum displayed one of each. I always marvel at the quality of the taxidermy that one sees in these places, but the Victoria museum's work was the best.

Natural history is more than plants and animals. Many of the displays showed how indigenous people lived in the arctic, walrus hunts, Beaver trapping, native peoples' hunting tools.

It was a very happy day for both of us, a priceless reminder of the beauty of God's creation and, for me, another unforgettable togetherness experience.

Chapter 38

God's Mysterious Ways

After four-plus years of utter happiness, it was almost beyond my comprehension when Joan began to show the first symptoms of dementia.

I'll never forget the very first of these. It was Mother's Day of 2009 and I was in the kitchen, making breakfast for her. She was nearby in our family room, arranging some flowers for the occasion, when out of the blue she said to me, "I don't like the way you've been treating me lately." I stopped what I was doing, walked over to her and asked why she had said that. She responded by pouting something like, "Well, if you don't know, you should think about it." I put my arms around her and told her, as I did every day at least once, how much I loved her, that I would never do anything to disappoint or hurt her. She accepted the hug, we kissed warmly, and that seemed to be the end of it. The whole scene lasted no more than a few moments and it was so unlike Joan. For many months following she was her old self.

But other things began to happen that were unlike her. For many years she had been a good bridge player, she loved the game and belonged to several groups that played together regularly, taking turns hosting each other in their homes. Getting ready for "the girls" to come to Joan's home for bridge was something she looked forward to. She had always been an excellent hostess, her table settings were masterpieces and she loved to cook, especially for guests. One day in January 2011 she was getting ready for "the girls" who would come for bridge the next day. Over the years Joan had collected many groupings of matching table sets, napkins, place mats, sterling silver, etc. On this day I noticed that she had been in the dining room for what seemed a very long time and as I watched her it was apparent that she could not decide which combination of napkins and placemats to use. She had been pondering this "problem" for at least fifteen minutes, a decision she usually would make in a matter of moments.

The next day, an hour or so before her guests were due to arrive, Joan still had not decided what to serve them for lunch. I offered to "help" her make a salad which she had used before and that I knew would be "safe," and she accepted my offer with a huge sigh of relief. She was pleased to let me prepare most of the luncheon. Again, a behavior completely unlike her.

The next day one of the women who had been at the bridge luncheon telephoned me to say that "the girls" were becoming worried about Joan—whom they had known for years—because she had become so very slow in responding to her cards and her bidding. I suggested, in response to this not-surprising news, that they simply stop reminding her of the next game. From that time forward Joan never received another reminder or an invitation to play bridge and she never said a word to me about this, as though an important part of her life had never happened.

The dementia gradually worsened, as it always does, and it re-appeared in an especially cruel way—in our church.

Joan had joined the Mercer Island Presbyterian Church in 1954, just a year after she and Cliff moved to the Island from Seattle. She quickly became a "do-er," arranging flowers, attending a weekly Bible study, leading a prayer group and, eventually, after Cliff died in 2003, singing second soprano in the MIPC choir. Just before we were married in 2005, I joined the choir in response to its plea for more male voices. Joan and I quickly became the "loving pair" in that congregation, everyone could see how much we loved each other (at age 75), always holding hands, kissing each other during the "joys and concerns" portion of the service.

So it was very disturbing to both of us when MIPC's leadership decided that it would adopt a new policy, proclaiming that the church would become "intentionally welcoming" to gay and lesbian people. We had always believed that anyone, gay or straight, was "welcome," but that this new policy would in effect paint a bulls 'eye on the back of anyone identifying him/herself as gay/lesbian. Worse, we believed, the church's leadership made it clear that it wanted, eventually, to see gays in the pulpit and to welcome gay marriage.

The issue was not new to the national Presbyterian Church. For years its annual General Assembly meetings had been inching toward this position. But for those of us Christians who could find no evidence in Holy Scripture to support these ideas, it was enough. About 50 of us voiced strong opposition to the new policy and at a December 15, 2010 meeting of the church's Session, or governing body, which Joan and I attended along with a dozen of our like-minded friends, the new policy was formalized. Our opposing views were not even considered. That was so disappointing that 15 of us "dissidents," as we soon began to refer to our group, left the church and began searching for new places to worship.

Joan and I visited a number of churches on Mercer Island. At one of these, a Lutheran church, we walked in one Sunday morning shortly before the service began and, as we did not know any of the folks who were already in the sanctuary, we introduced ourselves as "John" and "Joan," omitting our last name just to make things simple. After a few of these exchanges one of the Lutheran ladies asked Joan, "What is your last name?" Joan could not remember her last name. She turned to me, blushing and embarrassed, and asked, "I can't remember, what's our last name?"

In 1994 and 1997 Joan endured two radical mastectomies. Her surgeons assured her that there would be no need for follow-up chemotherapy or radiation treatments. "We got it all," they said. Whether that was true or not, the breast cancer reappeared in 2010, a little more than four years after we were married.

She had hurt her left shoulder, perhaps a result of her ever-faithful leadership of the three-times-per-week exercise class at our church. Rotator cuff surgery followed, along with the demanding and painful rehab routines, but at the end of this process, she still was experiencing pain in her left chest. Her family physician decided that a biopsy of that area would be a good idea. A week later he telephoned Joan with the bad news: Her breast cancer had returned. The good news, he told her, was that cancer treatments had improved significantly since her two mastectomies, there were now oral chemotherapy regimens available and that she "should be just fine."

Thus began a long series of trips from our Mercer Island home to a clinic in Seattle where Joan's newly-appointed oncologist worked. Once a month she received an infusion of a chemotherapy agent which was intended to reduce the risk of bone fracture. During these visits she also consulted with the oncologist who was monitoring her blood draws for signs that the oral chemo—a small yellow tablet called Femara, which she took once each day—was doing its job.

This monthly "routine" continued for about a year during which time I became even more concerned about the evidences of Joan's dementia, which were occurring more frequently. I was unwilling to talk to Joan about this because her physician had told me that Joan was exhibiting the well-known (to him) symptoms of denial and that a confrontation would be the worst thing I could do. So I contacted Joan's oncologist, who already knew about my concerns, and at our next visit to his office he suggested that she see a neurologist who could help her understand what she occasionally referred to as "my mushy brain."

Joan visited the neurologist only three times. During the first visit, he asked a young intern, who was participating in the consultation, what he thought about Joan's symptoms. It was the first time either

Joan or I had heard the word "Alzheimer's" spoken aloud in a doctor's office.

Later, during our drive home, Joan blurted out, with a sob, "It's time to die." For me this was a once-in-a-lifetime moment. How to respond? From behind the car's steering wheel it was impossible for me to wrap her in my arms, my instinctive reaction, so I said something like, "No, Sweetheart, we can beat this thing." I've wondered if my words were very convincing. A few minutes later, after we had arrived home and entered the house, she turned to me, hugged me with her head on my shoulder and said, "It's just going to get worse." That was the only time throughout Joan's long and difficult ordeal that she seemed to understand what was happening to her.

We visited the clinic a few more times, and at one of those meetings, Joan's oncologist told us that his review of her latest biopsy told him that the cancer had "escaped;" it no longer was being held in check by the oral chemo. As if to add more pain to that day, Joan's dementia again reminded me of the impossible burden she was carrying. As we drove along the familiar route to the clinic, before reaching the I-90 floating bridge that would take us into the city, Joan noticed some beautiful spring flowers along the roadside. They were the same color and kind that we had grown in her own garden and she had often complimented me on my ability to help her grow the flowers she so loved. She turned to me and said, 'You know, after Cliff died I married a man who - - -' and her voice trailed off. She was about to describe me to the man driving the car. In that moment of her demented confusion, she thought I was someone else.

The last of our visits to the clinic told me that there was no longer any hope that Joan could survive her recurring cancer and the dementia. The oncologist and his nurse agreed that no purpose would be served by her coming back. Over the next few days, in a series of telephone calls, I agreed that we should put Joan under the in-home Hospice care regimen administered by Seattle's Swedish Hospital.

Those Hospice nurses were among the most loving and

understanding women I have known. They visited Joan several times each week, others came to wash her beautiful hair, others to bathe her. One of them told me what to expect during Joan's final days. While waiting for the inevitable, I was able to control her pain. The nurses had taught me how to give her an oral morphine solution and to apply another pain medicine with a small skin patch. Even though she could no longer speak, it seemed certain that her pain was no longer a problem for her.

Two days before Joan died, Pastor Greg Asimakoupoulos, of the Mercer Island Covenant Church, came to our home, went downstairs to our bedroom and prayed for Joan. Neither of us could be certain that she was aware of his presence but that didn't matter. From a small bottle of oil he anointed her and then sang a hymn in his strong baritone voice. The following day one of Joan's neighbors came to the house and prayed over Joan for nearly an hour. These were two profoundly-beautiful Christian gestures that I never could have provided, so deep was my grief.

The night of June 22, 2011, I got into bed beside Joan, as I had been doing for the past five and one-half years, wondering if she would survive the night. I hugged her and kissed her goodnight but she could not respond. Something wakened me about two-thirty the next morning. I heard her shallow breathing, then a soft gurgle and I knew it likely was her last breath. I got out of bed, walked around to the other side and softly called her name; I had heard that hearing is the last of the human senses to respond. She did not answer and so I closed her half-opened eyes, removed her wedding ring, and then telephoned her daughter, Libby. I walked upstairs, into the darkened family room in which Joan and I had spent so many beautiful evenings together, sat down and wept.

The Hospice Service had given me many pages of instruction about "final arrangements." I had earlier phoned the Sunset Hills mortuary in Bellevue, told them that we knew Joan would die within the next week or so. They were ready for my 3 a.m. phone call and an hour later they came to take Joan away. The next day I began planning Joan's memorial service at our Mercer Island Presbyterian Church (even though we were no longer attending services there) because her family wanted to have the service before the Fourth of July weekend. My son Mike, the lead pastor for the Evangelical Free Church in Austin, Minnesota, had agreed to come to Mercer Island to participate in the service. I met with the MIPC pastors and Joan's family and together we planned her memorial service.

Mike preached to a packed sanctuary and five of Joan's family and friends delivered beautiful eulogies, including one by "Coach" Magee and another by our life-long friend Frank Sato. The service's bulletin included a loving tribute to Joan, written by Pastor Greg. He titled it "A Portrait of Grace."

A Portrait of Grace

The spectrum of life's colors
was the palette she employed
as blank canvases became her works of art.
With beauty, grace and dignity
she framed what God allowed.
Joan's gifts revealed a most amazing heart.

With her smile she made sun breaks
in a cloudy sky of grey.
She could brighten every room in which she stepped.
Pressure turned this Kohl to diamonds.
What she suffered fueled her faith
in Heaven where her crown's securely kept.

Yes, God's masterpiece is finished.
What he visualized is through
A portrait of His grace is now complete.
On the easel of forever
Is a picture of Joan
bowed in worship (fully whole) at Jesus' feet.

By Pastor Greg Asimakoupoulos

From Joan's Memorial Service Bulletin
Mercer Island Presbyterian Church
June 30, 2011

Long before Joan's illnesses appeared, she had told me several times that when the time came, she wanted her ashes to be scattered over the surface of Lake Washington. That would be the last of those sad but necessary events that a widower is obliged to make happen. Joan's sister Barbara, widowed in 2004, had a friend who owned a small boat which he moored on the lake. In September, two-plus months after Joan's death, Barbara, her friend, Joan's daughter Libby and I, along with Pastor Greg, motored out to that part of the lake which Joan had looked out on for so many happy years. After I had scattered the last of her ashes, Pastor Greg offered a brief homily, another prayer and he sang a hymn. Then our boat returned to its mooring.

During the two months following Joan's death I found myself feeling bitterly angry at God. How could He possibly have allowed such a cruel ending to such a beautiful life? The cancer was bad enough, but Alzheimer's on top of it? It made no sense to me, none at all. Then one day I reminded myself that I used to teach a class in churches, with my PowerPoint on-screen presentations, that tried to explain "how God works." It was based on Paul Little's well-known Christian apologetic, *Know Why You Believe*. In that book, Little answers the ten most-asked questions about Christian faith, including one he titled "Why Does God Allow Suffering and Evil?" I revisited that chapter. Little explained, and I then reminded myself that it is true, that God cannot play favorites. He loves each of us equally and that only by loving Joan "a little bit more" than everyone else could He have spared her.

Along with God, all of us who loved Joan so dearly know that now she is in that Better Place. I know that someday I will join her. I wonder, as do many of those left behind to grieve, if I will be able to connect with her again, to recount and relive our happy times together. The Scriptures give us a few hints about this important question and I believe it will happen. In the meantime I know that Joan is with Jesus and that for her there are no longer pain, confusion or tears.

Part Eleven – Another Life

Chapter 39

Covenant Shores

Within a month or so of Joan's memorial service at Mercer Island's Presbyterian Church, it was time for me to try to put my grieving aside long enough to make plans for my future. I certainly did not want to stay in her beautiful home, with all its memories nagging me at every step.

Joan's will provided enough money for her daughter, Libby, to purchase the home from Joan's estate. Libby had grown up in the home and she could move back into it, a very familiar and comfortable arrangement. It would also save me the considerable effort involved in trying to sell all the home's furnishings, go through real estate listings, find a buyer, etc.

Just before Joan and I went to Honolulu to be married, in November 2005, we had visited the Covenant Shores retirement community, on the north end of Mercer Island, and put down a deposit. It was a commitment that when the time came that we could no longer manage our own home, we could count on moving to a nearby, comfortable retirement community. Mercer Island's Covenant Shores is just one of twelve retirement communities scattered throughout the United States, under the management umbrella of Covenant Retirement Communities, or CRC. It has a strong Christian tradition and is closely affiliated with the Evangelical Covenant Church of America.

When Joan died, our names had been on the waiting list for nearly six years. That meant that I would not have to wait very long to make the move to a new bachelor's apartment.

The Covenant Shores marketing department already had an available apartment they thought I would like and they invited me to come have a look. On first inspection, I thought it was just right. It was a two-bedroom unit, the second bedroom small enough to serve as an office for me and my two computers. It needed a lot of refurbishing and that would take a few months but that was okay. I could wait.

While I was waiting, I began looking through Joan's home, in places I hadn't paid much attention to during our married years. One of these was her "storeroom," an unfinished part of the building's ground floor, home to its furnace, water heater, freezer and an ancient work bench. There, off to one side and under a cluttered shelf, I saw a long row of Joan's paintings, more than a hundred of them, stacked on edge and apparently untouched for many years. I had been vaguely aware of this "collection" but Joan never talked about it and, for me, it was "out of sight out of mind."

When I began to look carefully at each of these paintings, I realized that here was the work of a very talented artist, whose efforts would never see the light of day unless I did something with them. Each painting was different and each had a story to tell: What inspired it, how much time did it take her to finish it, why did she choose this or that particular medium, where did she paint it, why are a few unsigned and/or without titles? Whatever the answers to those questions, those paintings represented at least 40 years of devoted artistry, perhaps more. I quickly determined that Joan's paintings would indeed see the light of day, on the walls of my new bachelor pad.

The Covenant Shores managers told me I could begin moving things into my building, even though the apartment wouldn't be ready for another three or four weeks. Each apartment had its own storage space, a small locker on the ground floor. So for several weeks, each time I moved a few things from Joan's home to my storage room, I made sure to take with me four or five of her paintings, in the trunk of my car. I was able to squeeze 61 paintings into that storage room and, eventually, every one of them found a place on the walls of my apartment.

Every apartment in the Covenant Shores community has the name(s) of its occupant(s) on a metal plate on the entry door. Mine has my name and just below it another plate that is inscribed "Jo-an's Gallery." Indeed it is her gallery, and I feel surrounded by her love in every room.

I finally moved out of Joan's lovely home in mid-October, 2011. It was like saying good bye to a cherished friend. We had had so many beautiful times together, so many intimate evenings by her fireplace, so many hugs and kisses on her family room couch. I would soon discover what life was going to be like, alone and a widower.

The "alone" idea was misplaced. My new neighbors accepted me with open arms and I soon discovered that this community—there are about 380 people living on its campus—considers itself to be one huge family.

Within a week of my moving in, I received a call from the campus chaplain, Marlowe Shoop. I had first met Marlowe in 2006 when I did a PowerPoint presentation in the CS Fellowship Hall. The presentation was about the fundamental differences between the Christian and Muslim faith systems and apparently had been well received by my audience. Marlowe remembered this and our conversations that had led up to it.

Marlowe asked me to come to his office, just across the drive from my new apartment, and he began describing to me a Christian outreach program called BeFriender Ministry. The program already was in place on ten of the CRC's 12 campuses and the Covenant Shores managers had asked Marlowe to make it happen here. To do that, he needed to put together a leadership team which would then receive the specialized training required to put the program in motion. Marlowe already had recruited Mary Nehring, a widow who had moved to Covenant Shores a year earlier. When I said yes to his invitation, Marlowe had his leadership team: himself, Mary and me. We would fly to San Diego in January for a week of intensive training, come back to Covenant Shores and begin our befriending "in our own backyard."

The BeFriender Ministry program is pretty simple in its concept but not so simple to execute. Its descriptive motto is "A Listening Presence." The idea is that, in a retirement community such as Covenant Shores or in a typical church family, there are a lot of hurting people, people who are grieving over the loss of a loved one, struggling with financial worries, misbehaving grandchildren, oncoming memory loss—the list is a long one. As an extension of the chaplain's sympathetic ear, the BeFriender *listens* to whatever is of concern to the person befriended. The BeFriender is trained never to offer advice or to try to "fix" the problem, but simply to listen and by doing so to establish a mutuality of trust with, and compassion for, the person befriended. The program's nationwide experience has shown that most people, if given a chance to talk about their concerns—knowing that their conversations will be kept in strict confidence—have the wherewithal within themselves to heal.

The BeFriender program operates on four foundational principles: God is present; caring, not curing; a non-judgmental presence; and active listening. Although each of the four is important, the first is fundamental. In St. Matthew's gospel, chapter 18, verse 20, Jesus tells us that "Wherever two or more are gathered *in My name*, I am with them." The BeFriender claims this promise to be trustworthy and tries to assure the person befriended—who usually is a believer—that he/she can rely on it, as well.

When our leadership team returned from San Diego to Covenant Shores we immediately set to work. The training had been intense, four eight-hour days, with homework in the evenings, but we needed to put it into practice, asap. The program requires that a paid staff person, either a pastor or, in our case, our chaplain, is the responsible leader. On a campus such as Covenant Shores the chaplain—who knows everyone as well as anyone can—is the one who determines who might benefit from a BeFriender relationship. As soon as he identifies someone who agrees to a BeFriender visit, the process is set in motion.

Mary and I very soon found ourselves visiting those folks whom Marlowe had identified as needing our "listening presence." There are two "rules" in play: The BeFriender is always paired with a person of the same sex: Experience has shown when this rule is not in play, sometimes "affairs of the heart" develop, which is not a good thing. The other "rule" determines that each BeFriender visit no more than two people at one time. Usually the visits last no more than an hour and take place about once each week.

Marlowe knew from the get-go that Mary and I would never be able to deal with the needs all by ourselves. We wanted to grow the team, to train others to do what we were doing. So in May, just five months after our own training, Mary and I repeated what we had learned in San Diego. Eight CS residents volunteered to become our much-needed expansion and they, too, as I write this, are offering a much-needed listening presence to their friends.

It was not long after I committed myself to become a disciple of Jesus, in the early 1970s, that I felt led to try to share my new-found faith with others. I had participated in my church's classes about "spiritual gifts" and it didn't surprise me that *teaching* was at the top of that list.

Over the next 20 years or so I developed several Bible study programs and for many years I met with about a dozen men from my church, every Tuesday morning at a local restaurant, for breakfast, prayer and Bible study.

Along the way I acquired my first-ever laptop computer. After toying with it for a few days, it seemed obvious that I could expand my teaching "reach" by mating the laptop to a projector. I knew about Microsoft's PowerPoint program but was never in a position to use it. Now, with the laptop-projector combination, that would change.

The next step was to do some serious research into the Bible stories I had been teaching for many years. When were they written, to whom, what were the issues they tried to address? I became especially interested in the life and times of St. Paul and learned as much as I could about this amazing evangelist, who probably saved Christianity from extinction in the few decades following Christ's death and resurrection.

In the 1980s and '90s, years before the attacks on the World Trade Center and the Pentagon, Islamist terrorism already had become an issue that concerned me a great deal and I researched the history of Islam, how it came to be held hostage by its radical fringe elements. Then, after 9/11, there was even more evidence that the United States was facing an implacable enemy determined to disrupt our way of life—especially our *Christian* way of life—and that the threat was likely to persist for a very long time.

It took me some time to uncover the mysteries of PowerPoint and its powerful visual tools, but eventually I put all of my research and new understandings into a series of on-screen presentations that were very satisfying to me and, as important, to the audiences that gathered to see them. Sometimes there were only a handful of viewers, other times as many as 30 or 40. The numbers didn't matter because every one of my "shows" carried with it a Christian message.

Within weeks after Joan's death, it became painfully clear to me that I now had a huge hole in my life. Could I possibly fill it? She had *been* my life for five beautiful years and now she was gone. I began asking myself, did God—who cannot play favorites and had no choice in the matter—take her from me and her many loving friends—in order that I could fill that void with ministries, ministries that likely would not have been open to me if she were still alive?

I don't have a clear answer to that question but I have heard it said that God works in mysterious ways. Perhaps this is one of them.

Chapter 40

Music Notes

To close out this autobiography on the upbeat, I should say a few words about my romance with classical music which, in a way, began before I entered grade school.

As I have said, when I was four or five years old, my mother thought of me as a precocious kid; my father may have had his doubts. When I was just five years old, she somehow persuaded Dad that I should take violin lessons. I have no recall about how this happened, only that one day I found myself with a violin and a bow in my hands. I still remember the scene, in the kitchen nook at 912 Thompson Avenue, in Sumner. There I am, screeching and scraping on those violin strings. I think this awful experience persisted for no more than a few months. My dad, who worked every day, would come home from his law office and ask Mom about my violin "progress." Of course, I was never privy to these conversations but, mercifully, she sent the rented violin back to the supplier and that was the end of that; for awhile.

Mom was not one to give up easily. By the time I was 11 years old, she decided I should take piano lessons. In the meantime, I don't remember how, a piano appeared in our living room. A very old upright, which my mom was able to play pretty well. She had learned how to do this as a young girl, while growing up in Iowa.

"Miss Blue," as the whole town knew her, was the only piano teacher in Sumner and I soon found myself on her doorstep, knocking timidly. She answered the door and I told her who I was, ready for my very first piano lesson. Fortunately, Mom had telephoned her a few days earlier.

Over the next few years, I apparently developed enough keyboard skill that Miss Blue was willing to risk having me be part of the annual recital that she put on. These recitals, of course, are attended mostly by the parents of the kids who are taking lessons, plus a few curious citizens who have nothing better to do. As I think back on the experience, it seems like a risky form of "advertizing" for the sponsoring teacher.

I believe the only recital I took part in was a halting rendition of Snow White and the Seven Dwarfs. Walt Disney's movie had become a huge success and it was being copied, in many formats, all over the country. Miss Blue must have had at least eight students, seven plus Snow White. I was assigned the role of Sneezy (or was it Grumpy?) and I was required to play something on the piano. Like all the other kids, I was pretty nervous but we seem to have done all right. Miss Blue told us later that she thought the recital was one of the best she had ever put on.

But after taking lessons from Miss Blue for several years, Mom decided that I needed a better teacher. So she arranged for Mr. Williston to drive all the way from Tacoma—12 miles away—to come to our home and give me lessons. Mr. Williston, as I soon learned, was himself a very good pianist, slowed somewhat by arthritis in both hands. It was under his tutelage that I began learning the first movement of Beethoven's Moonlight Sonata.

While all this was going on, my dad decided to try playing the piano. But he wasn't about to take lessons: He would teach himself. And he did. I still remember drifting off to sleep while listening to my father's rendition of Schubert's *Serenade,* seeping under my bedroom door.

About this time—I think I was 14 years old—our junior high school football team was looking for new players. The Sumner junior high Bobcats had had a bad season the previous year and the team needed help. I decided to turn out for the team, knowing that its practice schedule would prevent me from practicing the piano. Such a deal! Mother was not happy about this, fearing that her son might get banged up and, probably more important to her, the piano lessons were now in serious jeopardy. As I recall, about six weeks into the football season, Mom gave Mr. Williston the bad news: No more piano lessons.

Fast-forward now to a few days after my high school graduation. Every kid in the graduating class expected some kind of "super gift" from his/her parents. Mine—I remember opening it on the living room floor, right next to our piano—was a portable phonograph player. It played 78 rpm records, one at a time. Along with the player, Mom included a record of Beethoven's Fifth Symphony, a piece of music I had never heard of. (Understandably, Miss Blue and Mr. Williston had not said much to me about Beethoven, even though I had been trying to learn his Moonlight Sonata.)

I'm pretty sure I listened to that recording of "Beethoven's Fifth" many times. There was something about it that really got to me. I began to read about this composer, a man who lived and worked in Germany and Austria in the 18th and 19th centuries, who became stone deaf half-way through his working lifetime, who died 30 years before the beginning of America's Civil War. That kind of personal history, and the music he composed—what little I knew of it, then— seemed to me to merit "hero" status in my young mind.

Just two years later, at the University of Washington, I wrote a paper, for my English professor, about Beethoven's life, his music, his travails and triumphs. Researching that paper required me to learn something about "the Master's" life. He remains something of a hero in my mind to this day.

Many years later, while I was serving at the American Embassy in Moscow, I found myself in Vienna, Austria. My job at the embassy required me to come to a West European capital every six months, in order to be briefed on the latest news by someone from Headquarters. The day I arrived, I learned that the Vienna Concert Hall, that very night, would be hosting a performance of Beethoven's Ninth Symphony, something I had heard only from recordings.

I could scarcely believe my good fortune. The hotel concierge told me the performance likely was sold out but he encouraged me to go to the concert hall's ticket office. "Just hang around," he said, "Something good might happen."

So "hang around" I did. It was a cold winter night in Vienna and I watched hundreds of patrons file into the concert hall. Eventually, at about eight o'clock, the doors swung shut. I was still outside, without a ticket. But the two women, who had been selling and taking tickets, knew what I wanted: I wanted to get into the concert hall! I had just come from Moscow, had never heard Beethoven's Ninth, this was the only opportunity, probably, of my life, so *please*, there must be at least one seat in that huge auditorium.

Sure enough, there was one seat, in the very back of the hall. I had heard concerts performed in Moscow's concert halls, but never Beethoven and never Beethoven in Vienna. It was a good thing I was sitting in the far-back corner of the auditorium; no one could see the tears of joy streaming down my face.

My service in Moscow provided several memorable opportunities in the world of music. The American ambassador often hosted large receptions for visiting artists. His Spaso House residence was a perfect venue for these kinds of events and he asked (required) that everyone on his staff who could speak Russian come to these receptions to mingle with the guests, most of whom were Soviet citizens from Moscow's cultural world. It was a good way to "show the flag" and I was happy to be part of the action.

Artur Rubinstein visited Moscow while I was there. He was in his late 70s and he performed in Moscow's Grand Hall, needless to say to a packed house. That hall, named after Peter Ilyich Tchaikovsky, is the same venue in which Van Cliburn stunned the world in 1958, at age 23, by winning the first world-wide Tchaikovsky piano competition. Rubinstein and Cliburn were the two pianists most well known to and loved by Soviet concert-goers.

Leontyne Price was another American performer who came to Spaso House. Although roughly my age, she already had become one of America's super stars in the operatic world, with a soprano voice like none I had ever heard. I was able to speak with her briefly and remember her as a beautiful and gracious woman.

My most memorable "encounter," however, happened one evening at Spaso House when I was able to meet Aram Khachaturian, at the time an established composer with a world-wide reputation. I was unaware of the man's humiliating experience, during the World War II years, at the hands of his own Communist Party. He had been forced to apologize for his "formalist" compositions before a meeting of the party's congress. But later, he returned to favor and was awarded many of the Soviet Union's most prestigious prizes. Knowing none of this, I walked up to Khachaturian and in my "best Russian" told him how much I enjoyed his music, that I could personally vouch for the popularity of his music in the United States. He seemed genuinely pleased to hear this and said he would like to visit America one day. Left unsaid was the likelihood that he would never receive permission to do so, owing to his previous difficulties with the Communist Party.

Another musical memory that pleases me is a performance at the Seattle Opera House, probably sometime in the 1970s, by Victor Borge. I knew very little about the man at that time but his performance was funny and entertaining. Once in a great while, during his show, he would play enough of a piece, seriously, that one had to admire his artistry. Borge lived to be 91 and he performed up to 60 concerts each year, right through his 90th. Even today, I enjoy watching/listening to tapes of his shows.

When Joan and I were married in 2005, we had already decided how we would use our joint incomes: Joan would keep up the house, pay for the groceries, insurance, automobile maintenance, etc., etc. It would be my job to pay for our travel and "entertainment." That entertainment, we agreed, should include a subscription to Seattle's symphony orchestra. For the 2006-07 season, we decided to buy a seven-concert series and I hoped to find two of the best seats in Benaroya Hall. The hall, completed in 1998, was said to have some of the best acoustical properties anywhere and because of my deteriorating hearing I wanted to be as close to the orchestra as possible.

At our first evening performance, we found ourselves seated in a lovely box in the Founders' Tier, close enough to the orchestra for my hearing to cope. Through the 2010-11 season we repeated this routine. And we added the Sunday POPs programs to our music-going experiences. These performances, at 2 o'clock on Sunday afternoons, were always fun, especially when Marvin Hamlisch led the orchestra. He was one of America's foremost composers, conductors and entertainers, especially gifted with children. His untimely death in 2012 has left a large void in the world of music.

Not so "upbeat" is an explanation about why Joan and I stopped going to Benaroya Hall. About half-way through a concert in early 2011 she turned to me and said she hated the music. That was her word, "hated." Her dementia had become bad enough that she had lost her appreciation for music, although I doubt she realized what had happened.

We never went back to Benaroya Hall.

After Joan's death in June, 2011, it took me several months before I felt like practicing again on the lovely piano she had gifted me for my 80th birthday, just two years earlier. It wasn't long before I began taking lessons from Cheryl Storey, a very talented woman who had been the choir director at Mercer Island's Presbyterian Church. Joan had been a member of the choir for a number of years and soon after we were married I joined it, too. My so-so bass voice was well-hidden in the back row, along with some guys who could really sing.

To this day, Cheryl patiently guides me through my struggles with, yes, two Beethoven numbers, one his Moonlight Sonata. Mr. Williston had taught me how to play, more or less, the first movement of this beautiful piece and I was surprised at how familiar the notes seemed to be, after 65 years. However, the sonata's second and third movements—rarely heard today—are a different matter. Likewise with The Master's Sonata *Pathetique*. The first movement of this sonata will remain beyond me but the second, the *adagio cantabile,* is coming around—after two years! And Cheryl is helping me with a Chopin piece, the only one of Chopin's "easy" enough for me to even approach, his *Prelude*, Op. 28, No. 4.

As they say in the news business, "That's the wrap."

Prologue

In the New Testament of our Lord and Savior Jesus Christ, His apostle Paul tells his beloved congregation at Philippi that "to live is Christ, and to die is gain." Paul would rather be with Jesus but he knows he must remain on earth for awhile longer, to finish the work God has asked him to do.

Today, I feel the same way as St. Paul did those so-many years ago. To die is to be with our Lord Jesus but, in my case, not only with Jesus but also with my beloved Joan. I pray that it may it be so.

Finis

Afterword

The proceeds from the sale of this book will be donated to the Alzheimer's Association and the Fred Hutchison Cancer Research Center (in collaboration with the Seattle Cancer Care Alliance), worthy organizations whose purpose is to learn more about, and eventually how to defeat, the scourges that took Joan's life.

About the Author

John Sager is an avid fly fisherman and a retired United States intelligence officer, whose services for the Central Intelligence Agency, in various capacities, spanned more than a half-century. He now lives in the Covenant Shores retirement community on Mercer Island, Washington. There, the walls of his bachelor pad—he calls it Joan's Gallery—are adorned with her exquisite water color paintings, acrylics and batiks, ever-lasting reminders of the girl of his dreams.

The United States of America

Central Intelligence Agency

Citation

MR. JOHN SAGER

is hereby awarded the

CAREER INTELLIGENCE MEDAL

in recognition of his exceptional achievement with the Central Intelligence Agency for more than twenty-five years. Serving in positions of increasing responsibility both at Headquarters and overseas, he was consistently praised for his perseverance, high degree of competence, enthusiasm and dependability. Throughout his career, Mr. Sager displayed uncommon devotion to duty, imagination, aggressiveness and efficiency. His solid background and broad-ranging experience, coupled with his professional expertise and initiative, won the respect and admiration of superiors, colleagues and subordinates alike. Mr. Sager's outstanding career performance and record of accomplishment substantially contributed to the mission of the Central Intelligence Agency, reflecting credit on himself and the Federal service.

The United States of America

To all who shall see these presents, greeting:

This is to certify that the Director of Central Intelligence has awarded the

Career Intelligence Medal

To

John Sager

for exceptional achievement

Given under my hand in the City of Washington, D.C. this 6th day of May 1981

William J. Casey

Director of Central Intelligence

Appendix

This article appeared in The Osprey, *an official newsletter of the Federation of Fly Fishers, Issue 11, January 1991.*

IN SEARCH OF:
SOVIET STEELHEAD
_____John Sager

Our associate editor is a retired U.S Government Soviet affairs specialist who lived and travelled in the Soviet Union in the 1960s. John dreams of going back someday, fly rod in hand, to search for steelhead in waters yet unknown.

What a dream. My Koryak guide has just relocated our fish: *"Nyemnogo dal'she, chut-chut na pravo"* (a little farther out, a tad to the right), he whispers, pointing to the spot. Makhat is naturally soft-spoken and above the riffle's song it's hard to hear him. Worse, in the presence of fish, he *whispers*. I've told him steelhead don't hear human voices; he thinks I'm crazy to risk being wrong about it.

He probably also thinks *all* fly fishermen are crazy, but he knows they tip well and in hard green, so he keeps his opinions to himself, about my neoprenes, cleats and ten foot graphite.

His way, up to a year ago on this virtually untouched Kamchatkan river, was a skillfully placed stick of dynamite, routinely stolen from the Petropavlovsk city construction trust. But banging steelhead was only for food and not all that often. *Koryaki* are meat-eaters, fresh salmon and steelhead only a seasonal treat. Despite the occasional dynamitings, these steelhead runs are in marvelous shape, scads of good spawning grounds in the many streams never exposed to clear-cuts and logging.

I finish the swing and aim farther right, upstream. As the fly settles in, I think of the geographic and ecologic similarities to Pacific Northwest steelheading: rain-nourished forests, mountain brooks flowing to sparkling streams, rapidly seeking the ocean, moderating maritime temperatures, latitudes in the low-to-mid fifties. The differences, though, are huge. No roads, no pollution, certainly no crowds. Also, no facilities, no fishermen's streamside trails and, worse, maybe no helicopter to come back for us tomorrow afternoon.

Makhat wasn't too sure about that. The Soviet air force major who requisitioned the bird *thought* he could come tomorrow; but if not then, no later than noon the next day, assuming his squadron commander is satisfied with his cut of the dollar pool.

It's been several years since Makhat has seen this portion of the river. So although he won't admit it, he's not *certain* we can float the six kilometers to the next cascade, which he recalls to be too tough for boating. But there's a clearing there—an old trapper's *izba* and garden plot—where the chopper will pick us up. If the river's too wild between here and there we'll get out and walk, maybe carrying the two small Achilles rafts on our backs. If the walking is too tough, we'll cache them and Makhat will come back before the first paying group flies in to Petropavlovsk.

I'm thinking this kind of roughing it, plus the uncertainties, are about as much as I can handle. I've chided Makhat that he must remember that the older clients who have the largest wallets also have the weakest legs: He should heat up the logistics and cool down the adventure. But he insists that the local Party chief has quietly given his personal assurance for this joint venture, so long as it's kept quiet. It's his *chestnoye slovo* (trusted word): "You can promise your American friends that *all will be in order.* I inwardly wince at that one—*vse budet v poryadke*—having heard it hundreds of times, in pre-*perestroika* days, as a meaningless intonation.

Just as I spot the huge dorsal, the line tightens viciously. But the fish declines to run and immediately begins a violent thrashing-in-place. I drop the rod tip. Too late; he's popped the tippet and the retrieval comes in limp and fly-less. Makhat says this one was at least a meter, maybe more. No mental conversion needed here, that would be a twenty-pound-plus fish and it looked and felt like it, however briefly.

A slightly smaller steelhead had come to hand only an hour earlier and Makhat gave me that now-familiar look as I released the incredibly strong fish. He's beginning to understand why I insisted we carry freeze-dry for dinner. Like most clansmen of the native Far Eastern groups, he's friendly and direct, but curious and a little suspicious in the presence of light-skinned foreigners. He assumed I had no confidence in our catching fish. But I think he's beginning to see the long- term implications of accepting our Northwest conservation ethic. And he certainly understands green dollars.

"Davay, otdokhnut'," I suggest. We sit down on a convenient log so I can rid the shakes and retie and we talk about how to make these trips more profitable. Putting another man or two on the river, in one boating group, may pose some tough choices: bigger chopper? If so, were do we get it? And shouldn't *Aeroflot* (the state-owned commercial carrier) be providing the helicopter, rather than his cousin, who just happens to be in the air force? (There are no privately-owned aircraft in the USSR so one gets them "where they're at.") A larger inflatable, or several more one-man boats? And what about the clients ("your soft people," Makhat calls them) who expect the guides to do it all? Just finding Makhat, amidst all the self-claimed "river experts," was tough enough. I'm beginning to see that this deal will easily take another month, at least, to get the bugs worked out. That's a must before the advertising can begin.

Makhat talks about other fish-filled rivers he knows about, all within helicopter reach of this one. We're already thinking in terms of a fly-in base camp at the *izba* we're supposed to reach by dark.

I keep pressing him for river profile maps. As I feared, he rightly assumes they're treated as classified military documents in this sensitive coastal region of Kamchatka. I try to counter that that's not in the spirit of *glasnost'* and he should remind his military "partners" of this. An officer should be able to de-classify them on his own authority, I say, in the interests of promoting capitalism. Moscow would be proud. Makhat thinks that's a crock: Moscow never heard of this deal and it's better if it doesn't, at least not until we start making some real money and decide whether to keep the air force in or out.

If only we could *drive* to these rivers. But as far as I can tell, the few valleys that have roads are few and far between. There's only one continuous north-south "road" in the whole country and in some places it's too narrow for two trucks to meet head on. Helicopters likely are the answer but they're expensive, and renting one would give the deal away because they're all controlled by the Party. And these local party hacks would love to subvert this *Amerikanskiy Beeznees* to their own greedy ends and could easily disrupt everything to the point of preventing good fishing and reasonable accommodations. Keeping the Party out, with the needed exception of the chief's personal cachet, still seems an important goal.

I ask Makhat if he's heard of the American sports entrepreneur Bill Davies, who is operating thousands of miles westward in Soviet Kola country. No, he's never heard of him. So I explain how Davies has organized Atlantic Salmon fishing expeditions for rich foreigners. He's doing it with the open cooperation of the local Party committee but, as reported in *The New York Times* (September 23,1990), other Party locals want to cause trouble by undercutting Davies: They want to out-bid him with unrealistic promises to would-be competitors.

Makhat understands greed and politics as the Soviets have done it for 70 years. Now I have to tell him that venal American organizers will make natural bedfellows with the newly-liberated Soviet money makers.

Makhat's osprey eyes have spotted another good roll just below the next riffle. We quickly agree to stow the business talk until evening camp and once again we push off down the river.

So much for dreaming, ending, as it always does, with another good fish just downstream.

The reality is that not until 1990, that I'm aware of, has an American entrepreneur been able to put together a river sports fishing package in the Soviet Union. This is the above-noted Bill Davies and his Philadelphia-based Soviet Sports Connections (per the *New York Times,* above), on one Atlantic Salmon river on the Kola Peninsula. And he apparently spent *five years* working on it. If *perestroika* works at all, in time these things will become easier, but dealing with Russians is unfathomably slow and demanding.

The formula is simple: their resource for our cash. But the development of any sports fishing activity, when it eventually does come, should be cautious and strictly in tune with preserving the resource. Decades of Soviet central planning have left an abysmal environmental and conservation record and Western steelheaders should not go there and make it worse.

So, do we dream in vain? Maybe there are readers out there who might want to share ideas about putting something together beyond dreaming. If so, *The Osprey* could serve as an information central and catalyst.

We'd be happy to try.